ANIMALS AND CRIMINAL JUSTICE

ANIMALS AND CRIMINAL JUSTICE

Carmen M. Cusack, JD, PhD

Routledge
Taylor & Francis Group

LONDON AND NEW YORK

First published 2015 by Transaction Publishers

2 Park Square, Milton Park, Abingdon, Oxfordshire OX14 4RN
711 Third Avenue, New York, NY 10017

Routledge is an imprint of the Taylor and Francis Group, an informa business

First issued in paperback 2018

Library of Congress Catalog Number: 2014045547

Library of Congress Cataloging-in-Publication Data

Cusack, Carmen M., author.
    Animals and criminal justice / Carmen M. Cusack, J.D., Ph.D.
        pages cm
    Includes bibliographical references and index.
    ISBN 978-1-4128-5596-9

    1. Animals--Law and legislation--United States. 2. Animal rights--United States. 3. Animal welfare--Law and legislation--United States. 4. Police dogs--United States. 5. Criminal justice, administration of--United States. 6. Animals--Law and legislation. 7. Animals in police work. I. Title.
    KF390.5.A5C89 2015
    345.73'0287--dc23

                                                        2014045547

ISBN 13: 978-1-4128-5596-9 (hbk)
ISBN 13: 978-1-4128-6521-0 (pbk)

Cover art courtesy of Susan White

V: "—Hem! —Hem! dit le roi, je crois bien que sur ma planète il y a quelque part un vieux rat. Je l'entends la nuit. Tu pourras juger ce vieux rat. Tu le condamneras à mort de temps en temps."

Antoine de Saint-Exupéry

Contents

Introduction

Animals and Criminal Justice is designed to inform students, practitioners, and scholars about the wide range of definitions, laws, procedures, policies, and treatment of animals in human society. Human society attempts to regulate nearly every aspect of human interaction, production, consumption, and expression. Laws are used to standardize regulation and enforcement. Animals can be treated quite differently under the law depending on which animals, people, jurisdictions, and contexts are involved. Animals' roles under the law include but are not limited to property, quasi property, beings, members of the family, companions, officers, defendants, service members, and service animals. *Animals and Criminal Justice* discusses each of these roles in sufficient detail to make readers aware of the diversity of roles, and of how seemingly arbitrary some laws can be.

Although theories of evolution and scientific classifications group humans and animals into certain categories, the law does not. In some cases animals receive the benefit of laws and procedures that humans also receive, and sometimes they receive better treatment than humans. However, they frequently receiver lesser treatment because the law is designed to create ordered liberty among humans. Animals are considered in this context, which may subordinate their interests or benefits. Many people who see animals as members of the family, beings with rights, sentient, and/or citizens of earth believe that the criminal justice system should increase its concern for animals to reflect higher values. This book discusses those beliefs in chapter 1 and explains work undertaken to accomplish related goals in chapter 10. Depending on the reasoning behind why people want the criminal justice system to treat animals better, the extent of their demands will vary. For example, people who would like animals to suffer less may ask for laws that ensure animal welfare, but people who would like for animals to have access to the courts to legally sue people who abuse them may demand rights for animals. Some people may want all animals, ranging from primates to insects, to be treated equally with humans, while other people may only demand increased enforcement of existing laws. Though people who want to protect animals have attempted to create a special class of protection for them, as it stands, laws dealing with animals need only have a rational basis. This means that as long as laws are not totally irrational, then they are legal, even if protections are allegedly inadequate.

Throughout this book readers should pay special attention to how dramatically the definition of "animal" can change depending on the jurisdiction, to how "cruelty" is defined, and to types of activities involving "animals." These variations significantly affect legal requirements for human-animal relationships. For example, the definition of "animal" could include insects or could be limited to certain species. Definitions for "cruelty" are quite broad depending on whether animals are in nature, science, homes, farms, commerce, captivity, or entertainment. For example, "cruelty" against a mouse will depend on whether mouse is included in a particular law's definition of "animal" regarding a particular activity. Mice may specifically be exempt from some definitions, while other definitions may only protect enumerated animals, not including mice. Some jurisdictions' laws broadly encompass a variety of illegal activities that fall under anticruelty statutes, for example, "harassment" or "torture," while others tailor definitions of "cruelty" to different legal activities, for example, extermination or experimentation.

Readers should note how much influence private organizations and regulatory bodies have in animal-human relationships. Private entities play vital roles in monitoring abuses, in investigation, in communicating with law enforcement, and in prosecution. As watchdogs, they also help to deter members of society from committing infractions against organizational rules, municipal infractions, or crimes. Numerous private organizations are responsible for investigating cruelty and lawbreaking as well as for bringing law suits, sometimes against the government. These organizations have been extremely—if not always—successful, even before the US Supreme Court. Some private organizations are considered to be benevolent and are beloved, while others are considered to be overbearing or even terrorist organizations. Many private nonprofit organizations share information, strategies, and resources, but their public images serve different roles in society. They may act as leaders, bullies, caretakers, enforcers, or advocates, or they may act in other capacities to essentially create similar results, that is, improvements for animals. These differences help formulate public opinion about each group; however, as long as groups are law-abiding, then these differences ought not to affect how the court views the groups or their legal positions.

Animals and Criminal Justice discusses the complex role that animals play when they assume positions of authority above humans. K-9 officers, war heroes, witnesses, and executioners are some of the positions occupied by animals that make humans subject to animals. Animals have been used by governments to control people and crime for thousands of years. Today, animals assume places at the top of the food chain throughout the world as they serve on police forces, in the military, in courts, and in other prestigious capacities. This book does not endeavor to tackle whether animals are sentient in a philosophical sense; however, in the criminal justice system, their capabilities are often given broad discretion, respect, and authority. Their instincts/intuitions, work, and work products are of great value.

Animals may be physically or socially powerful in some contexts, but because animals in society lack political power and domesticated animals lack autonomy, animals and humans are prohibited from engaging in bestial contact by society. Traditional antibestiality laws tend to ban sexual contact out of moral concern for humans. This is discussed in chapter 1. The law does not carve out a right for humans to engage in sexual contact with animals, but some jurisdictions do not specifically ban any or all erotic contact. Under anticruelty laws, which vary, only "cruel" sexual contact may be banned. Nevertheless, because of power disparities and enforcement of traditional morals in society, the criminal justice system is extremely intolerant toward extreme acts of affection or callous acts of sexual abuse toward animals. Yet, in certain contexts, such as in industry-standard farming practices, animals' genitals can be manipulated and penetrated. In this lawful context, which is an exception within society to the taboo against creating sexual contact with animals' genitals, amorous or abusive actions and intentions must be absent. This is discussed further in chapter 16.

Because humans throughout the world identify with a broad range of emotions regarding animals' roles in society, civil societies are judged, both literally and figuratively, by their treatment of beloved animals. In some countries animals may not be as beloved as in other countries. For example, in the United States dogs receive vastly greater protection than other animals. However, they are skinned, eaten, and routinely abused in other nations. In contrast, cows are skinned, eaten, and commonly abused in the United States but are beloved in India. Distinctions like these may be grounds for political or cultural misunderstanding and judgment. They may also be the basis for attempts to create international regulations or impose certain cultural values onto foreign people (Cusack 2014). These attempts can be complex and are often unenforceable. However, if certain animals—for example, sharks—are popular enough, then the majority of countries may effectively pressure the minority of countries. On the other hand, if the majority of countries agree that a particular species—for example, pigeons—is not beloved, then their protections may be lower. These globalized efforts are not commonly described as ethnocentric interpretations of ethical behavior or animal welfare because treaties or other regulations attempt to apply to all nations equally. However, on occasion, they are described this way, particularly when a certain treatment of a certain animal is customary or long-standing. Attempts to save or preserve specific animals have been described as "speciesist," in addition to being called "ethnocentric." Sympathetic, human-like, or attractive animals may be singled out for heightened protection above all others.

Readers should consider whether, when, how, or to what degree the law should be used on behalf of animals or their human counterparts. Each chapter covers several subtopics that will raise these issues. The role of animals as officers, criminal justice employees, service animals, and rehabilitative aides will be discussed in detail throughout several chapters, including chapters 4, 5, 6, 8, and 18. Mistreatment of animals will be defined and discussions will be provided that illustrate how varied responses to cases of mistreatment can be. Mistreatment is covered in chapters 2, 7, 12, 15, 16, and 17. Examples like hoarding, abandonment, sexual violence, and domestic violence will be contextualized within the greater theme of variability. For example, this book will discuss which laws forbid violence against animals, but will note that definitions of "violence," like definitions "cruelty," depend on various jurisdictions and understandings of animals as property, companions, and family members.

Animals as nuisances, violators, and enemies of the state will be analyzed in historical and contemporary contexts of justice throughout chapters 13, 14, and 17. Innovations in forensic and criminal justice uses of animals and technology, discussed in chapter 20, will offer readers some insight into possible future directions for how the criminal justice system will continue to incorporate and interact with animals throughout the world. *Animals and Criminal Justice* will bring to readers' attention that in some areas the US criminal justice system is exemplary, yet in other areas there is room to grow. International examples are provided throughout the book to enrich chapters, and in chapter 19 comparative analyses highlight international and foreign policies that should be revamped and offer strong policy guideposts.

1

Introduction to Animals in Human Society

Introduction

Legal obligations to animals may arise due to private relationships or dealings with animals, or under a theory of public law in which society demands that all citizens treat animals in a particular manner. Private and public relationships could create either affirmative duties to treat animals in a certain manner or duties to refrain from acting in certain ways. Overlapping civil and criminal duties may result from moral, societal, and legal obligations and norms. Though the law attempts to draw bright lines wherever possible, under the separation of powers doctrine, the legislature and courts each contribute to the formulation, interpretation, and manner of enforcement of laws. Each jurisdiction must conform to governing state laws and federal laws. These could dramatically change how the same activity is dealt with in each situation and jurisdiction. One major and controversial variation occurs in animal euthanasia. Animals who are not adopted may be euthanized using different methods. Some jurisdictions partner with private organizations to increase attempts to adopt animals, but others do not. Some jurisdictions opt for more humane methods, though some use less humane methods. Methods that were once popular have been banned because they inflict excessive pain on animals. Even though unadopted animals are not companions, property, or employees, society is concerned about their suffering. The law is used to balance interests, that is, animals' suffering against society's needs, to create practical, ethical, and humane solutions and policies.

Interspecies Ethics

Ethics, law, rights, social obligation, standards, and morality are conceptually bound together. Though these concepts are patched together, ethics is the individual concept that has come to broadly encompass animal

1

legal issues. Ethics are defined by obligations. Obligations may arise from moral, societal, legal, or other considerations; therefore, the ethical treatment of animals may arise from any number of beliefs. For example, one may feel that ethical treatment of animals benefits human society, that humans should routinely practice compassion or avoid cruelty, or that animals ought to be treated ethically because they feel pain (Branham 2005; Halsall 1998). These reasons may inspire choices, passion, activism, and societal changes, but they do not directly influence the law's codification or enforcement of laws that regulate the treatment of animals. In fact, there is no singular rationale behind all animal laws. For example, children's issues are mostly guided by what is in the "best interest" of an individual child. This is called the best interest standard. Animal laws have no such central nerve. Thus, broad ethical standards guide and overlap. A common ethical standard surrounding animal treatment is the prevention of cruelty. However, for a number of reasons, the definition of "animal" or "cruelty" in a variety of situations curbs ethical obligations toward animals under cruelty standards, for example, treatment of cows slaughtered in US Department of Agriculture (USDA)–approved slaughterhouses versus treatment of a lab mouse or of a house cat. The second most common standard used to enforce the ethical treatment of animals is endangerment. "Endangerment" is a term used to enforce the ethical treatment of children as well. However, when applied to animals, it protects the treatment of certain "endangered" species, not all animals.

Quasi-ownership status of pets demands a high, if not the highest, ethical obligation. Apart from endangered species, society obligates people to pets more than any other animals (Bearup 2007). This may be due to pets' numerosity, pets' endearing qualities, animal companions' loyalty to humans, or other reasons. The rationale is irrelevant because criminal law, which codifies and enforces society's standards, requires compliance irrespective of one's personal reasons for complying. In addition to society's ethical obligation to avoid cruelty and punish those who inflict cruelty on animals, society recognizes an ethical obligation to humans' property interests in animals, including domestic animal companions. Many pet owners who would sooner be called companions or guardians consider animals to be part of the family, not property. Many animal lovers liken companion animals to children, and they would prefer for society and the law to treat domestic animals better than chattel and with the same considerations with which children are treated.

US history inseparably weaves the ethical treatment of animals and children together. The American Society for the Prevention of Cruelty to Animals (ASPCA) was established in 1866 (Rosenheim et al. 2002). The Civil War brought attention to overworking and abuse of animals. Local ASPCA chapters were established throughout the country as humanitarianism flourished for the first time. Nine years after the establishment of the ASPCA, the Society for Prevention to Cruelty to Children (SPCC) was established. This private organization became extremely important for the improvement of child labor conditions. Prior to the establishment of the SPCC, poor children were frequently treated like indentured servants in forced apprenticeships and were overworked by parents who virtually relied upon their enslavement. There were few, if any, organized, institutionalized, or philanthropic attempts to prevent abuse or cruelty. Henry Bergh, who founded both the ASPCA and the SPCC, designed the SPCC to be modeled after efforts toward the ethical treatment of animals. In response to an abuse case that spurred the foundation of the SPCC, Bergh said, "The child is an animal; if there is no justice for it as a human being, it shall at least have the rights of a cur in the streets. It shall not be abused" (Garbut 1962). Notably, the jargon is different today. The word "cruelty" is associated with animal mistreatment, while the word "abuse" is associated with child mistreatment. Each has its connotations about the quality and extent of the undesirable behavior and the proper response from society. The teased-apart verbiage might imply distinct ethical considerations, and certainly denotes distinct legal standards, even though "cruelty" and "abuse" sprang from the same concept, and the words are used interchangeably or side by side in some statutes.

In some senses, ethical and legal treatment of children remains relatively similar to the treatment of companion animals. Broad discretion and latitude is afforded to caretakers, but physical abuse, neglect, abandonment, psychological cruelty, and sexual indecencies are all regulated to some degree. Depending on the jurisdiction, community standards, applications of the law, and other factors, treatment of children may effectively be less regulated than treatment of animals in some situations. For example, in some places, people may be allowed to use corporal punishment on children but not on animals, yet ethical obligations toward children's shelter are typically higher than toward that of animal companions, for example, "outdoor" pets.

3

Society's ethical considerations of parents' rights are one of the main principles that legally distinguish children from animals. Most parents biologically create children. This creates a natural ethical obligation to care for them. From this natural obligation, which extends to adoptive parents, legal duty arises and accompanies parental rights to control their children (Halsall 1998). Animal companions are not legally obligated to care for their young. Humans do not biologically sire animals, and humans have no legal right to own companion animals apart from general property rights. Under the Fifth Amendment parents have a special right to raise their children stemming from substantive due process rights, but the only rights given to animal owners are procedural due process rights that limit unfair governmental interference with property. Pet owners have the right to recover for stolen pets in a way that parents do not have for kidnapped children. No general societal obligation arising from property laws exists to recompense parents for lost children because children are not property. Some state laws have labeled animal owners as "guardians" or companions for limited purposes, for example, domestic violence or cruelty. This language shift results from evolved ethical considerations toward animals, but mostly has the effect of increasing humans' rights as a result of animal-human relationships. The language brings people one step closer to being treated like animals' parents rather than their owners but does not necessarily or directly grant animals greater rights even if animals receive increased protection.

The other main ethical obligation arising from human-animal relations occurs when animals are threatened or endangered. Legislative history and endangerment laws have cited numerous reasons for using the law to defend animals from the possibility of extinction (16 U.S.C. §§ 1531–1544, 2013; 16 U.S.C. §§ 1361–1421h, 2013). These include biodiversity, ecology, conservation, species protection, animal beauty or value, cultural heritage, necessity, and other reasons. Many people who support this sort of legislation feel an ethical obligation toward animals, the environment, or certain species. However, these laws most typically enforce humans' interest, not animals' welfare. One reason that international standardization of endangered species treaties is difficult is that different groups define their interests differently even though powerful drafters, signatories, or enforcers define ethical obligations by certain standards. Thus, nonenforcement may become a serious issue. Nevertheless, federal legislation in the United States reaches some international crimes involving taking endangered animals and enforces international law. Domestically, federal endangered species laws may patch together with state and federal property and cruelty laws to form a formidable net with which to exclude many unethical behaviors from society. Thus, in criminal law and within the criminal justice system, the three main sources of ethical obligation—that is, property rights, cruelty, and endangerment of species—form the backbone of most regulated human-animal interactions. The most latitude is granted to humans under property rights, but the government is obligated to intervene whenever illegal behavior occurs.

Morality and Criminal Justice Policy

Throughout US history morality has been regulated by the government. Public morality continues to be regulated. The right to privacy under the Fifth and Fourteenth Amendments protects private morality and immorality to some extent (*Georgia v. Stanley*, 1969; *Lawrence v. Texas*, 2003). The right to privacy is not unlimited. Some important parameters of right to privacy are that (1) it protects consenting adults inside their homes, (2) it does not extend to public immorality, and (3) it does not protect behavior that harms oneself or another. Traditionally, the government has used police power to regulate morality to preserve marriage and nuclear families, restrain female sexual agency, and institutionalize heterosexual and patriarchal gender norms (Cusack 2013; Cusack 2014). Traditional definitions of "morality" and "immorality" strongly relate to sexual mores that predominated when the Constitution was drafted. Traditional police powers reflect longstanding presumptions that the government should regulate morality. The US Supreme Court has stricken laws designed to protect traditional morality because major cultural or political changes have altered governmental interpretations of its police power over morality or certain private activities. Changes included societal acceptance of some private decisions regarding birth control, pornography, and sodomy.

Regulation of morality has always, and may likely continue to, strongly overlap with the harm principle (*U.S. v. Williams*, 2008). The harm principle, popularized by John Stuart Mill, is described by the US Supreme Court in *U.S. v. Williams* 2008) and by Justice Ruth Bader Ginsburg in her dissent in *Burwell v. Hobby Lobby* 2014). Under the harm principle rights may extend until exercise of one person's rights harms another person (Cusack 2014). Application of this principle is evident in the government's rationale for criminalizing child pornography. Though child pornography is considered to be immoral,

5

it is criminalized because it harms children. Similarly, bestiality and crusher pornography are criminalized because they are immoral and because they harm animals. This is discussed further in chapters 2 and 16. However, eliminating harm to children is a compelling interest, but eliminating harm to animals is merely a rational interest. Thus, pornography laws may protect children more strongly than animals even though traditional morality may equally prohibit adults from having nonmarital sexual relations with minors and unnatural intercourse with animals. Congress could pass laws requiring heightened protection that give animals the same status as children.

The government has the power to use criminal law to regulate morality and eliminate immorality that affects animals. On its face, law does not traditionally offer morality as a rationale for prosecuting all forms of animal cruelty. Yet, abstention from violent or cruel, that is, immoral, treatment of animals is indoctrinated into some aspects of American culture and likely underlies some animal welfare and cruelty laws. Most people probably behave less cruelly and more kindly toward animals than the law requires, even when they do not believe in animal rights or moral treatment of animals *per se*. In describing the difference between following beliefs or following conscience, Justice Antonin Scalia said, "You have an obligation to form your conscience according to what is right. That's the issue. The issue is whether it's right, not whether you believe in it" (National Press Club 2014). Yet, the First Amendment provides that people do not have to believe or accept moral precepts that underlie law, are held by the government, or are espoused by members of the legislature. Individuals' acceptance of moral rationales or their sincere belief in morality is not necessary, but compliance with the law is required. Thus, citizens who wish to commit immoral acts against animals are required to abstain from acts criminalized by the legislature, but they may commit legal acts that they believe to be immoral. Those individuals who wish to more closely align law with morality may attempt to change the law by raising issues, which may come before the judiciary or the legislature.

Morality is relevant to criminal justice analyses in terms of constitutionality of laws and police powers, and in terms of how morality's role in law and lawmaking could be extended or minimized through democratic processes. Morality-based animal protection laws only need to be rationally related to a legitimate governmental goal to be upheld if laws do not interfere with constitutional rights. Codified moral obligations to animals that broadly impinge on any constitutional rights would likely be invalid; thus, passing overly broad moral legislation to protect all animals in every circumstance may likely violate the Constitution. Yet, narrowly tailored laws could survive heightened judicial scrutiny. If laws survive, then they are implicitly rational, if not important or necessary. Constitutional rights may be impinged if all animals immediately received equal status with people. For example, if animals could not be bought or sold, then some people would allege deprivations under the Fourteenth Amendment and Fifth Amendment and violations of the right to contract. Yet, a superseding constitutional amendment could specify that animals have rights, moral consideration, legal standing, and so forth. Thus, while in some senses philosophical rationales for protecting animals are tangential to analyses of criminal justice policies that affect animals, nevertheless, legal scholars, legislators, and members of the criminal justice system may be influenced by morality and moralist arguments explicating why animals deserve greater legal protection.

Moral reasons for protecting animals can include animals' intrinsic value and maintenance of human morality to benefit human society and character. No singular reason or explanation has to govern or must be considered to be an ultimate reason. Each person, jurisdiction, and culture may hold various philosophies to be true or relevant depending on the issue, the animal, the species, the era, available information, and available resources. Yet, if legislators are persuaded by rationales, and rationales are supported by long-standing tradition, the Constitution, *stare decisis*, or other essential elements of US judicial and legislative processes, then particular rationales may be relevant to identify moral bases, for example, legislative intent, for protecting animals from harm.

Gary Francione argues that Western philosophy, in general, does not support the proposition that humans owe a legal obligation to animals, but he analogizes animals' possible future treatment to historical strides made by women and African Americans (Francione 2002). If law were to reposition animals in society in keeping with the courses taken by women's and African Americans' rights movements, then should animals receive special accommodations to repair historical discrimination? Justice Clarence Thomas said that attempting to create equality through favored treatment is as unfair as disfavoring one group. Justice Thomas has stated that equal and impartial treatment satisfy the "moral basis" for Constitutional Equal Protection (*Adarand v. Peña* 1995, 240). Francione specifies that animals should not have the same rights or opportunities as women and African Americans, for example, to matriculate at universities or to drive cars. Yet, for example, if animals could drive cars, then should they be permitted to do so (Minor 2014)? In New Zealand a nonprofit organization taught three dogs to drive MINI Coopers (Hayton 2012). Should animals be deprived of driving privileges if they are safe drivers simply because of their genetic attributes? Would it be fair to permit driving or deny driving privileges?

Rather than arguing for equality, Peter Singer argues that humans should treat animals humanely because animals suffer, that is, feel pain (Kerr et al. 2013). Inflicting pain on animals is immoral because humans also feel pain. Under a criminal justice analysis, egalitarian principles may be supported by state police powers to regulate morality, though these principles could conflict with retributive penological theories of capital punishment. However, Singer's argument approaches suffering through the lens of farmed animals, not through analyses of animals' culpability and punitive treatment of criminals. Animals' sentience is evaluated by Singer as being worthy of consideration, yet Singer allows for animals to be killed when it spares them from suffering. In limited circumstances this could overlap with criminal justice capital punishment policies. For example, if animals harm others because they are severely ill, for example, with second- or third-stage rabies, then humans may be justified in killing them to terminate their suffering, which potentially may also satisfy retributive aims (*Atkins v. Virginia*, 2002; *Hall v. Florida*, 2013). Capital punishment is discussed in chapter 13.

"Cruelty," a legal standard that varies throughout legal codes and case law, is generally defined as intentional or wanton infliction of pain or disregard for suffering. Generally, animal cruelty is prohibited by law, but laws do not protect all kinds of animals in every circumstance. Thus, adoption of Singer's idea by every jurisdiction would certainly help to uniformly define "cruelty"; however, legislatures could not be forced to adopt a single definition unless federal law bound them regarding a federal issue. Potentially, Congress could declare that animal suffering is a federal matter that permits them to bind states because animals enter into the stream of commerce, and interstate commerce is regulated by Congress. Congress has enacted popular laws with moral bases on behalf of animals. Congressional intent for prohibiting crusher laws incorporates, to some extent, Singer's argument that animals' suffering is immoral (Cusack 2014).

Social contract theories may underlie constitutional principles. Jean-Jacques Rousseau explained that humans were originally free and lived in harmony with nature, but humans devised a social contract to promote human survival (Tamir 2014). The social contract called for the collective to create civility by enforcing policies against individuals at the expense of moral freedom. Thomas Hobbes, whose philosophies likely influenced a number of US founders, believed that individuals may destroy one another to survive and achieve success. Rather than use their natural right to war, humans agree to refrain from destructive behaviors and invest those rights into a sovereign power, for example, the state. Stoicism, which values divine reason, and Rawlsian principles, which promote contractualism, hold that humans are capable of undertaking obligations under a social contract, but animals are not. Thus, animals may not be entitled to any place in the human community or full measures of justice because they cannot understand the exchange, for example, they cannot rationalize sacrifice, protection, and punishment (Huss 2002). St. Thomas Aquinas wrote that punishment may not be justified when it is and end in itself; the purpose of punishment is to right wrongs (Tamen, 1999). Thus, animals, who may be incapable of immorality but are capable of harm, could be part of a social contract that does not punish them, yet rights their wrongs. For example, reasonable labor terms could be imposed to right wrongs. Emmanuel Kant proposed that humans should avoid cruelty because it decays human virtue. Kant viewed animals as irrational, and thus not capable of entering into the social contract as a class. Kant argued that humans must consistently behave in a manner that upholds human moral precepts. This argument is somewhat like the government's traditional police power to regulate private morality because public decency may decay in conjunction with widespread private immorality. When people abuse animals, they lose opportunities to behave virtuously. In this way they could develop arrogance, violence, antipathy, and apathy (Bartlett 2002). A model penal code may incorporate Kantian perspectives with regard to cruelty (Francione 2002). Thus, under social contract theories, animals could be protected or exempted from cruelty or punishment for moral reasons or to preserve humans' best interest, civility, and social order.

Animal welfare philanthropy developed before child welfare philanthropy and subsequent legal protection for children. One morality-based argument may be that animals are owed legal protection because society identified them as being in need prior to development of child welfare (Rosenheim et al. 2002). Children have received vast amounts of attention, but only after animals opened the door. Aristotle described nature as organized in a hierarchy called the "Great Chain of Being" (Huss 2002). Divine beings are elevated above rational humans, who are ranked above other conscious creatures. Aristotle's philosophy supports the idea that groups can be ranked. In US history animals' needs were, at one time, ranked above children's needs perhaps because animals suffered more or perhaps because people cared more about animals. Either way, some animals may be owed the same amount of welfare interests given to children over the past century.

Animals and children both contribute to economic growth and social stability. However, one major outcome of the child welfare movement was restrictions on child labor (*Prince v. Massachusetts*, 1944; Rosenheim et al. 2002). Some working animals have been protected by law, but animal welfare–oriented labor reform may have been pushed aside because animals receive no monetary compensation other than room and board. Yet, because animals are immensely useful, they may deserve or be morally entitled to greater protection under the law. Their contribution to society is important; thus, perhaps they ought to be granted status commensurate with their value. Morally and legally, perhaps equal protection would not be required among humans and animals, all classes of working animals, or all species (Leiter 2013). For example, legal status may be required among animals who contribute to society, and certain status could be denied to those who detract from society, for example, infestations, as discussed in chapter 17.

Morality may be implicated by designating levels of protection and the effects on human-animal relationships. Protecting all classes of animals equally may benefit humans. For example, the Marine Mammal Protection Act (MMPA) seeks to protect animals to maintain biodiversity for humans. Yet, once biodiversity is achieved, then culling may be justifiable even though some critics find it to be immoral. Culling is discussed in chapter 17. Furthermore, maintaining biodiversity by protecting all species equally may only add marginal value to human society and environments. Therefore, it may be more moral for animals only to receive legal protections when their interests naturally or coincidentally align with human interests, such as Taoism (Satz 2009). Justice Stephen Breyer said that "ultimately, the point of law is to satisfy a human desire that's probably 10 or 20 thousand years old . . . people, of course, want justice . . . and they expect, ultimately, that the law will help them achieve that very basic and noble end" (Ishmael 2012). Perhaps law may expand to protect animals nobly or morally whenever expansion practically satisfies human desires.

Precepts annunciated in the Declaration of Independence could underlie humans' treatment of animals. Tom Regan believes that animals have natural rights, which endow nonhuman animals with moral rights. All animals are inherently valuable. Their value is not created by work, pleasure, reason, or human-animal relationships. Moral rights are vested in each animal. Thus, for animals to have moral rights they need not be granted particular status, for example, personhood. To believe that humans are without any moral, ethical, or legal obligation to protect animals may be pure prejudice or speciesism (Bartlett 2002). In general, legislatures tend to make laws acknowledging that many animals have value, but there is some variation in criminal justice responses to threats against these values. For example, value may derive in different circumstances through animal ownership, suffering, emergencies, and so forth, and responses must be appropriate for the circumstance. Implementation of Regan's idea to protect all animals' natural rights may require systemic parity that is only capable of being achieved through a constitutional amendment or federal legislation on a constitutional issue.

Personhood could be granted to animals without requiring animals to independently and autonomously participate in a social contract. For example, corporations are legal persons. They can be prosecuted, contribute to political campaigns, and practice the religion exercised by their owners and board members (*Burwell v. Hobby Lobby*, 2014). However, they cannot commit or be held liable for all classes of crimes, and they cannot vote. They are legal persons who have standing, but they cannot sit on a bench as judges. These examples illustrate that corporations enjoy personhood, but only a modified version. Similarly, animals could be endowed with personhood. They could have modified rights, like children and corporations, and their interests could be protected by guardians or corporate officers. This may raise moral questions: for example, whether animals who are legal persons could practice religion or choose to abstain from practicing religions practiced by their owners, for example, animal sacrifice. Corporations can be dissolved at the discretion of their corporate boards. Thus, could corporate dissolution policies be applied to animals? Could their personhood be liquidated and dissolved, for example, dispatched, as long as proper laws and ethical considerations are followed? Would personhood be in animals' best interests if it obligated them to pay taxes, like corporations? Animals' legal obligations are discussed in chapter 13.

Justice Stephen Breyer aptly summarized the relevance of moral considerations to the criminal justice system when he said, "In criminal law . . . if law goes one way and morality goes the other, think twice. It's not supposed to work out that way. Sometimes, you can't help it, but in criminal law . . . the rules for law are supposed to, in general, trace moral rules. So if you get something immoral in the laws, there's something wrong somewhere and you try to see why is this going wrong; and where is it; and maybe you can do something about it; maybe you can't" (Harvard Law School 2013). Infusing the law with greater moral consideration for animals may be beneficial or required in the future if the government decides that morality and law have gone in two separate directions.

Defining Interspecies Relationships: Civil and Criminal Crossover

Animals are not required to obey human laws, but they are subject to them. In addition to the criminal justice system, animals might be subject to civil law, family law, administrative codes, and immigration law. Very frequently, these bodies of law overlap. They mainly complement one another but at times can seem incompatible.

Family law is civil law that crosses over into criminal law at times. Child custody battles usually involve disputes about what is in the best interest of a child. At times, courts may consider the presence of animals living on a property as a factor weighing against in favor of custody (Paek 2013). Many aspects of criminal law, including animal cruelty, domestic violence, and child neglect may be relevant. On rare occasions, family law courts may consider the best interest of companion animals and their custody even if the animals are not in danger of cruelty. Bankruptcy matters could become relevant in criminal proceedings, family disputes, or other civil disputes. Bankruptcy courts are much more willing to consider animals as independently relevant by exempting household pets from property liquidation, even though animals are technically property.

Animals are frequently included in wills (Paek 2013). People who care about the well-being of their animals after their deaths can establish trusts that provide for their animals. These trusts are effective, though courts have limited exorbitant amounts of money that have been left in trust for animals. Differing slightly from that limitation is another limitation that occurs when the government takes money from a dead criminal who obtained the money through criminal activity. Criminals may leave money in trusts for animals, but if the government discovers a connection between trust money and crimes, then the money will be forfeited (Edwards 2011). Unfortunately, animals lack standing, therefore they are unable to enter as parties in forfeiture proceedings or enforce trusts. This means that transferees cannot be required to use the money held in trust for a pet (Beyer 2000).

In most jurisdictions animal owners can be held civilly liable for damage or injuries caused by animals to another person or property. In addition to any criminal or administrative proceedings that will be discussed in chapters 9 and 18, animal owners can be forced to pay civil damages. In some states—for example, Florida—a dog's bite makes an owner strictly liable. This means that if a dog bites any person who is privileged to be on a property at the time of the bite, then the owner will be responsible for all damage caused by the bite even if the dog was under the owner's control. Tough civil remedies may serve as more effective means of inducing compliance and caution from pet owners than light administrative consequences resulting from ordinance violations. For example, after a horse with no history of attacks bit a child's face in Connecticut recently, a judge declared that all horses are inherently vicious and should be restrained (MSN 2013). This response puts all horse owners, horse insurers, and the public on notice. Not all jurisdictions hold owners strictly liable for animal bites. Some courts make inquiries about whether an animal was wild or domestic, vicious, or owned or harbored lawfully (Fugate 2006). Baiting is a defense to dog bite liability when a dog bites in response to provocation, and in some jurisdictions harassing animals can be a criminal offense. Even when baiting fails to be proven in civil court, harassment still may be proven in criminal court. Thus, two courts could hold two somewhat opposing points of view about the same bite.

People are responsible for working animals. Police officers and other state actors are immunized from personal liability for injuries caused by working animals in the course of duty performance. However, if animals injure others due to police negligence, for example, then individuals may be liable for damages if the activity was beyond the scope of employment (Fugate 2006). An animal owner would not typically have any criminal claims against a person who accidentally kills an animal (Paek 2013). Accidentally killing a police animal, however, can carry civil as well as criminal consequences. For nonworking companion animals, the appropriate remedy would be damages amounting to the replacement value of the animal, that is, restitution. In a few states emotional distress or other similar civil claims are possible, but these are rare.

A large number of films portray abuse or killing of animals ranging from mice to endangered species. However, animals are almost never harmed in actuality. Even where the law is silent, for example, killing fish or bugs, moviemakers go to great lengths to avoid any semblance of true cruelty or killing. For example, fly fishing is the backdrop to the film *A River Runs Through It* (Graglia 1996). However, no fish were harmed during the movie even though fish are not considered animals under many cruelty statutes and, generally speaking, can be killed merely for human amusement. Mistreatment of wild animals and the topic of animals in entertainment are discussed in chapter 7.

Kosher slaughterhouses are permitted to slaughter animals using one swift slice of an animal's necks with a very sharp blade. When the appropriate procedures are not followed and cruelty results, criminal cruelty violations could be charged without civil fines. However, some jurisdictions enforce hefty fines to deter owners from falling below industry standards. For example, in Florida, the kosher slaughter violations carry a maximum of $10,000 civil fine per day (Wisch 2006). The statute also classifies kosher slaughter violations as a criminal misdemeanor. Religious slaughter and kosher killing are discussed in chapter 3.

Animals in traffic could raise civil and criminal liability. One commonly witnessed infraction is unsecured dogs in the beds of pickup trucks (CT ST § 14-272b). Dogs usually must be secured in carriers or by other devices. If a dog who is in the bed of a pickup truck bites a person, then the vehicle owner's auto insurance may be forced to pay (*Diehl v. Cumberland Mut. Fire Ins. Co.*, 1997). If a motorist strikes a domesticated animal, for example, a cow, who is in the roadway, then the animal's owner and the owner's insurance company could be liable for damages (*Honeycutt v. State Farm Fire & Casualty Co.*, 2004). The owner could possibly face criminal charges depending on the animal owner's actions leading to the collision. However, seemingly negligent actions are sometimes completely legal. For example, allowing a dog to cruise while seated on a driver's lap seems to be lawful in every state except Hawaii (Hawaii Revised Statutes § 291C-124, 2014).

Immigration is a field of law that blends many different kinds of law together. Entering the United States illegally is a civil violation. However, criminal law and family law frequently become part of cases. The crossover commonly occurs when aliens have criminal records, commit crimes in the United States, are victims of abuse, or have immediate relatives in the United States. Immigration law also involves animals. Undocumented residents may live with companion animals. When undocumented residents are faced with deportation, they may be forced to surrender their animals (Immigrant Pet Owners 2013). Sometimes this vulnerable population is easily threatened or blackmailed due to their status and love of their pets, especially when their companion animals are a source of tension, for example, dogs barking or rabbits chomping vegetation. People who are harmed by animals belonging to undocumented residents may trigger immigration proceedings by reporting. Undocumented status may limit a victim's recovery in the long run if a pet's owner is deported. Undocumented residents who travel into the United States with animals may be deprived of veterinary care if they cannot produce proper records. As a result, they may be forced to break municipal codes requiring vaccination.

Warehousing or Murdering: Between a Rock and a Hard Place with Homeless Animals

A homeless animal living within human society has only a few fates. A homeless animal may live an abbreviated and difficult life as a feral animal. A feral animal's lifespan will be cut short by hardship, starvation, disease, injuries, accidents, and competition. For example, a feral cat only lives about two years, whereas a domesticated cat usually lives into its teen years or even its twenties. A feral animal may be caught, then spayed or neutered, and released under trap-neuter-release programs (Smith 2009). This measure prevents breeding and subsequent creation of additional feral animals, but it does little to accommodate feral animals who already exist. Another option for dealing with strays and feral animals is to humanely exterminate them. From a practical standpoint society assumes a risk when animals roam public and private areas. These risks are not necessary to human survival or progress like some other risks, so they may not be worth taking. These extraneous risks could be limited by systematic eradication of free-roaming animals. From a compassionate standpoint, feral animals are likely to suffer throughout their entire lives. They also risk inhumane and cruel fates if they are poisoned, tortured, or attacked by other domesticated animals. Communities usually do not have sufficient resources to create ideal and safe environments for all homeless animals. Humane extermination guarantees an end to their suffering and ability to reproduce. Many counties and animal control agencies expeditiously and humanely exterminate animal populations. Some authorities actively trap and kill animals, while others only pursue animals who present a nuisance. Animals who are captured are given a small window to be rescued

15

by their families, if they are strays, or to be adopted into a new family. Since some domesticated cats might partially live outdoors, families may not have sufficient time to realize that their cats have been captured before that time window closes. Animals who are not taken into homes during that time window will be euthanized. During this window, which may be a few days at most, organizations often attempt to rescue animals from "death row."

No-kill organizations will make efforts to adopt animals. They also may attempt to capture animals or receive rescued strays or feral animals for adoption. These organizations may work with animal control, may substitute for animal control, or may effectively work against animal control's approach. Animal control is further discussed in chapter 9. No-kill organizations receive tremendous public and financial support. Many will only euthanize animals who are suffering and cannot be treated. No-kill facilities will provide animals with surgeries, amputations, vaccinations, and other services until an animal can be adopted. However, many animals are not promptly adopted. Animals at no-kill shelters usually live in wire kennels for the duration of their time in the shelter. Some animals spend decades or their entire lives living in rooms crowded with numerous animals stacked in kennels (Fivecoat-Campbell 2013). These conditions may be less than ideal. Though volunteers walk and play with animals, some critics suggest that the animals and society would be better off if animals were humanely euthanized (Smith 2009). Some jurisdictions require one approach or another, or leave room for both and allow private organizations to operate under both philosophies.

Holes, Loopholes, and Ends That Don't Meet: Unaddressed Animal Issues in Criminal Justice

Unresolved or inadequate encounters between the criminal justice system and animals are endless. Due to lack of resources, forces of nature, human error, depravity, politics, changing legislation, competing commercial interests, and a number of other factors, unpredictable or unsolvable encounters develop and manifest routinely. For example, some underaddressed issues include (1) insufficient statutes regulating or banning cosmetic animal mutilation or docking by amateurs, (2) unregulated or lawful feeding of small mammals to carnivorous reptiles despite cruelty laws and animal fighting laws that are not written to include exceptions, (3) emergency responses to insect infestation, (4) feral flocks of birds causing nuisances in towns or urban areas, and

(5) whether a person would be authorized to kill an eagle who attacks and injures several humans but not seriously (Rosen 2011). Depending on the circumstances, any of these could involve a crime or spiral into a criminal event. These few examples, like countless others, cannot be discussed with considering federal and state legislation affecting commerce, endangered species, animal welfare, hunting, and other issues and interests. Overlapping concerns better protect all animals and people through a patchwork of legislation, but competing interests can stymie formulation of new responses to problems since so many approaches can be taken and there are so many ramifications to be considered. When citizens feel concerned about unaddressed encounters involving animals and the criminal justice system, making an appointment with a congressional representative, local police representative, an association or corporate board member, or animal control to discuss the problem may generate problem-solving strategies or inspire grass roots lobbying or activism.

Conclusion

Many aspects of civil and criminal law allow society to act on behalf of animals' interests. Families and individuals who own or cohabit with companion animals may become involved in range of civil or criminal matters. Legal matters may be voluntary, for example, wills and trusts, or may be imposed by the state, for example, civil penalties and forfeiture. Civil matters may relate to criminal matters arising from the same set of facts. Depending on the circumstances, however, there may be no legal remedy for some situations, or legal remedies may not be equipped to respond equitably to every scenario. Gaps in the law may be ignored, exploited, or challenged. Despite significant civil and criminal overlap, legal gaps and jurisdictional variations demonstrate the possibility for abundant gray areas in the criminal justice system.

References

16 U.S.C. §§ 1531–1544 (2013).

16 U.S.C. §§ 1361–1421h (2013).

Adarand v. Peña. 515 U.S. 200, 240 (1995).

Atkins v. Virginia. 536 U.S. 304 (2002).

Bartlett, S. J. 2002. "Roots of Human Resistance to Animal Rights: Psychological and Conceptual Blocks." *Animal Law* 8:143.

Bearup, B. J. 2007. "Pets: Property and the Paradigm of Protection." *Journal of Animal Law* 3, no. 1: 173.

Beyer, G.W. 2000. "Pet Animals: What Happens When Their Humans Die?" *School of Law, Santa Clara University* 40:617.

Branham, A. 2005. "Quick Summary of Philosophy and Animals." *Animal Legal and Historical Center.* http://www.animallaw.info/topics/tabbed%20topic%20page/spusphilosophy_animals.htm.

Burwell v. Hobby Lobby. 573 U.S. ___ (2014).

CT ST § 14-272b (2012).

Cusack, C. M. 2013. "To-Get-Her ForEVEr: A Man Hater's Right to Same-Sex Marriage." *Journal of Law & Public Policy* 10, no. 1: 63–98.

———. 2014a. "In Opposition of Cultural Iof speech following U.S. Intervention into Foreign Governments." *Barry Law Review* 19, no. 2.

———. 2014b. *Pornography and the Criminal Justice System.* Boca Raton, FL: CRC Press/Taylor & Francis.

Deport the Statute. 2013. "New Film to Feature Immigrant Pet Owners Facing Deportation." June 12. http://deportthestatue.us/new-film-to-feature-immigrant-pet-owners-facing-deportation/.

Diehl v. Cumberland Mut. Fire Ins. Co. 686 A.2d 785. N.J.Super.A.D. (1997).

Edwards, S. 2011. "$6.9M of Assets Seized from Dead Drug Lord's Girlfriend." *Columbia Reports,* October 25. http://colombiareports.co/69m-of-assets-seized-from-former-drug-lords-ex-girlfriend/.

Fivecoat-Campbell, K. 2013. "Dog Still Seeking a Home after Eight Years in the Shelter." *Yahoo! News,* September 20. http://shine.yahoo.com/pets/dog-still-seeking-home-eight-years-shelter-202700783.html.

Francione, Gary. 2002. "Remarks: The Legal Status of Nonhuman Animals." *Animal Law* 8:1–76.

Fugate, R. 2006. "Survey of Texas Animal Torts." *South Texas Law Review* 48:427.

Garbut, R. G. 1962. "SPCC Founded Nine Years after ASPCA." *Virgin Islands Daily News,* July 24. http://news.google.com/newspapers?nid=757&dat=19620724&id=2HJhAAAAIBAJ&sjid=qUQDAAAAIBAJ&pg=6410,3570876.

Graglia, L. A. 1996. "Church of the Lukumi Babalu Aye: Of Animal Sacrifice and Religious Persecution." *Georgetown Law Journal* 85:1.

Hall v. Florida. 572 U.S. ___ (2013).

Halsall, P. 1998. "Modern History Sourcebook: John Kocke (1632-1704), Some Thoughts concerning Education, 1692." *Fordham University.* http://www.fordham.edu/halsall/mod/1692locke-education.html.

Harvard Law School. 2013. "A Conversation with Justice Stephen Breyer." *YouTube.com,* October 4. https://www.youtube.com/watch?v=i9RPOQjlGKQ.

Hawaii Revised Statutes § 291C-124 (2008).

Hayton, B. 2012. "Driving School for Dogs in New Zealand." *BBC News,* October 4. http://www.bbc.com/news/world-asia-20614593.

Honeycutt v. State Farm Fire & Casualty Co. 890 So.2d 756 (2nd Cir. 2004).

Huss, R. J. 2002. "Valuing Man's and Woman's Best Friend: The Moral and Legal Status of Companion Animals." *Marquette Law Review* 86:47.

Ishmael, P. 2012. "Antonin Scalia and Stephen Breyer Debate the Constitution." *YouTube.com,* May 14. https://www.youtube.com/watch?v=_4n8gOUzZ8I.

Kerr, J. S., M. Bernstein, A. Schwoerke, M. D. Strugar, and J. S. Goodman. 2013. "A Slave by Any Other Name Is Still a Slave: The Tilikum Case and

Application of the Thirteenth Amendment to Nonhuman Animals." *Animal Law* 19:221.

Lawrence v. Texas. 539 U.S. 558 (2003).

Leiter, B. 2013. "The Boundaries of the Moral (and Legal) Community." *Alabama Law Review* 64:511.

Minor, S. 2014. "Sheriff: Drunk Man Says Dog Drove Him to Store." *WPBF*, July 7. http://www.wpbf.com/sheriff-drunk-man-says-dog-drove-him-to-store/26823920#!bbUqJl.

MSN. 2013. "Owners Appeal after Conn. Court Classifies Horses as Vicious Animals." September 25. http://now.msn.com/horses-are-vicious-animals-rules-connecticut-court.

Paek, E. 2003. "Fido Seeks Full Membership in the Family: Dismantling the Property Classification of Companion Animals by Statute." *University of Hawai'i Law Review* 25:481–524.

Prince v. Massachusetts. 321 U.S. 158 (1944).

Rosen, Y. 2011. "Bald Eagles Attack Post Office at Alaska Port." *Reuters*, June 14. http://www.reuters.com/article/2011/06/15/us-alaska-eagles-postoffice-idUSTRE75E07P20110615.

Rosenheim, M. K., F. E. Zimring, D. S. Tanenhaus, and B. Dohrn, eds. 2002. *A Century of Juvenile Justice.* Chicago, IL: University of Chicago Press.

Satz, A. B. 2009. "Animals as Vulnerable Subjects: Beyond Interest-Convergence, Hierarchy, and Property." *Animal Law* 16:65.

Smith, V. R. 2009. "The Law and Feral Cats." *Journal of Animal Law & Ethics* 3:7.

Stanley v. Georgia. 394 U.S. 557 (1969).

Tamen, M. 1998. "Kinds of Persons, Kinds of Rights, Kinds of Bodies." *Cardozo Studies in Law and Literature* 10:1–32.

Tamir, M. 2014. "Law and Yoga." *Journal of Law and Social Deviance* 7:1–79.

U.S. v. Williams. 553 U.S. 285 (2008).

Wisch, R. F. 2006. "Table of State Humane Slaughter Laws." *Animal Legal & Historical Center.* http://www.animallaw.info/articles/ovusstatehumaneslaughtertable.htm.

2

Violence as Entertainment

Introduction

"Entertainment" is aesthetic or emotional amusement or appreciation directed at an activity or phenomenon. Entertainment is a multibillion dollar industry. For thousands of years animals have been used to entertain people. With the institutionalization of different cultural values and new definitions of "humaneness," some forms of entertainment are no longer considered to be entertaining and may be criminal. Yet, animals continue to be involved in a variety of entertainment industries. Some legal forms have been described by animal welfarists as "cruel," and the legality of certain industries and practices is often challenged. Other activities undergo an abundance of internal regulation to authoritatively rebut accusations of cruelty. Explanations for why animals involved in entertainment are treated differently under the law include legal ambiguity, lack of proof of injury or neglect, unenforceability of some international policies, breeding or hunting practices, loopholes, jurisdictional variations, species-specific polices, and other factors.

Illegal Violence in Legal Entertainment

The vast majority of jurisdictions around the world permit animals to be used for entertainment. The most prevalent uses of captive animals in entertainment are within zoos, (se)aquariums, circuses, safaris, rodeos, and the like. Animals may be employed performers, may be captive, or may be free-roaming depending on legal requirements and licensure. Animals are routinely victimized by violence in entertainment industries. Violence may be designed to make animals perform, or violence may results incidentally from animals' habitation or occupation of entertainment establishments. Unfortunately, undercover surveillance and governmental investigations fail to result in criminal charges against the majority of abusers, who remain undetected because their illegal violence is couched within legal activities.

Animals may become the victims of violence at zoos. Each year zoo employees around the world are charged with cruelty or in connection with abuse or killing of animals. In some cases violence may be incidentally related to entertainment, but prioritization of entertainment establishments' needs of the over an animal's welfare evidences patently callous attitudes toward animals and violence that frequently result in criminal behavior. For example, in Virginia, Meghan Mogensen, the daughter of a zoo owner, was sentenced to a month in prison for drowning a wallaby named Parmesan (Roberts 2013). Parmesan had suffered a simple eye injury that failed to heal and worsened in severity. The original injury was sustained by the wallaby while he played in his pen. When the injury required for Parmesan's eye to be removed, the zoo owner ordered him to be destroyed rather than be treated. Mogensen, who served as the director, drowned Parmesan in a bucket of water and then discarded his body in the trash. When questioned by authorities, Mogensen claimed to have euthanized Parmesan humanely. However, the zoo was not licensed to use the chemical that she claimed to have used, and a necropsy proved that Parmesan suffered injuries resulting from drowning. In several other instances, the US Department of Agriculture has investigated the same zoo owner, who owns several other animal enterprises (Greenwood 2012). He has been fined $10,000 for violating the Animal Welfare Act (AWA) at least twice and was fined nearly $3,000 on another occasion. Parmesan's death was not an isolated act of violence but is part of a greater pattern of neglect and abuse.

Under the auspices of entertainment, animals easily become victims of violence in circuses ("Circuses" 2013; Sinpetru 2013). Over the years circuses have notoriously abused animals, especially elephants. Laws that regulate treatment of exotic animals and cruelty statutes prevent circus trainers from intentionally inflicting pain on exotic animals, but no governmental agency monitors animal training in circuses. In undercover surveillance videos large cats and bears are dragged, beaten, and prodded, while chimpanzees are kicked and swatted with riding crops. Elephants, who are featured in countless mainstream and roadside circuses around the world, are commonly electrocuted, whipped, chained, and beaten. Elephant trainers have repeatedly been documented hitting elephants on their bodies and faces; piercing and prodding elephants with large, sharp bull hooks; and threatening animals with other weapons. Animals at zoos often suffer from neglect, but the intentional infliction of violence to gain submission highlights the use of illegal means to produce legal forms of entertainment.

Though violent training methods may be commonplace throughout the industry, when abuse is documented, circuses inevitably distance themselves from employees who are caught using violence, or they fully deny accusations by claiming that the video evidence does not show animals being beaten, but instead shows a trainer tripping or accidentally striking an animal. They have also evaded justice by claiming that undercover videos were created in cahoots with disgruntled employees or with undercover activists posing as circus employees. In jurisdictions allowing private prosecution, for example, the United Kingdom, animal welfare groups have brought private actions against trainers (*Telegraph* 2011). In other jurisdictions the government has prosecuted cruelty among trainers. The abuse of animals in circuses is so routine that some jurisdictions have completely banned the use of any animals in the circus. For example, in India, Bosnia and Herzegovina, Cyprus, Greece, and Costa Rica, use of animals in circuses is completely forbidden (ADI 2013; Mathew 2013). Throughout the United Kingdom, United States, and other jurisdictions, dozens of local laws criminalize use of any animals in circuses.

Horse and dog racing are legal forms of entertainment that routinely participate in illegal cruelty toward animals (Interstate Horse Racing Act, 15 U.S.C. 57 §§ 3001–3007, 1978). Animals are not actors and do not benefit from much industry oversight apart from that of state-contracted veterinarians, who monitor animals for cruelty and doping violations (Grimm 2014). Animals often become injured in the course of training and racing. Animals may have lower age limits before which they should not race; trainers may wait until just after animals' bones are sufficiently developed, then train and race animals against best practices. Horses and dogs are frequently pumped with pain medication and steroids that have the effect of pushing animals beyond healthy limits. On average, twenty-four horses and several dogs die weekly at American race tracks. In one case a man was discovered with the bodies of two thousand Florida racetrack greyhounds on his property. The man had been paid a total of $20,000 to kill and bury the dogs. Racetracks in Florida are not required to assume an enforcement role on behalf of the state.

The government's main interest in regulating horse racing relates to gambling, not animal cruelty. Animals are often doped just prior to racing, and drugs may become undetectable by the ends of races, as veterinarians usually screen animals for drugs after races. Gamblers are unaware of which animals are doped prior to placing their bets.

Trainers who dope may not be suspended from the sport for years after the discovery of an offense due to lengthy procedures (Shipley 2012). Trainers and owners may not fear misdemeanor-level charges for doping because prize money is usually in the thousands (Miller 2012). The state attempts to create fairness in betting but does not proactively attempt to eliminate animal abuse by reforming doping laws and imposing stiffer regulatory oversight. Federal and state felony fraud charges may be greater deterrents but only indirectly protect animals (FBI 2013). In 2011 the Interstate Horseracing Improvement Act was introduced, but the bill died after being referred to a committee. The proposed law would have banned administration of medication on race day and prohibited horses from racing while medicated or doped. It also proposed stiffer punishments for cheaters and increased safeguards for fair drug testing. The legislation aimed to improve the horse-racing business but included no reforms to benefit animals directly, for example, anticruelty measures.

Legal Violence as Entertainment

Real violence can legally be a form of entertainment. Though humans engage in violence, for example, boxing, they consent and are protected by professional and legal regulations. Animals do not consent, yet the government regulates violence against animals. Violence against animals as entertainment is regulated by various governmental agencies, state laws, and local regulations depending on the activity and the kind of animals involved (Chandola 2002). The majority of state laws are not designed to regulate entertainment *per se*, and quite frequently, violent entertainment is an exception to wildlife regulations or cruelty statutes. Most regulation and enforcement occurs at the municipal level. Municipalities must enforce state laws, but they enforce other regulations that do not oppose state laws.

Violence against certain animals, for example, fish, as a form of entertainment is largely unregulated. In most states and municipalities, fish are neither protected nor considered to be "animals." and yet, in other jurisdictions, fishing is an exception to cruelty laws. Under the Fish and Wildlife Act, every citizen and resident has the right to fish for pleasure, enjoyment, and recreation 1956). The most common limitations on fishing are quantity, season, species, and size. Certain species of fish, especially endangered or threatened fish, are protected (Graves, Mosman, and Rogers 2012; Nowicki 1999). For example, shark-finning is banned in certain states. The manner in which a person may handle most fish is unregulated despite the law's willingness to protect so many other vertebrates (Challener 2010). For example, fish may be pierced, harpooned, dragged, strangled, suffocated, pummeled, bludgeoned, shot, gutted, or consumed alive (Shafer 2012).

Except on federal lands, state agencies manage wildlife as natural resources (Vesilind 2013). The Endangered Species Act (ESA) and the Marine Mammal Protection Act (MMPA) regulate wildlife to prevent extinction of certain animals (16 U.S.C. §§ 1531–1544, 2013; 16 U.S.C. §§ 1361–1421h, 2013). ESA's interest in in ecological sustainability is enforced even though legislators originally enacted in response to a brutal and bloody roundup of numerous Californian orcas that resulted in the captivity of Lolita, an orca currently living at the Miami Seaquarium (Welch 2010; Schmahmann and Polacheck 1995; Madeline 2000). Unlike the Animal Welfare Act (AWA), these acts do not mention animals' pain and suffering as legislative reasons for curbing human practices. However, under the AWA fish are not considered to be "animals" even though debate still exists about whether fish experience pain because some studies have shown that they do (Bryant 2007; Reppy 2005). Yet, some jurisdictions, like California, extend anticruelty protection to endangered species or otherwise protected fish (Nowicki 1999). Restrictions on manner, quantity, and location of hunting are more common than proscriptions on fishing. However, some jurisdictions do carefully regulate the manner in which people may entertain themselves with the execution of animals. For example, deer may be hunted, but they may not be rammed and run over with snowmobiles (Vesilind 2013). Entertainment exceptions to cruelty statutes do not necessarily create a free-for-all that permits humans to unleash every cruel fantasy upon wild animals.

Legal hunting is not restricted to excursions into nature involving game and guns. Various jurisdictions allow a wide range of activities. Popular, lawful forms of entertainment include small game hunting, for example, killing turkey, quail, squirrels, rabbits, hares, raccoons, and coyotes with different kinds of guns or ammunition; shooting turtles with bullets or arrows; hunting using dogs; and falconry, which involves releasing trained raptors to hunt small game (DEC 2013). Captive hunting occurs on a game ranch or preserve (Graves, Mosman, and Rogers 2012). Animals are bred into captivity and fed by groundskeepers. Patrons pay for the experience of killing a tamed or semi-tamed exotic animal without having to hunt the animal. Many shooting preserves only charge for animals that are slaughtered, not for the rounds fired or opportunity to shoot. More than one thousand hunting preserves, mainly located in Texas, are in operation throughout the United States, though the majority of states ban this form of hunting. Many compare captive hunting to Texan remote or internet hunting. During Internet hunting an animal is restricted to an acre of land, and customers shoot the animal using a camera and computer (Humane Society 2013). Animals are trained to approach a feeding station at certain times each day. When customers pay, they can shoot the animal using virtual crosshairs at the appointed time. Then the animal is stuffed, mounted, and mailed to the customer.

Animals may be legally released into the wild to be hunted. The use of "clay pigeon" disks has largely replaced the practice of launching live pigeons (Present 2012). To this day, some shoots still involve trapping and launching pigeons into the air to be skillfully shot so that they land in a designated scoring zone. Besides the archaic use of pigeons as objects, a problem arises when pigeons are maimed but not killed. Injured pigeons may scamper into the wild and live with injuries. When animal control officers in Pennsylvania attempted to initiate cruelty charges because partially maimed pigeons' necks were being broken by hand at shooting ranges, the court ruled that animal control had no power to force prosecutors to prosecute. Only the State of Pennsylvania allows the release of pigeons for hunting, and the court in that case described the practice of launching pigeons as "truly shocking." Yet, wild pigeons are commonly hunted for entertainment, and urban pigeons may even be hunted for sport or food in metropolitan areas provided that weapon and hunting laws are not broken (Huffington Post 2012).

Pigeons legally provide another form of entertainment, though the amount of violence involved in debatable. Pigeons are entered into all-weather races that span hundreds of miles at approximately forty-five miles per hour (Shafer 2012). According to PETA, this sport is violent because it exhausts pigeons and because they are exposed to predatory birds. A winning bird can be sold for hundreds of thousands of dollars. Gambling practices involved may be illegal, but the potential violence inflicted is likely to be fully legal according to state and federal guidelines. Mike Tyson's TV show *Taking on Tyson* has brought some attention to the sport. The show demonstrates that violence toward animals, including racing, hunting, and fishing, may be aired on television for entertainment. Violence toward animals is not only legal because it relates to the procurement of food, but it is legal because some forms of violence are deeply rooted in culture (Coleman 2009; *Daily Mail* 2008; Nagulapalli 2009).

For the most part, rodeos are a traditional and legal form of entertainment that is predicated on inflicting violence upon domesticated farm animals (ALDF 2013; Chandola 2002). In fact, rodeo is the official state sport of Wyoming, South Dakota, and Texas. The AWA does not extend protection to animals in rodeos because they are competitive events involving cattle. By and large, state cruelty statutes do not outright bar the use of animals in rodeos. Thus, under most state laws, when it would be illegal to rope a puppy, it would be legal to rope a calf. The Professional Rodeo Cowboy Association (PRCA) establishes guidelines for rodeos. In some jurisdictions a licensed large-animals veterinarian must oversee the use of animals in a rodeo even though the American Veterinary Medical Association does not condone the PRCA's treatment of animals. The lawfulness of violence in rodeos ranges jurisdictionally. For example, varying laws may ban use of certain apparatus or equipment like the following: electric prods; whips; twisted wire snaffles; unpadded bucking straps; unpadded flank straps; wire tie-downs; clubs; sharpened spurs; irritating constrictors around animals' sexual organs; injurious chemicals or mechanisms; bristle or tack burs; or prods with nails, tacks, and sharp points (ALDF 2013; Chandola 2002; Larson 1998). Physically injuring, tormenting, or causing suffering may also be prohibited under rodeo or cruelty statutes. Animals are most seriously injured by roping, tripping, wild animal roundup, and wrestling maneuvers. Some of these activities might be banned in certain jurisdictions even though they are regulated by the PRCA. Special gear has been utilized to reduce injury or comply with the law in certain jurisdictions. For example, breakaway ropes might be used so that roped calves do not suddenly stop and fall. When animals are injured, veterinarians have complete authority. If the veterinarian suspects that an illegal activity, that is, cruelty, occurred, then an animal control officer must be notified in writing. While rodeos are legal throughout most of the country, they are partially or completely banned in a number of states and municipalities.

Cockfighting

Cockfighting is thousands of years old (Humane Society 2013; Hirsch 2003). In Southeast Asia more than three thousand years ago, jungle birds were pitted against each other in death matches. Human fascination with birds' ferocity perpetuates through the sport of cock-fighting in Southeast Asia, East Asia, India, Spain, Latin America, North America, and US territories (Hirsch 2003; Nagulapalli 2009). In the United States cockfighting became popular in the early 1800s but was already being banned across states by the end of that century (Nagulapalli 2009). Historical figures such as George Washington, Andrew Jackson, Abraham Lincoln, and Benjamin Franklin openly participated in cockfighting in contravention of their contemporaries' disparagement of the sport (Coleman 2009; Hirsch 2003; Nagulapalli 2009). Cockfighting has been banned for so long in the United States that to some it now seems as if US cockfighting laws disproportionately affect immigrants (Nagulapalli 2009).

Annually around the world during cockfighting season, which typically spans from Thanksgiving to July 4, people invest around one billion dollars on betting whether roosters can claw each other to death (Burnett 2013). A debate exists about whether cockfighting is lucrative. In some cultures cockfighting is fueled by passion, and cock-fighters claim to participate because they are animal lovers (Coleman 2009). Yet, in other jurisdictions cockfighters claim to be motivated by substantial rewards (Burnett 2013). The sport sometimes is tied into drugs, prostitution, and other forms of gambling. These activities connect much more money to the sport. Because the majority of cockfighting is underground worldwide, calculating revenue has been very difficult, and the amount of criminal activity surrounding the sport in speculative.

Cockfighting mainly involves roosters pecking and clawing at each other. Back spurs are located behind the roosters' front claws and are lethally sharp (Hirsch 2003). Sometimes people add gear to the roost-ers' claws to make the roosters even more lethal. Frequently, people strap gaffs to roosters' legs. Gaffs are razor blades designed to be worn by the birds. With or without use of the gaffs, birds commonly suffer from punctured lungs, broken bones, and punctured eyes. Abandoned or seized cocks often need to be euthanized because of the severity of their injuries (Grissom 2010). Brutal injuries stand in stark contrast to well-groomed cocks entering the ring. Cocks are fed healthy diets, often have the bottom of their bodies shaved, and are suntanned in order to maximize their physical beauty (Coto 2013). Serious injuries do not necessarily cause a match to stop or disqualify a bird. A winner is declared if an opponent dies, runs away, or does not get up after one minute. Cocks are not generally violent, but they are fiercely competitive, and they are bred and trained to fight.

The Animal Fighting Prohibition Enforcement Act is federal legislation that criminalizes cockfighting within interstate or foreign commerce (Ortiz 2010). This federal legislation makes an exception for cockfighting occurring legally within states. Currently, cockfighting is legal in US territories but is illegal in the District of Columbia and all fifty states (Coto 2012; Humane Society 2013). In most states cockfighting is a felony, and related activities are also illegal. These include attending or marketing fights, or possessing a bird, equipment, or a cockpit for fighting (Humane Society 2013; Hirsch 2003). In addition to cockfighting laws, prosecutors rely on cruelty statutes and gambling statutes to prosecute cockfighting (Hirsch 2003; Burnett 2012). Local law enforcement agencies work closely with animal welfare agencies that typically go undercover to track and expose fights (Grissom 2010). One serious limitation for law enforcement has been that some *botanicas*, which are stores that sell religious supplies, secretly house cockfights. Stores claim to sell birds for religious sacrifice but operate underground as rings. Gathering evidence against these establishments is more difficult because merchandise, patrons, activities, and profits are shrouded by legitimate religious activities.

Dogfighting

On August 20, 2007, Atlanta Falcons star quarterback Michael Vick was convicted by the federal government of conspiracy to travel in interstate commerce for dogfighting (Shafer 2012). Vick bred, trained, fought, and killed dogs for sport and entertainment. Vick's shocking crimes included participation in the slaughter of eight low-performance dogs and training of thousands of dogs over the course of thirty years. Bad Newz Kennels, run in Smithfield, Virginia, was likely named after Vick's hometown, Newport News, where Vick claims that he struggled to avoid street gangs as a youth. When authorities searched Vick's properties, they discovered sixty-six dogs, rape stands, treadmills, and pry bars. They also found bloodstains that attested to Vick's involvement in this lethal form of animal entertainment.

Before dogs fought each other for human entertainment, dogs attacked and killed other animals (Ortiz 2010). As early as the twelfth century, dogs fought bulls, bears, lions, and elephants to entertain all classes of people (Coleman 2009). In the eighteenth and nineteenth centuries, British working classes replaced blood sports, like bull baiting, with dogfighting (Ortiz 2010). Confined by their environments, they could host dogfights in small quarters indoors but were unable to accommodate larger animals. Dog breeders, looking to capitalize on gambling, crossbred and refined bulldog and terrier mixes to develop the modern fighting dog, the pit bull. The dog became popular as a farm dog, guard dog, and companion because pit bulls are willing to fight fearlessly as well as reengage despite being injured or overpowered. Because England criminalized dogfighting, links between gambling and dogfighting became clandestine in the United States not long after the pit bull became a breed. Despite its long-standing illegality, the industry takes in around half a billion dollars annually.

The lure of fast money, the exhibition of masculinity, and the benefits of criminal brotherhood are some of the main reasons that people engage in dogfighting. Dogmen view their organizations as fraternities, which are organized by hierarchies. Their hierarchies overlap with other organized criminal activities, like illegal drug and weapons trafficking. Dogmen maintain a group psychology that not only justifies cruelty but imposes demands for loyalty and acceptance from the master onto dogs. This psychological demand aids in transforming dogs into killers. For example, pitmen prey on the dogs' desires to belong and please; pitmen engage in a diabolical dance as they shift positions throughout dogfights so that they can remain in a dog's view at all times. Their emotional and physical presence motivates their dog to fight ruthlessly.

There are three types of dogfighters: professional dogman, hobbyists, and street fighters. Professionals run national and international games with high stakes. Breeding and betting are extremely selective and secretive. Specific information is critical to these operations and is a source of bonding for members. Professionals must be informed about dogs' bloodlines, fighting history, and training. Remote fight locations can remain secret until hours beforehand, and individual prizes can reach a hundred thousand dollars or more. Hobbyists are regional enthusiasts who occupy abandoned buildings in urban settings. Finally, street fighters demonstrate little preparation and may engage in unfettered, spontaneous fighting; they are interested in developing a "street" reputation and may go to extremes to pursue their goal. Street fighters might throw two pitbulls into the trunk of a car, go for a drive, and bet on dogs' fates. They may also imprison several dogs in a room with only a small amount of food and bet on which dog will survive. Professionals and hobbyists breed dogs for fighting ability, while streetfighters are likely to breed dogs for size because larger dogs look more intimidating to other gang members. Street fighting is so common that the Humane Society of the United States (HSUS) offers dogfighting and cruelty training programs to members of the criminal justice system, including animal control officers, throughout the nation (Ortiz 2010).

The federal government criminalized dogfighting in 1976 through an amendment of the Animal Welfare Act (AWA). The Animal Fighting Prohibition Enforcement Act, enacted in 2007, also criminalizes fighting that spans interstate or foreign commerce or uses the US mail. No two animals are allowed to fight for sport, commerce, or wager, unless the activity is considered to be hunting. Though the bloodsport-oriented philosophy behind fighting and hunting is the same in the broadest sense, the line drawn by the law could not be brighter. The bright line rule, as it stands, is that animals cannot kill or be killed for entertainment or sport, except during hunting. Though federal legislation succinctly bans dogfighting and was supported by several hundred law enforcement agencies and animal welfare groups, the provisions have virtually gone unenforced since 1976. Under state laws dogfighting is a felony in every state. In forty-eight states, all except Montana and Hawaii, attending dogfights is also a crime. Possessing dogs for fighting is also a crime in every state, but certain laws may not sufficiently cover every kind of animal involved in dogfights.

In addition to pit bulls, dogfighting training frequently involves bait dogs. Bait dogs are stolen, stray, or weak dogs that are used to train pit bulls. They do not pose a threat to pit bulls as they are being trained because bait dogs are much weaker or more docile. Bait dogs are permitted to be attacked repeatedly until they are ultimately killed. Bait dogs are bitten again and again throughout their lives, develop scars on their faces and bodies, and experience extreme terror over the course of their short lives as they are subjected to torture. Pit bulls can be kind, friendly, vivacious, happy, and loyal dogs who are not naturally inclined to kill bait dogs, but who do so to please or to avoid failure, that is, execution. Dogs who are injured will be shot, drowned, hanged, electrocuted, or otherwise put down inhumanely. Very frequently, bait dogs and pit bulls are abandoned by dogfighters. Dogs might be abandoned when gang members move out of the area, operations are shut down or are under investigation, natural disasters occur, dogs require veterinary care, and a host of other reasons. Sometimes rescued pit bulls can be adopted into good homes, but unfortunately, they are routinely destroyed because no one wants to adopt them, because agencies fear that they are dangerous, or because agencies suspect that the dogs would otherwise be adopted by predatory gang members for dogfighting.

Pit bulls are banned in some jurisdictions, like Ontario, Canada, and Miami-Dade County, Florida (Hanson 2006). These bans weigh against and in favor of pit bulls' survival and happiness. Weighing against the breed is society's misconception that pit bulls are aggressive. People develop prejudices against pit bulls that may make these dogs seem less sympathetic and loveable, more difficult to adopt, and more vulnerable to labeling and destruction. Where street fighting is rampant, pit bulls may behave aggressively on the streets, effectively validating negative stereotypes. In a Detroit neighborhood, for example, street fighting was so prevalent that it became too dangerous for postal workers to deliver mail and service was temporarily suspended (Ortiz 2010). This sort of scenario could easily lead to a ban and the extermination of numerous dogs. On the other hand, breed-specific bans can have the effect of reducing pit bulls' chances of becoming involved in dogfighting in certain communities. Bans may prevent gangs from organizing massive fighting rings in areas where ownership of pit bulls is illegal or blatantly engaging in street fighting at hot spots. Though some might argue that criminalizing ownership only forces fights further underground and contributes to the reduction of humane living conditions for dogs, overall the bans are designed to increase deterrence. Unfortunately, when bans take effect, jurisdictions may not "grandfather in" pit bulls living in the community, unless the pit bulls are working as certified service animals (Neil 2013). In some cases people who are not disabled but who rely on pit bulls for emotional support may experience severe trauma because they are forced to part with a friend and face the loss of an emotional bolster (Hanson 2006). The bans, no doubt, uproot and traumatize some stable and loved dogs, despite the government's best intentions to protect the breed at large. For this reason, and reasons relating to due process, the American Bar Association and President Barack Obama have taken the position that breed-specific legislation, that is, pit bull bans, are inappropriate (Greenwood 2013). In addition to the problems that these bans create, breed-specific legislation has demonstrated little positive effect on public safety or the reduction of cruelty.

In 1999 the US government passed a federal law prohibiting the sale, possession, or production of all videos that depicted the torture of animals (18 U.S.C. § 48, 1999). The government's rationale was that because dogfighting and other similar tortures are cruel, memorialization of and participation in such events ought to be illegal. The problem with the law was that the government does not have the power to ban speech, for example, videos, unless it has a compelling reason (*U.S. v. Stevens*, 2010). When a defendant was convicted of selling dogfighting videos in 2009, he claimed that the government could not outlaw the videos simply because they depict cruelty. The US Supreme Court agreed and struck the law prohibiting the sale of dogfighting videos. They struck the law for two reasons. First, the law, which was very broadly written, prohibited some types of lawful speech. Second, at the time that the law was struck, cruelty to animals was not a class of speech that could be restricted, like other classes of restricted speech such as child pornography or obscenity. The government argued that illegal and extreme cruelty is a compelling reason to ban the videos even if cruelty is not specifically a class of speech that can be restricted. The US Supreme Court somewhat agreed but still struck the law, noting that cruelty and videos of cruelty are different. The day after the law was struck, Congress initiated legislation specifically written to ban crusher films. That legislation became law, but the law only bans pornographic depictions of cruelty, which constitute obscenity. The law lists the prevention of cruelty to animals as a compelling government interest that qualifies the restriction on free speech independently of obscenity bans, but this area of law remains to be tested further (Malisow 2013). Irrespective of speech bans, animal welfare groups have invested resources into discovering the identities of perpetrators of cruelty in these films and turning over offenders' identities to the police. People identified as participating in dogfighting or other acts of cruelty on film have been prosecuted for cruelty.

Though the slightly gray area created by US Supreme Court seems to sidetrack anticruelty efforts in the area of dogfighting, one major development in favor of animal protection resulted from Vick's sentence. Often when pit bulls are seized by the government, they are euthanized. Dogs who were confiscated from Vick received veterinary care and were adopted through animal rescue organizations (Chiesa 2008a). Vick struck a deal with prosecutors that included restitution to the government and welfare agencies for the cost of caring for dogs and humanely euthanizing those who could not be rescued. The required restitution included all costs for long-term care, totaling nearly one million dollars. Vick agreed to pay the money because the government's plea deal required compensation for victims. Those organizations assuming care for the dogs would have been victimized by the expenses had Vick not repaid their costs. Yet, by the same token, the dogs who received care were restored by Vick because they were victimized by him. Restitution is normally reserved for persons under the law. In this case, pit bulls received the benefits of restitution. The terms of Vick's plea deal may implicitly recognize dogs as victims of dogfighting on a new and improved level.

Bullfighting

Bullfighting is a sport in which a human fights a bull for the entertainment of spectators (Coleman 2009). In some senses, bullfighting differs from other animal fights in which both participants are animals. Because one participant is human, bullfighting is much more like lawful activities, for example, fishing or hunting. In other senses, bullfighting can be considered to be crueler than animal fights because bullfighters are disproportionately powerful and virtually guaranteed to win each time.

Fighting bulls are thoroughbred animals that live organically and graze on ranches with other bulls (Velez 2010). Calves are weaned and separated from their mothers at eight months old. A few months later calves are branded. When calves are two years old, they will be repeatedly tested by the rancher for potential bravery. Between the ages of four and six years, bulls will be chosen for fighting. Chosen animals are prodded from the field into a narrow transport crate. They are driven by truck directly to the bullring by a person with whom the bull in unacquainted. The bull is bated from the crate into a dark holding pen until it is his turn to fight and die. When the bullpen door is opened, the bull is released from the dark pen. The bull is forced to run directly into a lit, loud, full, and unfamiliar arena (Fusfeld 2007). The entire event is choreographed and quite predictable (Rappaport 2008). The fight will be an orchestration of prancing and pageantry woven to tell a tale of masculine poise and power (Asay 2003; *Miller v. Civil City of South Bend*, 1990). It is designed to appear as a torturous ballet and a blitzkrieg on the bull.

The crowd witnesses pomp, antiquity, violence, danger, and grace in a bullfight. The bull experiences the sight of a horse and a man, called a *picador*, charging toward him as the man jams and then plucks a sharp stick from the bull's neck (Fusfeld 2007). Another horseback rider repeats the infliction, and blood draw from the bull serves to dramatically foreshadow the bull's death to the audience (Velez 2010). The bull charges, and a man, called a *banderillo*, impales the bull's shoulders with wooden *banderillas* (Fusfeld 2007; Velez 2010). For the audience the wooden spears are decorative and culturally commemorative. The matador gallantly waves a cloth in a series of *suertes* that hypnotize the audience and tease the bull (Velez 2010). The onslaught of injuries causes the bull's head to droop, which signals to the matadors and the audience that the *suerte suprema*, the moment for execution, has arrived. Due to exhaustion and blood loss, the bull suffers from blindness at this point in the sport. The matador kills the bull by extending a sword over the bull's horns and into the bull's heart between his cervical vertebrae to server his aorta (Fusfeld 2007; Velez 2010). If the matador accidentally punctures the bull's lungs, then blood will flow from the animal's face (Velez 2010). Approximately ten thousand bulls are killed this way each year. Following their deaths their bodies are certified by a veterinarian, and their corpses are butchered for human consumption.

Under federal law bullfighting is illegal in the United States. For those who insist on synthesizing lawful versions of animal fighting, bloodless bullfights have been attempted. Bloodless bullfights involve the use of Velcro at the ends of *banderillas* and other ceremonial adaptations (Velez 2010). These implementations supposedly reduce the elegance of bullfighting to the status of a glorified rodeo, and matadors have been reluctant to participate because the bulls retain their strength and pose a much greater danger. The danger in traditional fights must not be great since Spanish records show that only eight matadors have died from bull goring since the 1800s.

Bloodless fights have disguised traditional bullfights in the United States (Velez 2010). Undercover investigations have demonstrated the illegal use of *banderillas* at some supposedly bloodless events. Portuguese religious customs that involve bullfighting have been kept alive through the bloodless fights, especially in California. When undercover surveillance has demonstrated that cruelty is occurring at bloodless fights, prosecutors have been reluctant to prosecute church officials. In general, the bloodless fights have attempted to strike a balance between old-school tradition and US law. However, animal slaughter laws, which are designed to be compatible with animal cruelty laws, do not preclude the legal slaughter of bulls immediately following bloodless fights. Killing that occurs outside the bullring is consistent with the Portuguese bullfighting style, and thus compliance with bloodless rules does not seem to be the sole motive for killing the bull after the fight outside the arena (Chiesa 2008b).

The relationship between bullfighting bans and decreased interest in bullfighting is not unidirectional (Velez 2010). As people lose interest, bans become easier to enforce, and the reduction of access to fights causes the number of interested persons to continue dwindling. Internationally, bans have widely resulted from localized efforts, though animal welfarists, tourists, and governmental agencies have placed political pressure on nations where the sport remains popular. Under the Treaty of Amsterdam, European nations are encouraged but not required to adopt uniform animal welfare legislation (Donnellan 2007). In some regards, like animal testing or genetic modification bans, Europeans have been forerunners for anticruelty policies, but in this area of the law, Europeans have been reluctant to fully ban this traditional form of entertainment.

Some Spanish and Mexican regions have banned bullfighting, while other countries, like China, have intentionally stymied proliferation of the sport but have not gone so far as to criminalize it (Velez 2010). In Roman Catholic, Latin American nations, like Peru, Mexico, Venezuela, Ecuador, and Columbia, traditional bullfighting is popular, and bulls are killed within the ring (CAS International 2013). Bans in Spain have been culturally monumental and somewhat controversial. Some have suggested that the bans were designed to encourage tourism and reduce controversy created by animal welfarists, which has been the government's motivation in China. However, others have argued that the bans authentically reflect Spain's leadership position in animal welfare. Certain Spanish regions may have banned bullfighting because of their evolving respect for animals—which, surprisingly, has included granting the legal status of personhood to primates (Chiesa 2008b; Favre 2010). Though there are no wild apes in Spain, Spain was the first nation in the world to take this huge step. Thus, perhaps Spaniards are focused on the criminalization of bullfighting out of concern for bulls. In neighboring France the Constitutional Council recently declared bullfighting to be fully legal nationwide, though regional bans remain in effect (BBC 2012). The council's reasoning was that bullfighting is not a crime because it does not harm humans' constitutional rights.

Crusher Laws

Crusher films are pornographic films in which animals are crushed to provide the crusher or the viewer with sexual gratification. Nonhuman mammals, birds, reptiles, or amphibians are intentionally crushed, burned, drowned, suffocated, impaled, tortured, or seriously injured by tools, for example, stiletto heels, knives, or fists. Some of the animals may die instantly, but many animals wriggle in fear and agony as their bones and organs are defiled and disfigured.

For more than two decades, these films have been the subject of legal battles. Most recently, crusher films have been banned because they constitute obscenity. Congress and President Obama outlawed crusher films in the Animal Crush Video Prohibition Act of 2010 (H.R. 5566, 2010). Any interstate sale, marketing, advertising, exchange, and distribution of crusher films is illegal because they are obscene. In all fifty states and the District of Columbia, intentional acts of extreme animal cruelty, such as intentionally crushing, burning, drowning, suffocating, or impaling animals for no socially redeeming purpose, for example, science or art, is illegal. When outlawing these films, the government stated that it has a compelling interest in preventing intentional acts of extreme animal cruelty. Creation, sale, distribution, advertising, marketing, and exchange of crusher videos relates to extreme animal cruelty. The law states that the government's compelling interest authorizes it to place the necessary speech restrictions on these films to prevent the sort of abuse inflicted in these films.

The government also has the power to prevent people from producing or distributing obscenity. Obscenity is any depiction that appeals to a prurient interest in sex; is patently offensive; and lacks serious literary, artistic, political, or scientific value (Cusack 2014). Crusher films are defined by the government to be obscene. Because these videos constitute obscenity, the perpetrators of the animal cruelty typically remain anonymous and therefore cannot be brought to justice in the appropriate jurisdiction. Thus, for several reasons, the government has criminalized crusher films.

Crusher videos cannot be distributed, sold, marketed, advertised, exchanged, created for, or distributed in interstate commerce or foreign commerce in tangible or digital form. US law is written to have jurisdiction over foreigners who intend to transport the videos to the United States, its territories, or its possessions online or through the mail. However, crusher films are produced in other countries, for example, the Philippines. Thus, the US government cannot regulate obscenity in other countries if obscene material is not intended for distribution to the United States (PETA 2013). Violation of US federal law carries a penalty of up to seven years in prison. Depictions of customary veterinary or agricultural husbandry practices, like artificial insemination; slaughter of animals for food; or hunting, trapping, or fishing are specifically excluded from prosecution under the Animal Crush Video Prohibition Act of 2010.

Despite the government's desire to completely eliminate production of and distribution of crusher films, one caveat in obscenity jurisprudence may make it legal for US audiences to view crusher films. Under US law merely possessing obscenity is not a crime (*Stanley v. Georgia*, 1969). The definition of "possession" could be subject to interpretation, but in principle, it would be legal to watch a crusher film as long as the film was not exchanged or purchased in interstate commerce or through state commerce in contravention of state obscenity law. However, because of the cruelty component to the crusher films, viewing or possessing the films could potentially violate laws other than obscenity laws depending on the circumstances and jurisdiction involved.

Rattlesnake Roundup

Each year, dozens of groups hold rattlesnake hunts called roundups or rodeos. Though they are called roundups and rodeos, these events are more like hunting than traditional rodeos involving farm animals because rattlesnake roundups are not regulated by cruelty statutes. Rattlesnake-human interactions may be regulated by statutes that limit wildlife possession, prohibit cruelty toward pets, designate location of collection or hunting, delimit commercial animal or skin trade, prevent habitat destruction, or protect certain endangered species, but these issues are mostly tangential to roundups (Warner 2013; TPWD n.d.). Generally, roundups involve activities that would be illegal to perform on a cow but are fully legal to perform on a rattlesnake. Roundups occur around the country from January to July in Georgia, Texas, Alabama, Oklahoma, New Mexico, and Kansas (Rattlesnake Recipes 2006). Though states may not have laws that restrict roundups, state agencies may oversee roundups.

The Sweetwater Rattlesnake Roundup, the country's largest roundup, attracts approximately thirty thousand spectators to Texas over the course of one weekend each year (Owen 2009). As hunters capture rattlesnakes, the animals are placed in a weigh-in pit, where they are measured and weighed. Then rattlesnakes are transferred to a milking pit, where their venom is expressed (Owen 2009). People at roundups believe that the milk is collected into vats and donated for research and to produce antivenom. This myth is false. Captive produced, lab-certified venom copiously exceeds market demand for antivenom; furthermore, antivenom must be regulated by the government (TPWD n.d.). After rattlesnakes are milked, spectators are encouraged to pet the snakes, which are held still by hunters (Owen 2009). Armed with protective Kevlar coverings, snake hunters walk within the pit that contains thousands of snakes (Hollister 2010; Owen 2009). Apparently, a rattlesnake's bite feels comparable to being stabbed by two searing pokers (Wideman 2006). The Kevlar insulates the hunters since snakes' fangs cannot penetrate the material (Owen 2009). Some snakes are brought to a demonstration pit that is intended to teach safety awareness to crowds. Finally, the snakes are decapitated and skinned in the skinning pit. Their bodies and skins are donated, traded, and sold. These events are typical of the majority of roundups. Hunters earn five dollars per pound of snake delivered to the pit. Hunting teams earn thousands of dollars over the weekend as thousands of pounds of snakes are harvested during the festival. Since the beginning of the Sweetwater Rattlesnake Roundup, hundreds of thousands of snakes have been taken without any regulation.

The process of hunting the snakes in Texas has been reviewed and may become a regulated activity in the future. During festival weekends hunters set out into the wild in search of holes dug by burrowing creatures, like porcupines, skunks, and rodents (Owen 2009). Rattlesnakes take over these holes and use them as their own dens. When a hunter finds a den, he or she will pump gasoline fumes into the hole to poison and annoy snakes enough to force them to exit their dens (Owen 2009). The Texas Parks and Wildlife Department has considered criminalizing the use of gasoline to kill or capture rattlesnakes indiscriminately because gassing impacts nontarget wildlife and their habitats, including federally protected and endangered cave-dwelling invertebrates (TPWD n.d.). Thus, under federal law gassing may already be a crime that has not been prosecuted due to cultural or state-level pressures. Texans politicians have attempted to stop federal protection for sand dune lizards, lesser prairie chickens, and other animals because legislation interfered with oil and gas enterprises (Mildenberg 2014). At least twenty-nine states have banned gassing because it endangers more than twenty-six species of animals and insects. Proposed regulatory changes would restrict gassing for killing, but legal and licensed collection may not be affected (TPWD n.d.). Gassing restrictions may reduce the numbers of rattlesnakes driven from their dens by as much as 80 percent (Mildenberg 2014). In addressing public concerns about proposed regulations, the Texas Parks and Wildlife Department stated that no data demonstrates that rattlesnakes would become overabundant as a result of reduced taking (TPWD n.d.). To the contrary, the commission has expressed some concern about the quantity of snakes being killed in roundups and whether appropriate restrictions can be enacted (Texas Parks and Wildlife Commission 2007).

Data tends to show that roundups are not ecologically sustainable (TPWD n.d.). The Texas Parks and Wildlife Department has considered regulating roundups because of dwindling rattlesnake populations. Past roundups were determined to have eliminated 1 percent of the Texan rattlesnake population annually, but roundup patrons and state and federal officials have observed that populations are dwindling (Handwerk 2003). Not long ago, the US Department of Fish and Wildlife announced that the eastern diamondback rattlesnake, which is hunted in Georgia and Alabama, may qualify for protection under the Endangered Species Act (16 U.S.C. §§ 1531–1544, 2013; Giese 2012). If population trends continue, then criminal penalties may be imposed on taking specific snakes under certain circumstances that could affect roundup practices.

Self-regulation by roundup groups could preempt governmental regulation (Roberts 2012). For example, the rattlesnake roundup in Claxton, Georgia, was converted into a wildlife festival by the Evans County Wildlife Club. The half-century-old event will now celebrate reptiles and other wildlife while educating the public about habitat loss and conservation. Conservation groups will provide a modest amount of live snakes for public education, but hunting, milking, killing, and skinning will be completely eliminated.

Conclusion

Traditional forms of entertainment have evolved away from cruelty and will likely continue to evolve in response to changing moral, cultural, and ethical ideas about animals. As private organizations continue to influence the public and the government, society's demand for certain forms of entertainment may decrease while government oversight and intervention may increase. Because private and public actions vary by organization, jurisdiction, form of entertainment, and animals involved, new laws and attitudes may be incongruous or ineffective, but over time these developments may become more complete and be strengthened by increased attention so that, legally, society will only tolerate cruelty-free forms of entertainment.

References

16 U.S.C. § 1531–1544 (2013).

18 U.S.C. § 48 (1999).

Animal Crush Video Prohibition Act of 2010. H. R. 5566, 2010. http://www. gpo.gov/fdsys/pkg/BILLS-111hr5566enr/pdf/BILLS-111hr5566enr.pdf.

Animal Legal Defense Fund (ALDF). 2013. "Rodeo Facts: The Case against Rodeos." http://aldf.org/resources/when-you-witness-animal-cruelty/ rodeo-facts-the-case-against-rodeos/.

Animal Defenders International (ADI). 2013. "Worldwide Circus Bans." August 9. http://www.ad-international.org/animals_in_entertainment/ go.php?id=281.

Asay, A. P. 2003. "Greyhounds: Racing to Their Deaths." *Stetson Law Review* 32:433–67.

BBC. 2012. "Bullfighting Declared Legal in France." September 21. http://www. bbc.co.uk/news/world-europe-19673414.

Bryant, T. L. 2007. "Similarity or Difference as a Basis for Justice: Must Animals Be Like Humans to Be Legally Protected from Humans?" *Law and Contemporary Problems* 70:207–54.

Burnett, J. 2013. "Police: Cockfighting Season Begins." *Hawaii Tribune*, January 16. http://hawaiitribune-herald.com/sections/news/local-news/police-cock-fighting-season-begins.html.

CAS International (Comité Anti Stierenvechten). 2013. http://www.cas-international.org/en/home/suffering-of-bulls-and-horses/bullfighting/ bullfighting-in-latin-america/.

Center for Biological Diversity. 2013. "Outlawing Rattlesnake Roundups." http://www.biologicaldiversity.org/campaigns/outlawing_rattlesnake_roundups/.

Challener, D. J. 2010. "Protecting Cats and Dogs in Order to Protect Humans: Making the Case for a Felony Companion Animal Statute in Mississippi." *Mississippi College Law Review* 29:499.

Chandola, M. V. 2002. "Dissecting American Animal Protection Law: Healing the Wounds with Animal Rights and Eastern Enlightenment." *Wisconsin Environmental Law Journal* 8:3.

Chiesa, L. E. 2008a. "Of Persons and the Criminal Law: (Second Tier) Person-hood as a Prerequisite for Victimhood." *Pace Law Review* 28:759.

———. 2008b. "Why Is It a Crime to Stomp on a Goldfish? Harm, Victimhood and the Structure of Anti-Cruelty Offenses." *Mississippi Law Journal* 78:1.

Coleman, P. G. 2009. "Note to Athletes, NFL, and NBA: Dog Fighting Is a Crime, Not a Sport." *Journal of Animal Law & Ethics* 3:85.

Coto, D. 2012. "Puerto Rico Cockfighting: Legal Cock Fights in Danger in U.S. Territory." *Huffington Post*, July 24. http://www.huffingtonpost. com/2012/07/22/puerto-rico-cockfighting_n_1693362.html.

Cusack, C. M. 2014. *Pornography and the Criminal Justice System.* Boca Raton, FL: CRC Press/Taylor & Francis.

Daily Mail. 2008. "After the Horror of Horse-Fighting, the Sickening Images of Camel-Fighting." February 20. http://www.dailymail.co.uk/news/

article-516759/After-horror-horse-fighting-sickening-images-camel-fighting.html.

Department of Environmental Conservation (DEC), New York. 2013. "Small Game Hunting." http://www.dec.ny.gov/outdoor/27801.html.

Donnellan, L. 2007. "Animal Testing in Cosmetics: Recent Developments in the European Union and the United States." *Animal Law* 13:251.

Federal Bureau of Investigation (FBI). 2013. "Indictments Unsealed Charging Four Individuals Associated with Penn National Racetrack Fraud." November 11. http://www.fbi.gov/philadelphia/press-releases/2013/indictments-unsealed-charging-four-individuals-associated-with-penn-national-racetrack-fraud.

Favre, D. 2010. "Wildlife Jurisprudence." *Journal of Environmental Law and Litigation* 25:459.

Fish and Wildlife Act of 1956 (16 U.S.C. 742a–j).

Fusfeld, L. 2007. "Sterilization in an Animal Rights Paradigm." *Journal of Animal Law and Ethics* 2:255.

Giese, C. A. 2012. "Eastern Diamondback Rattlesnake Closer to Endangered Species Act Protection: World's Largest Rattlesnake Threatened by Habitat Destruction, Persecution." *Center for Biological Diversity*, May 9. http://www.biologicaldiversity.org/news/press_releases/2012/eastern-diamond-back-rattlesnake-05-09-2012.html.

Graves, P., K. Mosman, and S. Rogers. 2012. "2011 Legislative and Administrative Review." *Animal Law* 18:361.

Greenwood, A. 2012. "Meghan Mogensen, Reston Zoo Director, Charged with Animal Cruelty for Treatment of Sick Wallaby." *Huffington Post*, June 25. http://www.huffingtonpost.com/2012/06/25/meghan-mogensen-reston-zoo_n_1625560.html.

———. 2013. "Obama Comes out against Dog Breed-Specific Legislation, Joins the Fight for Pit Bulls." *Huffington Post*, August 20. http://www.huffington-post.com/2013/08/20/obama-breed-specific-legislation_n_3785911.html.

Grimm, F. 2014. "Fred Grimm: Florida's Outdated Gambling Laws Must Be Updated." *Miami Herald*, February 19. http://www.miamiherald.com/2014/02/19/3946996/fred-grimm-floridas-outdated-gambling.html#storylink=cpy.

Grissom, B. 2010. "Loopholes Allow Cockfighting to Thrive." *Texas Tribune*, December 26. http://www.texastribune.org/texas-issues/gaminggambling/loopholes-allow-cockfighting-to-thrive/.

Hanson, B. 2006. "Dog-Focused Law's Impact on Disability Rights: Ontario's Pit Bull Legislation as a Case in Point." *Animal Law* 12:217.

Handwerk, B. 2003. "Rattlesnake Roundups Draw Crowds, Complaints." *National Geographic*, March 10. http://news.nationalgeographic.com/news/2003/01/0130_030130_snakeroundup_2.html.

Hirsch, V. 2003. "Legal Protections of the Domestic Chicken in the United States and Europe." *Animal Legal and Historical Center*. http://www.animallaw.info/articles/dduschick.htm.

Hollister, J.O. 2010. "Roundup. Herpo Enterprises: Reptile Hobbyist." *King Snake*, April 3. http://www.kingsnake.com/roundup/.

Huffington Post. 2012. "Eating Pigeons in NYC: Jackson Landers Hunts and Eats Invasive Species in the Big Apple." September 27. http://www.huffingtonpost.com/2012/09/27/eating-pigeons-in-nyc-jackson-landers-hunting-invasive-species_n_1920973.html.

Humane Society. 2013. "Cockfighting: State Laws." http://www.humanesociety.org/assets/pdfs/animal_fighting/cockfighting_chart_2013.pdf.

Humane Society. 2013. "Internet Hunting." http://www.humanesociety.org/issues/internet_hunting/

Interstate Horse Racing Act, 15 U.S.C. 57 §§ 3001–3007 (1978).

Kamarudin, Y. 2012. "The Annual Texas Rattlesnake Massacre." *Environmental Graffiti*. http://www.environmentalgraffiti.com/news-texas-insane-rattlesnake-festival?image=1#Ameluj0mrb20sMi9.99.

Larson, P. W. 1998. "Fourth Annual Conference on Animals and the Law: Rodeo Is Cruel Entertainment." *Pace Environmental Law Review* 16:115.

Lokke, M. 2013. "The Sweetwater Rattlesnake Roundup." *New Yorker*, March 21. http://www.newyorker.com/online/blogs/photobooth/2013/03/slide-show-matt-eichs-photos-of-the-sweetwater-rattlesnake-roundup.html#slide_ss_0=1.

Madeline, B. A. 2000. "Cruelty to Animals: Recognizing Violence against Nonhuman Victims." *University of Hawai'i Law Review* 23:307.

Malisow, C. 2013. "Open Season: Do Laws against Animal Crushing Videos Violate Free Speech?" *Houston Press*, May 15. http://www.houstonpress.com/2013-05-16/news/ashley-nicole-richards/.

Mathew, A. P. 2013. "Animals to Be Banned in Circus." *Times of India*, August 8. http://articles.timesofindia.indiatimes.com/2013-08-08/coimbatore/41200228_1_circus-industry-circus-shows-tigers-and-lions.

Mildenberg, D. 2014. "A Not-So-Popular Plan to Protect Rattlesnakes." *Bloomberg Businessweek*, January 27–February 2, 26.

Miller, M. E. 2012. "Cheaters Prosper at Calder Race Course." *Miami New Times*, August 8. http://www.miaminewtimes.com/2012-08-09/news/cheaters-prosper-at-calder-race-course/.

Miller v. Civil City of South Bend. 904 F.2d 1081, 1097 (7th Cir. 1990).

Nagulapalli, K. 2009. "Strictly for the Dogs: A Fourteenth Amendment Analysis of the Race Based Formation and Enforcement of Animal Welfare Laws." *Rutgers Race and Law Review* 11:217.

Nash, J.C. 2013. "Rattle Snake Round Up Festivals in Texas." *USA Today*. http://traveltips.usatoday.com/rattle-snake-round-up-festivals-texas-61591.html.

Nowicki, C.L. 1999. "The Animal Welfare Act: All Bark and No Bite." *Seton Hall Legislative Journal* 23:443.

Neil, M. 2013. "Judge Says 2 Cities Can Maintain Pit Bull Bans That Accommodate Service Animals." *ABA Journal*, August 5. http://www.abajournal.com/news/article/judge_says_2_cities_can_maintain_pit_bull_bans_that_accommodate_service_ani/.

Owen, A. 2009. "The World's Largest Rattlesnake Roundup." *American Festivals Project*, March 18. http://americanfestivalsproject.net/2009/03/18/the-worlds-largest-rattlesnake-roundup/.

People for the Ethical Treatment of Animals (PETA). 2013. "Circuses." http://www.peta.org/issues/animals-in-entertainment/circuses.aspx.

People for the Ethical Treatment of Animals (PETA). 2013. "Urge Philippine Officials to Stop Horrific 'Crush' Videos and Hold the Perverts Who Make Them Accountable." http://www2.peta.org/site/R?i=MgDHjdabQx7byLmCTsImJg.

Present, B. 2012. "Humane Officer Loses in Pigeon Shoot Case." *Pittsburg Post-Gazette*, September 3. http://www.post-gazette.com/stories/business/legal/humane-officer-loses-in-pigeon-shoot-case-651677/#ixzz2bjmdEPFe.

Rappaport, B. 2008. "A Shot across The Bow: How to Write an Effective Demand Letter." *Journal of the Association of Legal Writing Directors* 5:32.

Rattlesnake Recipes. 2006. "Rattlesnake Roundup Locater [sic]." http://www.rattlesnakerecipe.us/roundup.htm.

Reppy, W. A. 2005. "Citizen Standing to Enforce Anticruelty Laws by Obtaining Injunctions: The North Carolina Experience." *Animal Law* 11:39.

Roberts, C. 2013. "Virginia Zoo Director Going to Jail in Connection with Drowning of Wounded Wallaby." *New York Daily News*, January 3. http://www.nydailynews.com/news/national/zoo-director-pleads-guilty-animal-cruelty-article-1.1232473#ixzz2bdFMiXPX.

Roberts, N. 2012. "Reptile Victory: From Rattlesnake Roundup to Wildlife Festival." *Care2 Make a Difference*, January 26. http://www.care2.com/causes/reptile-victory-from-rattlesnake-roundup-to-wildlife-festival.html#ixzz2bp4zbxPs.

Schmahmann, D. R., and L. J. Polacheck. 1995. "The Case against Rights for Animals." *Boston College Environmental Affairs Law Review* 22:747.

Shafer, M. L. 2012. "Perplexing Precedent: United States v. Stevens Confounds a Century of Supreme Court Conventionalism and Redefines the Limits of 'Entertainment.'" *Villanova Sports and Entertainment Law Journal* 19:281.

Shipley, A. 2012. "Florida Lags in Racehorse Doping Regulations." *Sun Sentinel*, December 1. http://articles.sun-sentinel.com/2012-12-01/news/fl-horse-racing-drug-testing-20121201_1_tampa-bay-downs-horse-industry-richard-sams.

Sinpetru, L. 2013. "Elephant Abuse Video Leads to Top Circus Being Charged with Animal Cruelty." *Softpedia*, April 16. http://news.softpedia.com/news/Elephant-Abuse-Video-Leads-to-Top-Circus-Being-Charged-with-Animal-Cruelty-345732.shtml.

Stanley v. Georgia. 394 U.S. 557 (1969).

Telegraph. 2011. "Circus Elephant Owners Charged with Cruelty over Beatings." November 10. http://www.telegraph.co.uk/news/uknews/crime/8880863/Circus-elephant-owners-charged-with-cruelty-over-beatings.html.

Texas Parks and Wildlife Commission (TPWD). 2007. "Regulations Committee Meeting: Proceedings." January 24. http://www.tpwd.state.tx.us/business/feedback/meetings/2007/0125/transcripts/regulations_committee/index.phtml.

Texas Parks and Wildlife Commission (TPWD). n.d. "Gassing As a Means to Collect Nongame Wildlife." https://tpwd.texas.gov/faq/huntwild/gassing.phtml

U.S. v. Stevens. 559 U.S. 460 (2010).

Velez, A. N. 2010. "Ole, Ole, Ole, Oh No!: Bullfighting in the United States and Reconciling Constitutional Rights with Animal Cruelty Statutes." *Penn State Law Review* 115:497.

Vesilind, P. 2013. "Local Food Global Food: Do We Have What It Takes to Reinvent the U.S. Food System?: Preempting Humanity: Why National Meat Ass'n v. Harris Answered the Wrong Question." *Maine Law Review* 65:685.

Warner, C. 2013. "Owner of Abandoned Snakes Arrested." *Union Daily Times*, July. http://www.uniondailytimes.com/view/full_story/23008446/article-Owner-of-abandoned-snakes-arrested.

Welch, C. 2010. "Smart and Fast, Marine Mammals Are Guarding Our Military Bases." *Seattle Times*, August 28. http://seattletimes.com/html/pacificnw/2012662209_pacificpdolphins29.html.

Wideman, T. 2006. "Texas Rattlesnake Tales." Abilene, TX: State House Press.

3

Animals, Religion, and Criminal Justice

Introduction

Historical practice of religion has been foundational to societal development of morals, ethics, customs, and law. Around the world nations have developed laws and order in response to traditional religious norms and the evolution of morality in society. Many customs, attitudes, and policies directly relate to or are suspected to relate to religious undertones and influence. Despite separation of church and state, in the United States many laws have been created, interpreted, and enforced in alignment with values traditionally held by Anglo-Protestants. Religious principles and the right to practice religion are essential to the American notion of ordered liberty. Throughout US history members of society and people within the government have occasionally targeted religious practices that they perceived as an affront to Protestantism. Some religious outsiders have been prosecuted but have prevailed in court. Other outlying sects or practices have continued to be excluded from religious protections. Though religious targeting is illegal, the government has successfully prosecuted certain religious adherents under generally applicable laws. Some religious groups that have important ties to mainstream Protestantism, such as Jehovah's Witnesses and Christian Scientists, have been given additional protections, and certain religious practices have been excepted from general criminal provisions, for example faith healing (Cusack, 2015). Typically, exempted practices are highly regulated and are exempt from certain provisions because adherents have demonstrated that their practices are neither cruel nor dangerous to humans, animals, or the community, or that these practices are limited in scope. Because the law must only bear a rational relationship to the government's goals, interests, and powers, laws are legal if they do not violate constitutional rights, excessively entangle the government in religion, or inhibit lawful religious practice. However, laws that directly and exclusively target certain religious practices violate the Constitution.

Religion and the Constitution

Free exercise of religion is guaranteed under the US Constitution. The constitutional right to practice religion is guaranteed by the First Amendment. Under the First Amendment the government cannot force people to practice or abstain from practicing religion, or to worship in a particular manner. The government can only enforce laws that are constitutional; thus, enforcement of laws that infringe on First Amendment rights will be enjoined or such laws will be stricken. Many times practitioners have sued the government to enjoin it from enforcing laws that infringed on the constitutional free exercise clause. Courts strictly scrutinize any laws that impinge on First Amendment rights. Under the Religious Freedom Restoration Act (RFRA), the government cannot pass laws that substantially burden religious practice (42 U.S.C. § 1996[a], 2004). Usually, when laws limit free exercise, courts will side against the government. Yet, over time the government has presented to the US Supreme Court many necessary reasons for impinging on First Amendment rights. Certain religious activities compel the government to impose highly tailored laws that effectively or directly restrict particular religious practices. Laws are written as narrowly as possible in order to prevent harm while leaving the remainder of harmless religious practices undisturbed. In a handful of cases, courts have upheld restrictions that have usually served to protect practitioners, their families, or the public from seriously dangerous religious practices. In other situations the government will create exceptions to laws that allow practitioners to practice freely. These exceptions do not create a conflict between church and state because the government is not endorsing or forcing a religion or practice. The government is simply permitting generally prohibited practices to occur in limited doses for religious reasons.

The Endangered Species Act protects the Florida panther, which was threatened with extinction (*U.S. v. Billie*, 1987). In 1987 a beginner practitioner of medicine who was also chairman of the Seminole Tribe in Florida killed a panther roaming on Seminole Tribe land. The federal government prosecuted the practitioner under the Endangered Species Act. Until that point no one had ever been prosecuted for killing a Florida panther (Shabecoff 1987). Seminole Tribe members testified that they generally preferred to have panther claws accessible for medicinal use during healing ceremonies. They also testified that they believed that cramps are best healed by panther claws, though claws are not the exclusive means for healing cramps. The defendant testified that before he killed the panther, he did not plan to use the panther's carcass in a particular manner. After the fact, he decided to humble himself by gifting the carcass to an experienced medicine man with the hopes of learning more about medicine. The court held that taking panthers was not necessary or regularly part of his religious practice. Possessing panther parts was not critical to healing even though possessing such parts was preferable. Weighing the defendant's religious interest against the government's compelling interest in protecting the Florida panther, the court held in the government's favor.

The Bald Eagle Protection Act criminalizes golden eagle and bald eagle hunting. However, the secretary of the interior may grant hunting permits to Indian tribes so that they can use eagle feathers in religious ceremonies. The taking of feathers is regulated and limited. If everyone were to hunt eagles indiscriminately, then eagles would likely become extinct, but if Indians could not have any eagle feathers, then those particular rituals would be completely eradicated from their religions and cultures. Thus, the government carves out a small exception to accommodate and balance ecological and religious needs.

Practice of religion substantially underlies culture and law. Many religions explain and dictate humans' relationships with animals. However, people increasingly adopt secular understandings of human-animal relationships, and increasingly attempt to separate law from morality. Yet, religious communities continue to help evolve constitutional and criminal law as practitioners exercise rights to handle animals in certain ways or as practitioners impermissibly fall below society's expectations for animal-human relationships.

Religion and Animals

Animals have coexisted with humans since before the inception of criminal law. Over time religious laws that regulated the treatment of animals were imbedded into criminal laws. As nations developed, many retained connections between law and morals without a religious component. Religions like Buddhism, Hinduism, Islam, and Judaism have carefully regulated the treatment and killing of animals for centuries. In some nations where religion influences contemporary law, ancient religious requirements for dealing with animals may be incorporated.

Around a half billion people practice Buddhism worldwide (Ganeri 2003). The majority of practitioners are concentrated in the Far East. In countries like Bhutan, the judiciary openly links criminal law and procedure with Buddhist religious influence. The Royal Court of Justice specifically mentions the "indiscriminate killings of wild animals and destruction of marine life" as serious crimes that are forbidden by spiritual principles (Judiciary of Bhutan 2013). Yet, in other countries, such as Sri Lanka, the rich Buddhist heritage of nonviolence toward animals is put aside in favor of legal slaughter of fish, fowl, and cattle (Weeraratna 2013). In the Far East, Buddhist prohibitions have not been codified as criminal regulations as much as they have been maintained through moral authority. In China the state does not follow religion despite the major influence that Buddhism has had on the nation and culture (Tatlow 2013). China has few animal protection laws, and farming and horrific treatment of dogs and cats are prevalent. Animal mistreatment reflects broad and pervasive disinterest in protecting domestic or domesticated animals from cruelty. More than half of large animals in China are used for work, but they receive no protection. Perhaps some link exists between the conscientious elimination of religion from Chinese society and the extinguishment of the traditional Buddhist compassion toward animals and of the moral regulation of cruelty against them.

In Japan wantonly killing protected animals is a crime under Animal Protection Law Article 27 (Takahash 2004). The government feels that this law reflects Buddhist proscriptions against violence, but the ancient proscription may also indirectly contribute to a potential issue between humans and the feral cat population. Cats are protected animals, but there are no laws requiring care for cats. According to government surveys, it seems that the majority of people would be unlikely to bring feral cats to animal shelters where they might receive care if these persons believed that the cats would be euthanized. Some scholars have gone so far as to trace Japanese motives for this choice to the year 724, when Emperor Shomu first implemented six edicts against hunting and killing animals based on Buddhist principles. Feral cats may be viewed as wildlife, which has traditionally been protected by law and morality. Between 1685 and 1709, hunting, neglect, cruelty, and abandonment of animals could be punished by exile, death, and other penalties. Though these stiff punishments were abolished in favor of more contemporary jurisprudential approaches, moral prohibition against lethal actions possibly remain embedded.

Directly related to principles of nonviolence in Buddhism are principles of nonviolence in Hinduism. Principles of nonviolence toward the sacred cow and the holiness of cows in India are well-known to cultures throughout the world. Due to Hindu influence on society, the cow is thought of as a holy mother figure that should not be confined or abused. Like feral cats in Japan, under secular law in India, cows are permitted to roam freely through the streets and are loosely considered to belong to the community. Killing or injuring a cow can be punished severely in some regions (Bauman, Bohannon, and O'Brien 2011). Comparable with US law, which requires no duty to render care, Indians are not required to care for wild cows under cruelty statutes. Thus, the laissez-faire approach to the presence of cows comes with its drawbacks for cows. Neglected wild cows are not fed regularly and rummage through garbage; an average cow eats as many as three hundred plastic bags over a lifetime (Edwards 2011).

Though 80 percent of Indians are Hindus, in western regions of India, Islam is practiced. In these regions cows are not venerated, and killing cows is permitted or accepted. Much of the leather used in the United States and Europe is imported from India (Beckoff 2007; Islamic Concerns 2013; PETA 2013). First-hand accounts and undercover documentation has demonstrated that a large number of cows are tortured in brutal leather trade practices that are virtually unregulated in these regions (Islamic Concerns 2013; PETA 2013). Though Indian leather manufacturers violate principles of Article 48 of the Indian Constitution and cruelty laws, several factors have insulated offenders from prosecution or pressure to modify their practices, including very little enforcement, religious separation, financial concerns, and state sovereignty.

Since 2000 in the United States, Jewish and Muslim prison inmates' request for dietary accommodations under the Religious Land Use and Institutionalized Persons Act (RLUIPA) has been fairly common (Davis 2000; Johnson 2006; Larson 2007; Nelson 2009; Prisoner's Rights 2010; Stout 2010). One major issue for religious inmates is abstention from certain meats, for example, pork. While the state must honor requests for religious accommodations, including kosher and halal meals, prisons' inability to afford special kitchens or catered meals may effectively curb inmates' rights. In some cases, kosher-style meals, for example, vegan and vegetarian meals, which exclude prohibited foods but are not strictly kosher, may serve as a substitute. Unfortunately, a fruit cup, a vegetable, a granola bar, and a nutritional supplement may qualify as the only "kosher" meal available due to budgetary constraints. Some prisoners have subsisted on only bread and water for months at a time. Private organizations may supplement meal costs or deliver special meals to prisons. In one case, when a private Jewish organization provided Orthodox Jewish inmates with meals, Muslim prisoners were not entitled by law to those meals. If the state provides fully kosher meals, then under the equal protection clause the state would also be required to provide halal meals. However, religious accommodations do not extend to all dietary requirements. Inmates may likely be prohibited from preparing their own meals in a kitchen in a religiously prescribed manner. In one case a court held that the First Amendment was not violated when a prison ordered an Orthodox Jewish inmate to work with nonkosher food and ingest nonkosher odors in a nonkosher kitchen as part of his prison work.

Food Regulation, Cruelty, and Religion

Many Jews throughout the world obey Jewish law, which regulates slaughter of and cruelty toward animals. The US Department of Agriculture (USDA) regulates animal slaughter under the Humane Methods of Slaughter Act. The USDA requires that animals be rendered unconscious through captive bolt stunning or other methods prior to slaughter (9 C.F.R. § 313, 2013). An exception is made for animals killed in compliance with Jewish kosher laws in the United States, though this exception is not necessarily carved out by other nations with Jewish populations (FSIS 2003; *Huffington Post* 2013). Individual state laws also regulate slaughter and cruelty, but every state permits kosher killing. The exception to USDA regulations is made because kosher slaughter methods cause an animal to lose consciousness instantly when the carotid artery is severed with one swift and precise slice of the animal's throat.

An undercover investigation conducted by People for the Ethical Treatment of Animals (PETA) in 2004 found that an AgriProcessors, Inc. plant in Postville, Iowa, was slaughtering animals in a cruel manner that violated kosher requirements and USDA requirements (Cooperman 2014). As the largest kosher meat producer in the United States and sole exporter of kosher meat to Israel, the discovery of violations at AgriProcessors, Inc. prompted a strong response from Orthodox Jewish practitioners and the USDA. The USDA independently investigated and concluded that at least 20 percent of the animals were slaughtered in a manner that violated the law (PETA 2004). The USDA also reported that certain inspectors accepted gifts, engaged in misconduct, and failed to report violations. Yet, the assistant US attorney for the Northern District of Iowa declined to press charges against AgriProcessors owners, slaughterers, or inspectors. Without repercussions or penalization, it is difficult for society to enforce religious requirements that serve as an exception to criminal law. In this situation, on the surface, traditional morality was tightly intertwined with the law, but because the secular law had no teeth, only religious, reputational, or financial incentives motivate AgriProcessor's compliance with secular law.

Under Islamic *Sharia* law slaughter methods must be halal. In the eyes of state and federal law, halal slaughter is identical to kosher slaughter, and under Islamic and Jewish law, the overall processes are quite similar, while the actual killing is identical (Wisch 2006). The underlying rationale for both kosher and halal slaughter is prevention of cruelty to animals. In Judaism and Islam cruelty to animals is forbidden. Sometimes, when practitioners fail to obey religious law, the criminal justice system must intervene to prevent and punish cruelty toward animals. In 2004 the owner of the halal slaughterhouse located in Weatherford, Texas, was charged with cruelty to farm animals (*Qaddura v. State*, 2007). Local police investigated a complaint of a foul odor emanating from the slaughterhouse's property. As is commonly the case when police respond to foul odors, several improperly disposed of and rotting corpses were identified by the officer. A number of decomposing farm animals were found in proximity to scores of living but undernourished sheep and goats. Many animals' facial orifices were secreting mucus, and several animals were lame or immobile. Water was insufficient due to the fact that only one automatic watering device was hooked up to supply approximately fifty animals, and that container was half-empty. Some cows had no access to water. The only food material present was moldy, dry, and black hay that could not be accessed by the animals. No feed, leaves, or grass was available. The inspector warned the owner on several occasions that conditions must be improved, but the inspector's warnings were ignored. The owner went on vacation for several weeks. During that time conditions were not improved and animals were uncared for. Because the animals were first neglected then abandoned, a warrant was issued to seize the animals. Ninety-three weak, immobile, and hungry animals were seized. The owner was tried and convicted of cruelty to animals by the trial court, and the verdict was upheld by the court of appeals.

Many states make an exception for religious slaughter of any animal (Wisch 2006). Yet, Muslims, like Jews, only slaughter ruminant animals with cloven hooves. Neither group slaughters pig for consumption. *Sharia* law criminalizes it. *Tazir* crimes are like infractions that carry discretionary penalties (Slaughter 1993). In countries like Yemen and Saudi Arabia, where *Sharia* law predominantly guides criminal law and procedure, eating pigs is a *tazir* violation. Pig consumption falls into a class of crimes that violate society. Though eating pigs does not carry a definite sentence, it violates morality in society and can be punished with confiscation, counseling, and fines (Barkan and Bryjak 2010). Extremely *tazir* violations can be punished with house arrest or flogging depending on the seriousness of the infraction. Also, depending on the circumstances, selling pork or tricking others into consuming pig could potentially change the class of crime from *tazir* to *haad*. This would be a more severe class of crime that directly violates one's obligation to God. Severe violations would be accompanied by more stringent evidentiary standards, especially when more severe penalties are at stake. In one example a Muslim schoolmaster caned a boy in Malaysia for bringing pork fried rice to school for lunch in 2010 (Palmer 2012). This response was deemed to be excessive and severe by the community. Similarly, in ancient biblical times consumption of pork may have called for dozens of lashings, banishment, or capital punishment under Jewish law and custom. However, these punishments are obsolete, and pork consumption is not crime for Jews anywhere because of Jewish law. In fact, it is neither a crime nor a civil violation to import nonkosher meat into Israel (Shachar 2009).

Church of the Lukumi Babaluaye, Inc., et al. v. City of Hialeah

Religion involves animal sacrifice. Many religious adherents around the world decline to sacrifice animals, yet they retain a connection to the practice through textual descriptions and metaphoric sacrificial rituals. The Yoruba religion began in and around the area of Africa that is presently Nigeria. During the European imperialist invasion of the Americas, Africans were enslaved and relocated to the New World. There they were forced to adopt Christianity to survive. Rather than fully relinquish their religious practices, a syncretic religion developed whereby slaves masked their religious devotion with Catholic rituals and saints. The result was a blend of Yoruba and Catholic rituals, beliefs, deities, and saints. Santeria is a specific syncretic religion that developed in Cuba, though distinguishable forms, such as voodoo, developed elsewhere. Santeria spread to other Latin American nations, for example, Puerto Rico (*Merced v. Kasson*, 2009).

A variety of Santeria ceremonies designed to invoke and please spirits may incorporate animal sacrifice. Santeria centers around *orishas*,
which are divine spirits that represent the supreme deity. Santeria
rituals honor and involve spirits in material affairs by transferring life
energy, called *ashe*, from animal blood to *orishas*. Birth, marriage, illness, death, and the initiation of priests involve sacrifice. The initiation
of priests, which usually occurs in the initiates' homes, involves the
sacrifice of numerous animals including the following: five to seven
lambs or goats, a turtle, a duck, ten to fourteen chickens, five to seven
guinea hens, and ten to fourteen doves. Following the sacrifice, animals
used for rituals other than death or illness are cooked and eaten. The
will of the *orisha* determines where ceremonies will occur, for example,
at temples or shrine sites. Only two temples, located abroad, serve to
accommodate Santeria's two hundred fifty thousand practitioners,
making the home the most routine and crucial site for sacrifice.

Under the First Amendment *santeros* have the right to sacrifice
animals. The First Amendment protects free exercise of religion to
the extent that neither the state nor municipalities can pass laws that
outright ban animal sacrifice, though some municipalities have tried
to enforce certain laws that prevent religious practitioners from practicing animal sacrifice. Unless the government is able to show that its
laws are so narrowly tailored that they accomplish a compelling governmental goal by enforcing the fewest restrictions as possible, then
the US Supreme Court will rule that restrictions that impede animal
sacrifice are not necessary.

In *Church of the Lukumi Babaluaye, Inc., et al. v. City of Hialeah*, the
US Supreme Court held that the government cannot pass ordinances,
such as animal cruelty laws or health codes, that have the effect of
unfairly targeting the practice of religious sacrifice 1993). The Church
of the Lukumi Babaluaye began an uphill battle to become fully permitted and licensed in the City of Hialeah in 1987. Within weeks after the
church legally became operational, the city held an emergency meeting
to discuss its concerns about the church. Resolution 87-66 expressed
Hialeah's concern with religious practices that were inconsistent with
public morals, peace, or safety. The State of Florida's attorney general
assured the city that animal sacrifice was against the law in the state.
The result was local Ordinances 87-40, 87-71, 87-52, and 87-72, which
addressed the city's concern about the church. The ordinances did
not specifically mention Santeria, but they did effectively ban animal

sacrifice of the kind practiced by the church. The city opposed slaughter, abandonment of animal carcasses in public places, and consumption of uninspected animal flesh, which can be crucial elements in the practice of Santeria. The city's first ordinance echoed Florida's animal cruelty statutes in criminalizing unnecessary or cruel animal killing. The city claimed that rituals are not necessary for food consumption, and therefore, sacrifice is cruel. Although practitioners may consume carcasses, the primary purpose is sacrifice, not consumption. In Hialeah it was a crime to possess an animal for sacrifice or slaughter an animal in any ritual. The remaining ordinances defined sacrifice and slaughter to mean that it was illegal to kill an animal for food outside of a licensed restaurant or slaughterhouse located in an area zoned for such activities. However, the ordinance permitted a small number of domesticated animals to be slaughtered. This exception likely contemplated traditional festivities in Hialeah involving backyard slaughter and barbeque. A violation of any of the ordinances was punishable by fines of up to five hundred dollars or imprisonment not to exceed sixty days, or both. The church sued the city for breeching their right to freely exercise religion. Although the lower court and the court of appeals sided with the city, the US Supreme Court heard the case and agreed with the church. Before the lower court, the city cited prevention of public health risks, which could occur from the abandonment of carcasses, and cruelty to animals. It said that it could not regulate the church's sacrifices more narrowly than a total ban because adherents were secretive and would flout the ordinances in home ceremonies. The district court acknowledged that the church was targeted by the ordinances, but held that the government offered compelling reasons for criminalizing sacrifice, slaughter, and cruelty. The US Supreme Court said that "the principle that government may not enact laws that suppress religious belief or practice is so well understood that few violations are recorded in our opinions" (*Church of the Lukumi Babaluaye, Inc., et al. v. City of Hialeah*, 1993). This case was one such violation. Thus, the court found suppression of the practitioners' rights to be evident especially because fishing use of live rabbits to train greyhound dogs, euthanasia of stray animals, and pest extermination were all legal or free of prosecution. Thus, the effect of the statute was not neutral or generally applicable.

In *Merced v. Kasson* the president of Templo Yoruba Omo Orisha Texas, Inc. brought suit against the City of Euless, Texas, for violating Texas Religious Freedom and Restoration Act (TRFRA) (*Merced v. Kasson*,

2009; Lammoglia 2008). Merced, who had been practicing Santeria in Euless since 1990, was informed in 2006 that he could not sacrifice animals within city limits. Merced claimed that the city's enforcement of six ordinances substantially burdened his free exercise of religion (*Merced v. Kasson*, 2009). The appellate court agreed with Merced that under TRFRA, a Texas act that mirrored the federal First Amendment, the Euless government failed to demonstrate that it was necessary to impeded Merced's rights to further a compelling governmental interest in the least restrictive manner.

In Merced's lawsuit against the city, the court found that city ordinances suppressed animal sacrifice in several ways. Slaughter was criminalized as a separate misdemeanor on each day that it occurred, animals and birds could not willfully be harmed, animals could be impounded for misdemeanor violations if a person committed cruelty, keeping more than four animals was illegal, it was a crime to keep livestock within one hundred feet of any human habitation or within an enclosed area of less than one-half acre per animal, and only certain kinds of animals could be kept. The city said that enforcement of these ordinances against *santeros* was necessary to protect public health and safety by eliminating runoff of urine and feces, pestilence, injuries resulting from interspecies conflict in tight quarters, offensive odors, and disease transmission. The government stated that carcasses attract predators and insects. Contradictorily to their position, evidence showed that the city permitted hunters to return to Euless with large animal carcasses, and butcher and dispose of them within city limits, and it allowed restaurants to dispose of animal parts in dumpsters. Merced presented evidence that he could not initiate new priests unless he could perform sacrifices. The city failed to submit any evidence that Merced's slaughter methods had ever presented any threat to sanitation or public health, or caused any animals to suffer more than commercial slaughter practices would. Thus, the court found that Merced's free exercise of religion would be substantially burdened by enforcement of the ordinances, and that less restrictive means, for example, religious slaughter licenses, were available. Thus enforcement of these ordinances against *santeros* was enjoined.

When private individuals lawfully interfere with sacrifice, courts will not usually become involved (Bryan 2011). In 2011 a group of Muslims who belonged to mosques throughout the City of Sunrise, Florida, legally planned to sacrifice a goat on a farm situated in City of Sunrise. The sacrifice was intended to celebrate *Eid ul-Adha*, a festival honoring the story of Abraham's sacrifice. Sheila Alu, a city commissioner in Sunrise, knew that she could not use her authority as a commissioner to interfere legally, but she was intent on blocking the event because of her personal disdain for halal slaughter practices and the highly visible display of animal slaughter at a public event. As an animal lover, Alu placed a phone call to the landowner and asked the landowner to forbid use of the farm for sacrifice. The landowner agreed, and the scheduled event was canceled. However, the group found another private location where its members could perform the festive sacrifice. Because Alu called as an animal lover, not as a commissioner, and the land was privately owned, the interference was legal. Alu's lawful interference in the sacrifice raises a classic biblical example of interference in sacrifice that would be criminal by today's standards. In Matthew 21:12 Jesus is said to have overturned tables on which sacrificial doves were being bought and sold in the temple. If this occurred today, results might include any number of criminal charges, for example, animal cruelty, destruction of property, and felony burglary.

Snake Handling

In the Bible the Gospel of Mark (16:17–18) mentions that it will be evident that Christians believe in Jesus if they cast out devils, speak in tongues, lay hands on and heal the sick, take up serpents, or drink poison but survive. Based on this scripture the practice of wrangling live, poisonous snakes during religious worship services emerged in the United States. The Dolly Pond Church of God with Signs Following initiated snake handling in Grasshopper Valley, Tennessee, in 1909. George Went Hensely, who founded the church, was bitten nearly four hundred times before dying in 1955 from a final diamondback rattlesnake bite in Florida. During his lifetime Hensely spread his faith and rituals throughout the nation, but snake handling mainly caught on in the Appalachian region.

Snake handling's foothold has been explained by scholars as relating to faith, class, sexual psychology, desire for danger, maintenance of mountain culture, and a variety of other sociological motives. Snake handlers can generally be described as Pentecostal Christians who handle fire, wash feet, and drink strychnine (Daniel 1996; Penegar 1978). Like other mainstream Pentecostal groups, snake handlers speak in tongues; holler or sing effervescently; dance; cast out demons; practice hands-on healing; claim to bring some dead people back to life through the power of God; and adhere to a puritanical moral code that excludes wearing sleeveless shirts, drinking alcohol, patronizing bars, taking drugs, cursing, and premarital sex (Daniel 1996; Reed 2012). Women in snake-handling churches must wear skirts and grow their hair out, but they may not wear makeup or jewelry. Women do not usually handle serpents during church services.

Snake handling may compliment male pastors' personal interests. First, individual pastors may perceive an opportunity to become legends among practitioners if they accumulate an extraordinary number of bites (Tidball and Toumey 2007). For example, Dewey Chafin, a West Virginian pastor, became famous for surviving more than 120 snake-bites. Second, despite the fact that snakes are supposed to represent the devil, some pastors may love snakes. Part of snake-handling culture involves pastors enjoying snake lore and sharing information about how to deal with, feed, and care for snakes; snake ecology, biology, and chemistry; congregational need for certain snakes; where to acquire additional snakes; and how to dispose of their remains. Pastors trade and gift snakes among each other. They also buy them. This method is less common because it is risky, since many of their activities involve crimes. For example, Jamie Coots, pastor of Full Gospel Tabernacle in Jesus Name Church in Kentucky, became involved with the criminal justice system in Tennessee and Kentucky due to snake importing (UCN 2013). He purchased five rattlesnakes in Alabama and then drove through Tennessee, where he was charged with transporting illegal reptiles in improper containers. Snakes were seized and relocated to a zoo in Tennessee. Had he made it to Kentucky, he would have been in violation of Kentucky's laws. His snake permits had lapsed months before this incident, and thus he lacked any permit to import nonnative snakes into Kentucky. A few years prior to this incident, he was charged with trafficking snakes in Kentucky. Though he was barred from applying for permits following his conviction, he circumnavigated the law using relatives' permits.

To avoid these pitfalls, pastors sometimes capture wild snakes (Tidball and Toumey 2007). Much like snake roundups, handlers may hunt in groups. They grab wild snakes and place them into wooden snake boxes that are eighteen inches wide by thirty inches long and four inches deep. Snake boxes have air holes or mesh wire tops. Pastors may attempt to simulate a snake's environment in a heated holding pen filled with wood chips and logs. Pens are three feet by five feet by four feet. To transfer snakes from a snake box to a pen, handlers use a hooked pole, called a snake crook. In addition to their role in worship, snakes become pastors' pets. When snakes die, they may immediately be frozen to be stuffed by a taxidermist or skinned.

Some may argue that snake handling ought to be legal. Arguments are that (1) snake handling is not religiously inferior to Santeria's animal sacrifice, and (2) it is no less dangerous than recreational snake round-ups. Thus, the government ought not to have the power to criminalize it. First, the government and the Constitution do not endorse any religions through law. Laws must be designed so that they neutrally and generally apply to all religions. Second, the government can enact very narrow bans on particular aspects of religious practices if it presents compelling reasons demonstrating why there is no way, other than a ban, to accomplish a necessary goal. Preventing people from intentionally handling poisonous snakes in a manner that is known to be lethal has proven to be a compelling reason. In the *Church of the Lukumi Babaluaye, Inc., et al. v. City of Hialeah*, the US Supreme Court fully legalized animal sacrifice but distinguished sacrifice from snake handling because states have the power to protect people's health and safety from such likely and extreme danger. Though little data exists about the death rate from bites among snake handlers, in one case court evidence showed that within four months a single church handled snakes four times, and on one occasion a snake bit and injured a handler (*Swann v. Pack*, 1975).

Snake handling differs from roundups because people do not die from snakebites at roundups. If people are bitten by rattlesnakes during roundups, then they immediately receive medical treatment. Unlike organized roundup events, snake handling may be somewhat chaotic and often occurs in crowded sanctuaries (*Ventimiglia v. Sycamore View Church of Christ*, 1988). The day on which snakes may be handled during a service is somewhat random, though the event is indicated by the quickening of worship songs' rhythms, increased congregational volume and ecstatic singing, dancing, and heightened intensity that culminates when a wooden box is shaken and opened, and snakes are handled (Tidball and Toumey 2007). During handling snakes may be tossed between male pastors, caressed, and foisted in the air. Only a rope divides the audience from the snake-handling minister (*Ventimiglia v. Sycamore View Church of Christ*, 1988). Though some courts have refused to accept this proximity as a form of endangerment that merits the loss of child custody, other courts have found that snakes' threat to roaming or unattended children provides grounds for a ban (*Harris v. Harris*, 1977; *Ventimiglia v. Sycamore View Church of Christ*, 1988).

Handlers have been described by the court as being hypnotized and hysterical; thus, the danger arises in the manner of handling, not in the physical handling of snakes. The threat is so serious that in Tennessee those who are present during snake handling are guilty of aiding and abetting the handler, and of creating and maintaining a public nuisance (*Swann v. Pack*, 1975; *Ventimiglia v. Sycamore View Church of Christ*, 1988). This may be a heavy burden on church members, but for now criminalization of attendance seems to continue to be constitutional (Fraser 2003). As in Tennessee, in Kentucky religious snake handling is completely banned, though the penalty is merely a small fine (KRS § 437.060, 2013). Since the 1940s and 1950s, other states, like Virginia and Georgia, have banned snake handling, but arrests, imprisonment, and fines have had almost no deterrent effect on practitioners who continue to practice secretly or openly, as well as post to social media evidence of their potentially lethal activities (Daniel 1996; Reed 2012; Snake Handler 2012).

The threat of death surrounds and defines snake handling. Deaths from snake handling have been reported in West Virginia, Alabama, Kentucky, and a number of other jurisdictions. Several cases have been reported in which handlers died in a manner similar to their fathers, who also died from snake handling. Handlers in Holiness Serpent Handlers ("Holiness"), an Apostolic movement, have died from snakebites even though research on Holiness shows that snakes can be handled without incident (Holiness Serpent Handlers. 2008; Tidball and Toumey 2007). A researcher visited twenty-five different snake-handling churches involved in Holiness, and attended over three hundred services throughout Kentucky, east Tennessee, and southwest Virginia (Daniel 1996). The researcher was invited to handle serpents, and did so without being bitten. The researcher reported that apart from snake handling, practitioners were otherwise law-abiding and normal people by their local standards. However, exceptions exist. For example, a snake handler was recently charged with and convicted of attempted murder. A serpent handler in Alabama accused his wife, Darlene Summerford, of infidelity. Then the snake handler forced Summerford, at gunpoint, to place her hand inside a religiously inscribed wooden box full of rattlesnakes in his bedroom (Matthews 2009; Tidball and Toumey 2007). When Summerford reached in, she was bitten but survived (Daniel 1996). Her husband was sentenced to ninety-nine years in prison.

Conclusion

Nearly every religion transmits stories, rules, standards, explanations, or ideas about how humans should or should not interact with animals. Religion has been one of the most powerful influences on the development of contemporary society, morals, and law. To some extent animals continue to be subject to the influence of traditional religious authority. Yet, as societies become more secular and animals receive greater consideration under the law, tensions may continue to rise between religious adherents and the government. Competing agendas have resulted in some interesting case law, ambitious legal claims, illegal targeting, and aggressive lawbreaking. Society and law will likely become more and more secularized while accommodating as much religious practice as possible.

References

9 CFR § 313 (2013).

Barkan, S. E., and G. J. Bryjak. 2010. *Fundamentals of Criminal Justice: A Sociological View.* 2nd ed. Burlington, MA: Jones and Bartlett Publishers.

Bauman, W. A., R. R. Bohannon, and K. J. O'Brien. 2011. *Grounding Religion.* New York: Routledge.

Beckoff, M. 2007. *Animals Matter: A Biologist Explains Why We Should Treat Animals with Compassion and Respect.* Boston, MA: Shambhala Publications, Inc.

Bryan, S. 2011. "Sunrise Commissioner Blocks Muslim Sacrifice of Goats and Lambs." *SunSentinel,* November 2. http://articles.sun-sentinel.com/2011-11-02/news/fl-sunrise-politician-blocks-muslim-fest-20111102_1_sunrise-commissioner-sheila-alu-animal-sacrifices-sacrifices-for-religious-purposes.

Church of the Lukumi Babaluaye, Inc., et al. v. City of *Hialeah.* 508 U.S. 520 (1993).

Cooperman, A. 2004. "USDA Investigating Kosher Meat Plant Advocacy Group's Grisly Video Sparked Outcry." *Washington Post,* December 31. http://www.washingtonpost.com/wp-dyn/articles/A37569-2004Dec30.html.

Cusack, C. M. 2015. *Laws Relating to Sex, Pregnancy, and Infancy: Issues in Criminal Justice.* Palgrave Macmillan: New York.

Daniel, W. H. 1996. "Taking up Serpents: Snake Handlers of Eastern Kentucky." *Mississippi Quarterly* 50, no. 1: 141.

Davis, H. 2000. "Inmates' Religious Rights: Deference to Religious Leaders and Accommodation of Individualized Religious Beliefs." *Albany Law Review* 64:773.

Dubgyur, L. 2013. "The Influence of Buddhism on Bhutanese Trial System." *Royal Court of Justice: Judiciary of Bhutan.* http://www.judiciary.gov.bt/html/education/publication/buddhism.php.

Edwards, M. A. 2011. "Cultural Attitude toward Animals in India." *British Veterinary Association*. http://www.bva.co.uk/public/documents/os_grant_ menai_edwards.pdf.

Fraser, A. 2003. "Protected from Their Own Beliefs: Religious Objectors and Paternalistic Laws." *BYU Journal of Public Law* 18:185.

Ganeri, A. 2003. *Indian Culture*. Chicago, IL: Heinemann Library.

Harris v. Harris. 343 So. 2d 762 (Miss. 1977).

Holiness Serpent Handlers. 2008. "Official Website of Holiness Serpent Handlers." http://holiness-snake-handlers.webs.com/

Huffington Post. 2013. "Poland's Kosher Slaughter Ban Unacceptable and Harms Jewish Life Says Israel." July 15. http://www.huffingtonpost. com/2013/07/15/poland-kosher-slaughter-ban_n_3597550.html.

"Islamic Concerns." 2013. http://www.IslamicConcerns.com.

Johnson, M. F. 2006. "Heaven Help Us: The Religious Land Use and Institutionalized Persons Act's Prisoners Provisions in the Aftermath of the Supreme Court's Decision in Cutter v. Wilkinson." *American University Journal of Gender, Social Policy and the Law* 14:585.

KRS § 437.060 (2013).

Lammoglia, J. A. 2008. "Legal Aspects of Animal Sacrifice within the Context of Afro-Caribbean Religions." *St. Thomas Law Review* 20:710.

Larson, J. D. 2007. "RLUIPA, Distress, and Damages." *University of Chicago Law Review* 74:1443.

Matthews, J. 2009. "Review of *The Serpent and the Spirit: Glenn Summerford's Story.*" *Journal of American Folklore* 122, no. 484:230–32.

Merced v. Kasson. 2009 U.S. App. LEXIS 17027 (5th Cir. Tex., July 31, 2009).

Nelson, J. D. 2009. "Incarceration, Accommodation, and Strict Scrutiny." *Virginia Law Review* 95:2053.

Palmer, B. 2012. "Swine and Punishment." *Slate*, June 20. http://www.slate. com/articles/news_and_politics/explainer/2012/06/hebrew_national_lawsuit_what_happens_to_jews_who_eat_non_kosher_food_.html.

Penegar, K. L. 1978. "Survey of Tennessee Constitutional Law in 1976-77." *Tennessee Law Review* 46:120.

People for the Ethical Treatment of Animals (PETA). 2004. "Officials Agreed: Agriprocessors' Cruel Methods Had to Change." http://www.peta.org/ features/Agriprocessors-experts.aspx.

People for the Ethical Treatment of Animals (PETA). 2013. "The Global Leather Trade." http://www.peta.org/issues/animals-used-for-clothing/ global-leather-trade.aspx.

"Prisoners' Rights: Annual Review of Criminal Procedure." 2010. *Georgetown Law Journal* 39:993.

Qaddura v. State. 2007 Tex. App. LEXIS 1493.

Reed, E. 2012. "Liturgy with Bite? A New Generation of Snake-Handling Preachers Is Emerging." *Christianity Today/ Leadership Journal*. http:// www.christianitytoday.com/le/2012/summer/liturgywithbite.html.

Shabecoff, P. 1987. Killing of a Panther: Indian Treaty Rights vs. Law on Wildlife." *New York Times*, April 15. http://www.nytimes.com/1987/04/15/us/ killing-of-a-panther-indian-treaty-rights-vs-law-on-wildlife.html.

Shachar, G. 2009. "Food and Agricultural Import Regulations and Standards-Narrative: Fairs Country Report." *GAIN Report Number: IS9015: Israel*, August 3. http://gain.fas.usda.gov/Recent%20GAIN%20Publications/Food%20and%20Agricultural%20Import%20Regulations%20and%20Standards%20-%20Narrative_Tel%20Aviv_Israel_8-3-2009.pdf.

Slaughter, M. M. 1993. "The Salman Rushdie Affair: Apostasy, Honor, and Freedom of Speech." *Virginia Law Review* 79:153.

"Snake Handler." 2012. *Christian Century* 129, no. 13:8.

Stout, T. G. 2010. "The Costs of Religious Accommodation in Prisons." *Virginia Law Review in Brief* 96 (August 19):1201.

State ex rel. Swann v. Pack. 527 S.W.2d 99 (Tenn. 1975).

Takahash, M. A. 2004. "Cats v. Birds in Japan: How to Reconcile Wildlife Conservation and Animal Protection." *Georgetown International Environmental Law Review* 17:135.

Tatlow, D. K. 2013. "Amid Suffering, Animal Welfare Legislation Still Far Off in China." *International Herald Tribune*, March 6. http://rendezvous.blogs.nytimes.com/2013/03/06/amid-suffering-animal-welfare-legislation-still-far-off-in-china/?_r=0.

Tidball, K. G., and C. Toumey. 2007. "Serpents, Sainthood, and Celebrity: Symbolic and Ritual Tension in Appalachian Pentecostal Snake Handling." *Journal of Religion and Popular Culture* 17.

Urban Christian News (UCN). 2013. "Snake-Handling Pentecostal Pastor in Trouble with the Law." February 20. http://urbanchristiannews.com/ucn/2013/02/snake-handling-pentecostal-pastor-in-trouble-with-the-law.html#.Ug27LpK1GSo.

US Department of Agriculture Food Safety and Inspection Service (FSIS). 2003. "Humane Handling and Slaughter of Livestock." October 7. http://www.fsis.usda.gov/OPPDE/rdad/FSISDirectives/6900.2.pdf.

U.S. v. Billie. 667 F. Supp. 1485 (S.D.Fla. 1987).

Ventimiglia v. Sycamore View Church of Christ. 1988 Tenn. App. LEXIS 710.

Weeraratna, S. 2013. "Animal Friendly Cultural Heritage and Royal Decrees in the Legal History of Sri Lanka." *San Fransisco State University.* http://online.sfsu.edu/rone/Buddhism/BuddhismAnimalsVegetarian/Animal-FriendlySriLanka.htm.

Wisch, R. F. 2006. "Table of State Humane Slaughter Laws." *Animal Legal and Historical Center.* http://www.animallaw.info/articles/ovusstatehumaneslaughtertable.htm.

4

Canine Officers, K-9s, and Criminal Justice

Introduction

K-9 units contribute tremendous value to law enforcement, search and rescue organizations, and society. Dogs are experts in locating hidden people and objects, like cash, cadavers, narcotics, and bombs. Because of their expertise, dogs' participation in law enforcement has earned full respect from human peers. It has also garnered pushback from defendants who seek to challenge their training, reliability, and superhuman talent. In general, canine officers generate goodwill in the community and may improve public opinion regarding officers, especially among youth. Within law enforcement departments K-9 units may be costly and may be considered to be cliquish. However, their overall potency and efficiency is widely recognized and highly desirable.

Canine Officers

Police dogs are vital to law enforcement. They detect contraband, cash, accelerants, and cadavers better than any human officers, and they reflexively deal with threat more quickly than humans (Levy 2009). They can track missing persons or criminals, as well as conduct search and rescue operations. To their handlers police dogs are family, partners, weapons, and tools. To the public they are one of the most successful deterrents ever (USPCA 2013).

The presence of police dogs in communities lowers crime rates. In the public eye canines have become famous for their expert detection skills. For example, drug runners may avoid traveling through certain airports where canines are present. Another example is how the New York Police Department has heavily stationed police dogs at New York subways since the 9/11 attacks to deter terrorist attempts on the subway (Braverman 2013). Deterrence and detection may save taxpayers significant amounts of money, especially in comparison to the minimal cost required to maintain K-9 units (Wolfe 1999).

Records of cost, canines' health, training, and work activity must be scrupulously accounted for not only to demonstrate dogs' reliability but also to demonstrate K-9 units' cost-effectiveness. Training for dog and handler may cost approximately seven to fourteen thousand dollars (Geiger 2006). Equipment for a dog can cost several thousand dollars, and outfitting a police vehicle to become a K-9 unit adds to startup costs. Annual veterinary bills and food may cost several thousand dollars per dog. Handlers receive stipends for food as well as additional compensation for home and vacation hours spent with canines. Opportunity costs to a department may be valued at a few thousand dollars because officers must forgo other duties to receive initial handler training. Thus, the bulk of costs are front-loaded for a K-9 unit. Nevertheless, because dogs are not salaried officers, they outperform salaried human officers dollar for dollar throughout their tenures (Wolfe 1999). Their cost-effectiveness contrasts with increased paperwork required for K-9 units. Thus, opinions of their value may be polarized (Rouhib 2003). Yet, their strengths as cost effective crime fighters and community ambassadors cannot be overstated, even by those who are reluctant to accept them as officers.

Some canine training programs save money by adopting dogs from pounds or shelters and training dogs with positive feedback (Bird 1996). Adopted dogs may be admitted to the program, but those who are not admitted may receive the benefit of additional skills and socialization before being adopted by citizens.

Dogs are trained using games that culminate in field work. Dogs and trainers first use a towel as a toy. Eventually trainers wrap a scent in the towel; for example, narcotics may be hidden inside. This causes the dog to become accustomed to the scent and learn to search for the scent. Contraband, for example, drugs or cell phones, may be hidden in crates or stacks of boxes. K-9 officers may sniff up and down in a "V" pattern or use an off-leash pattern, which requires alerting by sitting next to detected contraband. Off-leash patterns are used to cover greater distances. Dogs who are off-leash may be tracked by helicopters using infrared collars, or they may be trained to locate contraband or temporarily seize suspects and wait for human officers to arrive.

To help the dogs develop acuity, the training process of locating scents is repeated numerous times using synthetic or actual scents, for example, marijuana or sweat. Trainers will conduct training in adverse conditions, such as noisy, snowy, rainy, or pungent environments. When dogs succeed under particular conditions, a detailed record is kept of their behavior and success. Training records are kept and will be used to support future field reports about the dog's alerts during adverse conditions, for example, certain wind patterns or high temperatures. The entire process lasts between two and six weeks. A dog's handler will be present during the dog's training and will also require additional training. Handlers receive between ten and sixteen weeks of training. This time is when a trainer initially develops a psychological bond with a dog. Recertification exercises recur throughout a dog's decade of service on the force.

Canines in K-9 units are officers. Dogs may be issued bulletproof vests or badges, and may be sworn in by barking. Killing, wounding, battering, and taunting police dogs are examples of crimes that elicit little mercy from the public police (Gilbert 2007; Novak 2013). In some jurisdictions killing a police dog may be a felony (Fla. Stat. § 843.19, 2013). If police dogs are killed, then they are buried by their departments. When they retire they may be adopted by and live with their handlers, though most departments will discontinue paying for the dog. Thus, canines do not typically receive police pensions, even though they work eight-hour days for the duration of their careers, just like every other officer (Levy 2009). However, some departments do provide mini-pensions in the form of lifetime basic veterinary and kennel expenses, which only cost taxpayers a couple of hundred dollars each year. The presence of canines reduces police use of weapons, which is another way that canines can reduce department costs. For example, when suspects are attempting to flee or fight, canines can subdue them without officers needing to rely on their weapons (Romero 2001). Sometimes officers improperly kill people, which results in lawsuits. If dogs properly subdue people, then those additional costs are avoided and dogs more than earn their mini-pensions (Weintraub 2001).

Unfortunately, police dog bites lead to lawsuits from time to time. For example, a suspect might sue police for shooting and killing his or her animal companion who runs at a canine officer (*Warboys v. Proulx*, 2004). Another example is when a suspect refuses to surrender, for example, hides. Officers will warn a suspect that a police dog will subdue and retrieve the suspect unless the suspect surrenders voluntarily (Weintraub 2001). When the dog is deployed, he or she will bite the suspect on the arm or leg and hold the suspect until other officers take control. In this case people may allege that officers improperly used unreasonable force or otherwise violated the Fourth Amendment, that is, illegal seizure. An individual officer, a department, and a municipality might be sued. More often than not, these suits do not amount to much since a municipality will not be held vicariously liable if proper procedures were followed, and an officer will likely receive qualified immunity. Nevertheless, for a number of reasons, including the announcement of the dog's deployment, the dog's adherence to training, and police's proper implementation of policy, lawsuits of this nature are frequently dismissed.

K-9 units generate tremendous amounts of goodwill for departments. They maintain a presence in schools and other locations within the community where dogs can be viewed as friends of the community—all while receiving affection and praise from the public (Weintraub 2001). This strategy is multilayered. As dogs endear themselves to the public and raise awareness to deter crime, public appearances help raise funds for K-9 units. Interested civic groups may conduct fundraisers if they buy into the overall value and importance of K-9 units in their communities (USPCA 2013). They may advertise desired donation goals and promote K-9 units to the public. They may also help arrange for the best training options or serve as liaisons. In exchange, civic groups may ask for K-9s to be available to them.

Dogs and handlers become extremely sensitive to each other. Dogs and handlers may be inseparable and always work as K-9 unit partners. For example, a handler may be able to sense the subtle effect that wind conditions are presently having on a dog's behavior (Annual Review of Criminal Procedure 2011; *U.S. v. Muñoz-Nava*, 2008). Policies that tolerate and incorporate these sensitivities may open the door to higher detection rates as well as increased policy challenges by defendants and the community. Psychological connections between a handler and a canine are lauded when they lead to successful search and rescues, but intuitive knowledge is questioned when searches for contraband are based on alert behaviors that do not strictly conform to training. Canine officers technically lack any professional discretion because they are not trained to make judgment calls in certain situations. Unlike human officers, canines must perform their duties in a routine manner each time. When they receive an order, canines must fulfill it immediately and accurately (USPCA 2013). As a result of this expectation, dogs may not actually be responsible for their mistakes. Handlers are responsible for dogs' and K-9 units' mistakes. Any variations in the field are likely to be blamed exclusively on a handler's incompetent training procedure. Generally, handlers must train with their partners for several hours each week. Training procedures must be documented in detail and thorough records must be kept of dogs' successful detections and alerts in a controlled environment in order to defend in-field alerts and procedures.

The importance of working dogs in criminal justice has amplified since the first use of war dogs on police forces sixty years ago. For example, police dogs are presently being used to detect sperm (Guibourg 2011). On one force dogs trained for a year before seeking evidence of semen in the field. Samples are collected when dogs alert to traces of semen at crime scenes. Forensic specialists then attempt to match collected samples to DNA samples taken from suspects, victims, or defendants. A special unit in Washington, DC, uses dogs to secure areas that will host the president, vice president, and visiting heads of state (Homeland Security 2013). Accident survivors may seem to disappear underwater, but trained volunteer rescue dogs can detect human scents up to one hundred feet below the surface (Gardner 2013).

Police dogs sometimes earn top honors for their valiance. For example, a veteran police dog retired in Spain after receiving the People's Dispensary for Sick Animals Gold Medal. He was honored because in 2009 he alerted to a bomb stashed under a car (MSN 2013). In New York a police dog was injured in the line of duty. Upon his release from the hospital, he was greeted with a K-9 Honor Guard (Masuike 2013). Spurred by the loss of K-9 officer Sirius on 9/11, the United States Police Canine Association is planning a National Law Enforcement Animal Memorial to honor all canines, horses, and other certified law enforcement animals who have died in service (USPCA 2013).

Canines and the Constitution

State, federal, and US Supreme Court cases have challenged the constitutionality of criminal procedures involving K-9 units. K-9 searches of private property have impacted US constitutional jurisprudence. Governmental searches of private property are forbidden by the Fourth Amendment of the Constitution unless the state has probable cause. Grounds for probable cause are constantly being challenged. On several occasions, the US Supreme Court has interpreted the Fourth Amendment and Fifth Amendments with respect to canines' superior ability to detect contraband. K-9 units' detection methods have been challenged because canines possess an ability to "x-ray" private property and because dogs are trained to alert their handlers.

Discussions about dogs' susceptibility to handlers' bias and unconscious cues have gone on for decades without much resolution. Critics have claimed that the value of a dog's alerts is inflated or fabricated because a handler may interpret a dog's behavior (Weiner and Homan 2006). Together the two operate as a team. Communication between a dog and handler may be subjective. Sometimes dogs alert in a manner that varies from their training. Officers have testified that their understanding of their dog requires a degree of mind reading or intimacy. That begs the following questions: (1) does an officer actually read a dog properly, (2) does a canine typically alert to what an officer believes is being alerted to, and (3) does a dog read an officer's expectation or desire to receive an alert and then alert?

For the most part, canine sniffs are not considered to be searches under the Fourth Amendment (*U.S. v. Jacobsen*, 1984). Canines' sense of smell penetrates exterior barriers and dogs detect contraband; thus, in some senses, they have a similar effect as searches. Dogs' acute detection abilities are precise, and yet, they do not detect noncontraband items. Thus, they disturb privacy far less than an officer rummaging through a person's possessions. Private articles that are intended to remain hidden are not turned out for public view during dog sniffs. Furthermore, sniffs are typically not searches because a container's exterior is not a reasonable place for a person to expect privacy. For example, a person does not expect that the public will not see the outside of a purse or pocket. Privacy rights are based on where a person can reasonably expect to have privacy. One's home is the most private place. Privacy rights are higher when one's home is involved because society expects a home to be private. The inside of a car may be somewhat private, but the outside of a car is visible to the public, just as the outside of a suitcase would be at an airport. A dog's sniff of exterior surfaces, for example, cars and luggage, does not violate any societal belief that a dog has infiltrated a private space without probable cause. Sniffs are not the same as opening a container for the world to see. However, probable cause to open and search a container would arise if the officer came to believe that a container contained contraband because a canine officer alerted to it.

In 1981 an assistant principal, a dog handler, a uniformed police officer, and fourteen German shepherds detained every junior high and high school student in one school for a massive dog sniff (*Doe v. Renfrow*, 1981). Each student was sniffed one by one over a period of more than two hours while members of the press watched. In response to this incident, the US Supreme Court stated that police dog sniffs were not searches as defined by the Fourth Amendment and the school had the right to "sniff-out" contraband. Police dogs could sniff students' bodies for drugs and alert handlers to drugs without probable cause. Furthermore, the alert could give officers probable cause to search, but not strip-search, students even if no drugs were found. During this school-wide sniff, police dogs alerted fifty times, but only seventeen students were found to possess marijuana, paraphernalia, or beer. Even when an alert was triggered by the lingering scent of a student's dog that was in heat, the alert and subsequent probable cause to search the student were valid. This use of dogs is not generalizable. For example, a road-block, which is like detention, cannot be set up in order to allow dogs to sniff every car in traffic (*Edmond v. Goldsmith*, 1999). For a number of reasons relating to the role that schools play in the community and the expectation of privacy held by students, systemic and warrantless sniffs are legal in this context.

Another constitutional question triggered by K-9s was whether permanent seizure of property is justified to permit police adequate time to relocate luggage to K-9 units. The Supreme Court analyzed whether police could take suspicious luggage from an airline passenger to bring it to a canine at another airport for a sniff test (*U.S. v. Place*, 1983). The answer was that although the exterior of luggage may be sniffed while it is in a passenger's possession, and luggage may be seized from passengers for a brief amount of time to be sniffed by a nearby K-9 unit, officers could not seize luggage without probable cause for a long period of time. Even though the passenger's privacy was not violated by the sniff test itself or would not have been violated by a brief seizure, the passenger's rights would have been violated by the officer's rummaging through the luggage without a warrant just the same as an extensive seizure.

During routine traffic stops canines may sniff the outside of any vehicle (*Illinois v. Caballes*, 2004). When a motorist is lawfully stopped by police pursuant to a traffic infraction, the motorist is seized under the Fourth Amendment. A seized motorist does not have a special privacy right to the outside of that vehicle. A motorist's privacy expectation while in a public place is much lower than in or immediately around his or her home. Even though there is privacy protection on the inside of one's vehicle, the outside of the vehicle is different. A free-air sniff of a vehicle's exterior can be conducted without a warrant (*Florida v. Harris*). If a canine alerts to the presence of contraband, then the officer has probable cause to search a vehicle without the driver's consent.

In 2013 the US Supreme Court decided that a search occurs when an officer brings a canine to a home's front porch to sniff for the presence of marijuana inside a person's home (*Florida v. Jardines*, 2013). The act of bringing a canine officer to the front porch is a governmental search of a person's home under the Fourth Amendment. Because a police dog's superior sense of smell can penetrate walls, the act of bringing the dog to a front porch would be the same as opening a closed door and rummaging through the house. The canine's odor-detection skills effectively penetrate a home in a way that is impermissible because of a society's high expectation for privacy inside one's home. Probable cause to search a home must be established under the Fourth Amendment before a K-9 unit approaches a front porch, not after the dog alerts for the presence of marijuana inside the home. One might argue that police dogs should not be excluded from approaching homes when all other leashed dogs may customarily be allowed to approach front porches. However, police dogs' training and purpose at the home is what precludes them from approaching under the circumstances. They are not excluded from approaching front porches in a manner that is customary in our society. Approaching a home to sniff for evidence is not customarily acceptable. In the line of duty, a dog works for the state, and thus, approaching a home to search it must be subject to the Fourth Amendment.

Simultaneous with the US Supreme Court's decision about front-porch canine searches, the court also decided that a canine's alert could give rise to probable cause for a lawful search of a car. The court held that irrespective of whether a canine gave a false alert, probable cause exists because a dog's reliability is dependent on the totality of the circumstances (*Florida vs. Harris*, 2013). In conformity with a defendant's constitutional rights, if a canine detects contraband and a suspect is arrested, then the defendant has a right to challenge whether the dog's alert created probable cause that led to a lawful search. At a probable cause hearing, the state would need to prove that a particular dog reliably detects drugs. The state can show that the dog is certified in drug detection or routinely detects drugs in controlled situations. In *Florida vs. Harris*, the defendant was pulled over for an infraction. The defendant, who appeared nervous and had an open container of alcohol, refused a search of his vehicle. A K-9 sniffed the outside of the vehicle and alerted. Though no drugs were found, numerous ingredients for cooking methamphetamine were found. The defendant was arrested. He admitted to cooking and using meth in his home. On another occasion the same dog detected drugs in the same defendant's vehicle during a traffic stop. No drugs or ingredients were found on that occasion. The defendant argued that the false positive demonstrates that the dog was not reliable. The defendant argued that because that dog was not reliable, the first alert did not legally give the officer probable cause to search and consequently arrest him. The court held that the totality of the circumstances goes to show probable cause. Cases should not turn on a single false alert.

If a defendant disputes the state's proof that a dog is reliable because the dog gave a false positive in one situation, then a court will weigh the evidence. The dog's reliability will come into question just as any witness's reliability would during a probable cause hearing. A history of false alerts will balance against the dog's certification, record of accuracy or field performance, and successful training maintenance. The totality of the circumstances will be examined to determine whether a particular dog's alert in a specific circumstance lawfully created probable cause to search a vehicle. In considering inconsistencies in field performance, the court supplied possible explanations for why well-trained dogs may seem to give false positives. For example, a dog could alert to narcotics odors on door handles that transfer from drugs handled at home, or a dog might alert to the presence of drugs that could not be found because they were too well hidden. Thus, a history of inaccuracy with a particular dog in a particular case goes to the totality of the circumstances in making a determination about probable cause in that particular case, but a false alert does not single-handedly taint the dog's reliability overall. Certification or training that is validated by a history of successful drug detection in controlled environments is enough to trust a dog's alert. Nevertheless, a defendant has the right to challenge the dog's reliability, training, and bias, even if a court rules that an officer had probable cause to search based on a dog's "false" alert because probable cause cannot be made in hindsight based on what is or is not discovered during the search.

One of the most controversial uses of canines is dog scent lineups (IPOT 2009; Taslitz 1990). Lineups are a polarizing aspect of justice because many feel that they are suggestive and fallible. For the same reasons, many people feel that dog scent lineups ought to be impermissible. In a dog scent lineup, an article or object is identified as belonging to the guilty party. A canine officer sniffs the article and matches the scent to a particular person in a lineup. The alert is admissible evidence. In one controversial case four officers (who were known to the dog) and the suspect were the only individuals standing in a five-person lineup. The dog alerted that the suspect's scent matched the article. The suspect was tried and convicted. This example was held not to violate due process, but in other cases due process has been violated when a suspect is the only person of a particular race, age, or other obvious demographic. These flaws are with the officers' designs of the lineups, not necessarily dogs' scent-detection capabilities. Yet, canines' susceptibility to suggestivity and bias has been called into question.

Criminal Justice Subculture and Canines

K-9 culture is close-knit. K-9 officers, K-9 units, and large K-9 departments invest a huge portion of their emotional and mental energy into psychologically connecting with dogs, training dogs, and engaging in bonding activities that strengthen K-9 subculture. Bonding occurs through discussion, shared leisure activities, and K-9 competitions. It almost always occurs to the exclusion of non–K-9 units. Though non–K-9 officers may love or respect canine officers, they may not be intimately involved with the dogs or any aspect of K-9 culture.

Local, regional, and national K-9 competitions draw passionate teams and reinforce K-9 culture or solidarity among officers and units (ACA 2000). In regional competitions scores of police and correctional teams may compete in indoor-location competitions and vehicle competitions. At competitions K-9 handlers might discuss the structure of their unit; the kinds of searches conducted, for example, special, targeted, or random; distinctions between police and corrections units; and variations in training among dogs. K-9 units could discuss detection of drugs in prison mail or airport parcels, how to keep prison populations moving safely in a group, how to detain groups, hidden-compartment detection in vehicles, night fires, one-hand shooting skill, and interrogation and interview techniques. Handlers will compare their unique experiences, including how one dog may be trained to close patrol car doors using a towel, while others may be trained to assist in first aid or helicopter deployment. During competitions or while working, handlers share information between teams, units, departments, agencies, and jurisdictions about how to procure reputable handlers; where to purchase specially bred dogs; how to acquire donated dogs; benefits of adopting from the Humane Society; and pros and cons of unit sizes, structures, and policies (USPCA 2013). Shared information may be useful, but many of the discussions are purely for bonding, enjoyment, and enlightenment.

Handlers ought to be intelligent, sensitive, good public speakers, stable family members, loyal, fit, patient, self-motivated, and sufficiently mature to maximize a dog's strengths and training (Forgues 2012; Rouhib 2003; USPCA 2013). Handlers cast their partners in the best light possible (Weintraub 2001). They use positive reinforcement to train dogs and avoid blaming their partners for any team mistakes. K-9 culture may encourage handlers to cover up dogs' mistakes and privately make adjust training. Some officers may be willing to bend rules or procedures to protect or defend their partners.

When a suspect is to be taken into custody but instead flees, K-9 units may be deployed to search for the suspect. When a suspect is located by a canine officer, the dog will bite the suspect and maintain a grip. Docile suspects are injured less than resistant suspects. Canine officers release when ordered by a handler to do so. If a suspect has run much faster than the handler, then a seizure may last between seconds or minutes until a handler is able to catch up. In one case an officer claimed that when he arrived at a seizure, a suspect was resisting by hitting his K-9 partner with a pipe. In response, the officer kicked the suspect in the head, face, and body while the canine continued to bite the suspect. Though the suspect did not prevail in his lawsuit, the court discussed the handler's breech of rules. In this situation the officer probably should have ordered the dog to end the seizure so that the handler could take the suspect into custody. This would likely have taken the canine and that suspect out of harm's way more expeditiously, but the handler likely felt protective and angry in response to the abuse. Incidents like these are equally common and possibly more serious within non–K-9 teams. Unfortunately, when K-9 units make mistakes, those who view dogs as a liability may take advantage of failures to implement sweeping policy changes. In one instance a deputy from the Los Angeles Sheriff's Department K-9 Unit took his partner to a park for a walk. The canine bit a man at the park. The department paid the man's medical costs plus a small settlement, but the entire jurisdiction was forced to undergo significant policy changes in response to the incident (Schwartz 2012).

K-9 handlers have been described by non–K-9 officers as cliquish and protective of their dogs. One complaint that non–K-9 officers may voice is that they are unsure of the extent to which they should insulate a handler and canine partner. Some non–K-9 officers wonder what should be done, for example, if a canine officer attacks a K-9 handler. Should a non–K-9 officer intervene with lethal force? Many handlers would likely discourage intervention. However rare, lethal force may be required to subdue a canine officer (Cullman County 2013). In those situations, a K-9 officer might prefer to pull the trigger, but only if it is absolutely necessary.

Another question is whether non–K-9 officers should blow the whistle on abusive handlers. Police culture demands brotherhood and secrecy. Whistleblowing is frowned upon. Yet, animal abuse is so repugnant, unconscionable, and outside the normal range of police indiscretions or abuses that officers may choose to blow the whistle. The best route for doing so would be an anonymous tip. However, if anonymity is breached, then a whistleblower may be ostracized. In one case an officer reported K-9 abuse to People for the Ethical Treatment of Animals (PETA) (Swift 2012). The officer believed that the tip was confidential, but PETA believed that they could use the officer's identification to substantiate the allegation that a handler repeatedly punched and kicked a canine officer, which is a crime. The whistleblower, who did not know that his anonymity had been breached, denied whistleblowing during an internal investigation, and subsequently had to resign for perjuring himself. The handler was never sanctioned or charged. In recent years PETA has become involved in a number of cases involving allegations of K-9 abuse (Mason 2013). Yet, handlers are rarely penalized unless a canine officer dies, for example, when a canine is killed by heat stroke while waiting in a hot car (Murdock 2013). Departments usually take note of scandals involving animal cruelty and attempt to adopt proactive measures. For example, after a few canine officers died from heat stroke, many K-9 units began using hot-dog car systems that may role down windows, turn on air conditioning, page officers, or sound alarms if hot temperatures are detected.

When police dogs die in the line of duty, they are honored; and when handlers die in the line of duty, canine officers mourn their fallen partners. They may show signs of depression or may keep vigil beside a coffin or location where a handler and dog bonded most within a home (*Huffington Post* 2013). Animal vigils are common in nature and among domesticated companion populations, but canine officers' public grief often consoles fallen officers' families or colleagues and generates goodwill from the public. Human officers' grief over the loss of their canine partners may be quite moving. In one case a canine officer's obituary spread rapidly throughout the Internet (Weir 2014). The human officer sadly described the experience of writing an obituary with "tears . . . flowing freely" for his partner who had detected more than one thousand grams of heroin, eighty-six hundred grams of cocaine, one thousand pounds of marijuana, and fourteen million dollars in cash over the course of twenty-three hundred K-9 unit rides.

Conclusion

Canines may have superhuman talents, but they are neither invulnerable nor infallible. Suspects may resist arrest, human officers may neglect or abuse canines, and defendants may attack K-9 units' credibility in court. While working—for example, in bomb detection, locating corpses, and contraband searches—dogs' and human handlers' lives are at risk. When canines have been killed in the line of duty, their deaths have been deeply regretted within departments. Yet, K-9 units are typically enthusiastically committed to law enforcement and the preservation of human life. They are cost-effective and create goodwill between police and communities.

References

American Correctional Association (ACA). 2000. "Maryland Division of Correction's K-9 Unit Wins National Championship." *Corrections Today* 62, no. 5 (August):122.

"Annual Review of Criminal Procedure." 2011. *Georgetown Law Journal* 40:1.

Braverman, I. 2013. "Passing the Sniff Test: Police Dogs as Surveillance Technology." *Buffalo Law Review* 61:81.

Bird, R. C. 1996. "An Examination of the Training and Reliability of the Narcotics Detection Dog." *Kentucky Law Journal* 85:405.

Cullman County. 2013. "Hanceville Officer Forced to Shoot K9 after Dog Attacks Him." June 24. http://cullmancounty.myfoxal.com/news/news/195583-hanceville-officer-forced-shoot-k9-after-dog-attacks-him.

Edmond v. Goldsmith. 183 F.3d 659, 665-66 (7th Cir. 1999).

Fla. Stat. § 843.19 (2013).

Florida v. Harris. 2013 U.S. LEXIS 1121; 568 U.S. ___ (2013).

Florida v. Jardines. 2013 U.S. LEXIS 2542; 569 U.S. ___ (2013).

Forgues, S. 2012. "Selecting the Better K9 Handler." *Officer.com*, December 13. http://www.officer.com/article/10841851/selecting-the-better-k9-handler.

Gardner, T. 2013. "There's a Good Buoy! Britain's First Underwater Sniffer Dog Can Find Submerged Bodies up to 100ft Away." *Daily Mail*, June 3. http://www.dailymail.co.uk/news/article-2335020/Sniffer-dog-trained-search-UNDER-WATER-bodies-100ft-away.html#ixzz2cUXxhaSo.

Geiger, B. 2006. "People v. Caballes: An Analysis of Caballes, the History of Sniff Search Jurisprudence, and Its Future Impact." *Northern Illinois University Law Review* 26:595.

Gilbert, H. 2007. "Man Charged with Killing Police Dog Could Get Life under 'Three Strikes' Law." *Oregonian*, October 25. http://www.freerepublic.com/focus/f-news/1916238/posts.

Guibourg, C. 2011. "Sperm-Sniffing Police Dog Snags Rapist." *Local*, July 16. http://www.thelocal.se/34986/20110716/.

Homeland Security Division. 2013. "Icon Protection Branch Canine Unit." http://www.nps.gov/uspp/Canpag.htm.

Illinois v. Caballes. 543 U.S. 405 (2004).

Innocence Project of Texas (IPOT). 2009. "Dog Scent Lineups: A Junk Science Injustice." September 21. http://www.ipoftexas.org/Websites/ipot/images/IPOT_Dog_Scent_Report.pdf.

Levy, A. 2009. "Police Dogs to Retire on Their Own Gold-Plated Public Pensions." *Daily Mail*, July 16. http://www.dailymail.co.uk/news/article-1204551/Police-dogs-retire-gold-plated-pensions.html#ixzz2cUAv1B50.

MSN. 2013. "Police Dog Gets Top Honor for Its Lifesaving Sniffing Skills." June 12. http://now.msn.com/ajax-spanish-police-dog-wins-award-for-bravery-from-british-animal-group.

Murdock, S. 2013. "Officer Robert Miller, Suspended for Leaving K-9 Partner in Hot Car, Leading to Dog's Death." *Huffington Post*, July 16. http://www.huffingtonpost.com/2013/08/16/k-9-tank-death_n_3767699.htmlHuffington.

Mason, M. 2013. "PETA vs. Fort Myers PD in Case of Officer Striking K-9 Partner." *Fox 4*, February 18. http://www.fox4now.com/news/local/191752021.html.

Masuike, H. 2013. "A K-9 honor guard for bear the police dog." *New York Times*, June 26. http://cityroom.blogs.nytimes.com/2013/06/26/a-k-9-honor-guard-for-bear-the-police-dog/?_r=0.

Novak, B. 2013. "Don't Mess with Slim: Woman Arrested after Allegedly Harassing Police Dog." *Madison.com*, August 19. http://host.madison.com/news/local/crime_and_courts/don-t-mess-with-slim-woman-arrested-after-allegedly-harassing/article_35a2024f-ce9b-56d0-a813-0e99798c0f02.html.

"Police Dog Figo Pays Lasts Respects to His Fallen Partner, Officer Jason Ellis." 2013 *Huffington Post*, May 31. http://www.huffingtonpost.com/2013/05/31/figo-jason-ellis_n_3367374.html?utm_hp_ref=mostpopular.

Romero, M. 2001. "From El Bandido to Gang Member." *Denver University Law Review* 78:1081.

Rouhib, G. T. 2003. "Implementing a Canine Unit in a Small Police Agency E.M.U. School of Police Staff and Command." *E.M.U. School of Police Staff and Command*. http://www.emich.edu/cerns/downloads/papers/Police Staff/Patrol,%20Operations,%20Tactics/Implementing%20a%20Canine%20Unit%20in%20a%20Small%20Police%20Agency.pdf.

Schwartz, J. C. 2012. "What Police Learn from Lawsuits." *Cardozo Law Review* 33:841.

Swift, A. 2012. "Lee Ex-Deputy's Suit vs. Peta in Whistle-Blower Case Heads to Trial." *Balmer*, January 7. http://www.naplesnews.com/news/2012/jan/07/k9-officer-peta-lee-sheriff-lawsuit-whistle-blower/?banner=1.

Taslitz, A. E. 1990. "Does the Cold Nose Know? The Unscientific Myth of the Dog Scent Lineup." *Hastings Law Journal* 42:17.

U.S. v. Jacobsen. 466 U.S. 109 (1984).

U.S. v. Muñoz-Nava. 524 F.3d 1137, 1145-46 (10th Cir. 2008).

U.S. v. Place. 462 U.S. 696 (1983).

United States Police Canine Association (USPCA). 2013. http://www.uspcak9.com/

Warboys v. Proulx. 303 F.Supp.2d 111 (D. Conn. 2004).

Weiner, J. S., and K. Homan. 2006. "'Those Doggone Sniffs Are Often Wrong: The Fourth Amendment Has Gone to the Dogs." *Champion* 30:12.

Weintraub, M. 2001. "A Pack of Wild Dogs? Chew v. Gates and Police Canine Excessive Force." *Loyola of Los Angeles Law Review* 34:937.

Weir, S. B. 2014. "K-9 Obituary Goes Viral: Pass the Tissues." *Yahoo.com*, January 29. http://shine.yahoo.com/pets/k-9-obituary-goes-viral-pass-tissues-184100011.html.

Wolfe, M. 1999. "A Study of Police Canine Search Teams." *United States Police Canine Association.* http://www.uspcak9.com/training/WolfeBuilding-Study.pdf.

5

Other Animal Employees

Introduction

Law enforcement is aided by animals on land, air, and sea. Some animals who are normally thought to be wild are either raised in captivity and trained or voluntarily contribute to law enforcement efforts. Feral cats may naturally offer mice-catching skills, while horses, dolphins, sea lions, and pigeons have been trained to perform specialized work. Like K-9 units, animals in government service often risk their lives by working with weapons, detecting terrorists, subduing rioters, and apprehending intruders. Typically, law enforcement departments embrace their efforts and reward them with admiration and additional protection.

Transportation Security Administration (TSA)

The Transportation Security Administration (TSA) created the National Canine Program (NCP) to train dogs to detect drugs, explosives, and other contraband ("TSA's Puppy Program" 2012). Dogs have worked in airports since the 1970s, but following the 9/11 attacks, the TSA began spending approximately half of a million dollars annually on breeding programs (Huddleston 2012). Each year since, the TSA has bred approximately eighty sturdy puppies that were not as susceptible to common ailments (Huddleston 2012; TSA 2007). More than five hundred genetically selected puppies have been bred since the program began, but the breeding program was closed in 2012 due to budgetary constraints. The TSA continues to fund one hundred twenty canine teams (Lovitt 2013). This is a fraction of the nearly one thousand canine units operating at transportation facilities throughout the country. Annually, each team costs taxpayers one hundred sixty-four thousand dollars in basic expenses, for example, veterinary care. Altogether, TSA budgets more than one hundred million dollars each year for detection services through the NCP.

To maintain cost-effectiveness, the TSA now buys puppies from sources other than their former in-house breeders; relies on hundreds of volunteers to foster puppies prior to their training; and trains puppies using more cost-effective methods, such as prisoner pet-training programs (Huddleston 2012). Puppies are fostered between the ages of nine weeks and fourteen months (TSA 2007; "TSA's Puppy Program" 2012). Once puppies are trained, they are paired with full-time handlers (Strunsky 2013). Trained dogs who are ill-suited for the National Explosives Detection Canine Team Program are adopted by private individuals (Jennings 2008; "TSA's Puppy Program" 2012). Because NCP dogs are trained at Lackland Air Force Base, the Department of Defense Military Working Dog Adoption Program will place retired detection dogs for adoption (Waac 2010). Almost all dogs that are adopted through Lackland Air Force Base programs are adopted by their former handlers.

Handlers may feel that TSA dogs are like partners and family members. The TSA pays handlers a yearly stipend for food, but handlers are fully responsible for their dogs every hour of the day (Lovitt 2013). Because of this full-time relationship, dogs are also required to behave like companion animals with the handlers' spouses, children, neighbors, and so on (Strunsky 2013). During their shifts dogs who are not actively working may behave like companion animals with their handlers, but when duty calls, dogs and handlers readily refocus.

German shepherds, Belgian malinois, beagles, and Labrador retrievers are some breeds of dogs that may be trained to detect bombs or contraband in cargo and on commercial flights (Aratani 2013; Strunsky 2013). The Federal Air Marshal Service, Homeland Security, and the Department of Defense may utilize dogs trained to patrol transportation facilities and detect explosives (Strunsky 2013). Implementation of passenger prescreening on commercial flights means that many passengers will be sniffed prior to passing through TSA security to eliminate shoe, liquid, and laptop removal procedures (Millstone 2013).

Unfortunately, working dogs occasionally incur some of the same issues as TSA employees. They may give false alerts, experience moodiness, or randomly attack passengers (Lovitt 2013). In 2013 a woman in Georgia claimed that a TSA dog bit her stomach for no reason. The bomb-sniffing dog passed her, jumped up, punctured and bloodied her abdomen, and then walked away. These events are rarer than allegations of abuse made against human TSA employees, yet they demonstrate that dogs are susceptible to stress and chaos that may come with the territory of working airport security. Further research is needed to determine optimal behavioral, physiological, and genetic markers of successful detection canines and best practices for de-stressing working dogs (TSA 2013).

Though unprovoked attacks are few and far between, an abundance of NCP deficiencies was brought to light in a 2012 study. A number of canine teams throughout the country were noncompliant with the TSA's monthly training requirements between May 2011 and April 2012. This may likely have affected the teams' proficiency explosives detection. Between September 2011 and July 2012, canine teams exceeded the requirement for screening cargo placed onto passenger aircrafts. This demonstrated that TSA was generally lax but could uniformly increase all air cargo screening or redeploy canine teams to actively screen more passengers using a risk-based approach. The report notes false alerts and teams' failure to detect some explosives odors. Finally, the study states that findings could have been put to better use, but data was not efficiently applied. In response to the report, qualitative research was conducted among handlers, who stated that TSA ought to improve consistency and objectivity in their evaluation processes so that they can accurately assess whether canines were properly and competently performing their duties. The NCP, which seems to be extremely successful and cost-effective overall, is still being researched to improve a number of its facets (TSA 2013). The program continues to expand annually at a rapid rate (Lovitt 2013).

Horses

Mounted police are a critical component of some police forces. Police horses mainly patrol streets, create police presence, improve community relations, provide transportation, and control crowds (Cooper 2011). Occasionally they have been used to run down other animals, including wild horses (Hodgin 2013). Due to their visibility, approachability, and public popularity, the presence of a police horse is estimated to be seven to ten times as effective as the presence of one human officer in terms of deterrence within crowds (Cooper 2011). Despite their effectiveness, police horses are rapidly being replaced by police riding bicycles, skateboards, and scooters. Though these methods of transportation are not as visible as police horses, they also create approachability and likeability. These methods require less time and money than police horses, who rarely spend all eight hours of their shifts on patrol. Police horses may cost around twenty thousand dollars annually for a couple of decades, while bicycles cost next to nothing. Though police horses receive large donations from the community, they cause departments to incur opportunity costs. While officers are prepping and bedding horses, they forsake other duties.

Horses acquired by police departments through donation or purchase undergo evaluation and training (Cusack, 2015). In Houston, which operates a large mounted patrol, initial training lasts for ninety days (Houston Police Department 2013). Horses are exposed to tarps, loud fireworks, and the presence of smoke. Their dispositions when encountering groups of people and other horses are assessed. During training they are exposed to a variety of situations, including parks, crowded city districts, major city construction projects, vehicular traffic, pedestrian traffic, changes in terrain, steps, and water obstacles. If they successfully pass the ninety-day training, then they are accepted onto the force. Police horses do not often participate in public swearing-in ceremonies, as some canine officers do. Once on the police force, horses routinely train. Training is unlike K-9 training because horses do not participate in searches. K-9 units must continuously train in constitutional and industry-standard detection techniques so that detected contraband can become legally admissible evidence. Equine officers' training mainly involves grounding horses to be ridden, riding practice, formation, crowd control procedures, and harassment and loud noise preparedness exercises. Horsemanship training may be conducted in addition to routine skills maintenance.

Various jurisdictions have increased ecological awareness of equine officers (Houston Police Department 2013). For example, the Border Patrol in Arizona incorporated horses, in part, because of the Border Patrol's concern for its carbon footprint in ecologically sensitive areas (Rotstein 2005). The patrol feeds equine officers special food produced from native plants so that horses' droppings do not disseminate and fertilize nonnative seeds throughout the region. The Houston Mounted Patrol initiated national interest in barefoot programs. Originally, a few mounted officers paid out of pocket for training in hoof trimming. They developed a technique whereby they trim their horses' hooves, then use hoof boots until equine officers' hoof strength is regained and sensitivity is eliminated. Under the barefoot program, barefoot police horses do not wear shoes; yet, they successfully work on all terrains and have very few physical problems.

Out-of-pocket expenses may overwhelm officers. In some cases officers have declared bankruptcy because, in addition to other expenses, they have had trouble paying thousands of dollars each year to maintain police horses after retirement (*In re Dorwarth*, 2001). Alleviation of care-related expenses could tempt creative judges to order offenders to contribute fines or services to equine departments. In one case an offender convicted of committing insurance fraud against horse trainers was ordered to perform janitorial services for horse stables belonging to the Baltimore City Police Mounted Unit (Morton 2001).

Police horses may vary between departments. Though some mares serve, police horses are usually gelded males, who have been castrated (Tierney 2007). Officers often switch horses, so the horses' subdued personalities make it easier for multiple horses to be ridden by several officers (Tierney 2007). In some police herds a single horse's care and supervision will be assigned to an officer (Mounted Patrol 2013). The length of a police horse's service depends on an individual's age and health. Some police horses are purchased, but others are donated. Horses may be donated when community members are unable to care for them. When horses retire they may return to live with the original donor. Oftentimes they are placed on farms belonging to officers' relatives (Tierney 2007). Arthritis or other conditions that onset in old age usually contribute to retirement. Police horses may receive pension in the form of hay and water (Cooper 2011). When a large number of horses retire from a herd around the same time, departments may strain to find enough suitable homes expeditiously (Tierney 2007).

Harming police horses is a serious offense that deeply bothers members of the police force. Killing a police horse could be a felony offense in some jurisdictions. In California merely interfering with a police horse can enhance sentencing (Sigal 2007). Despite serious charges associated with harming police horses, on-duty police horses face many dangers. Sometimes horses are accidentally or intentionally injured by drivers in traffic or drunk drivers (Cooper 2011; Moran 2013). Injuries caused by pedestrians may be intentional or result during crowd control (Moran 2013). In a highly publicized incident, a professional basketball player from Cincinnati was charged with assault for punching a police horse in the neck four times (*Inquirer* 1995). Police horses have also been vandalized, battered, and illegally released from their stables (Reimer 2012; Robol 2012).

In addition to horses receiving abuse from crowds, mounted police have been alleged to use questionable or violent crowd control tactics. Antiwar protests after 9/11 involved such allegations (Dunn 2005). The New York Police Department's (NYPD's) mounted unit was sued for allegedly illegally dispersing people peacefully assembled on public walkways. Specifically, a student claimed that he had been toppled and injured by a police horse. The student was arrested after the incident. He also claimed to have been beaten and detained for hours in a frigid police van. In that case the court held that the petitioner did not have standing, and thus, a determination was not made about the crowd control tactics employed by NYPD's mounted unit. During Occupy Wall Street protests, demonstrators in New York again claimed to have been abused by the mounted unit (Guelpa 2011). They claimed that police horses were used to abusively charge into crowds, mounted police tore apart tents and pepper-sprayed peaceful people, and units illegally blocked streets. The NYPD also claims that demonstrators abused horses during these protests.

When horses are killed in the line of duty, they are memorialized and sometimes mourned by thousands of attendees (Briggs 2006). When police horses survive great ordeals, they may be honored (Lawless 2012). For example, in London three equine officers were awarded medals for their service during World War II. In one situation a bomb exploded, sending glass and debris flying into a public area. A police horse was seventy-five yards from the bomb and was showered by debris during the explosion. The horse remained calm and assisted the rider in directing traffic until the situation was under control.

Dolphins, Sea Lions, and Pigeons in the Military

Dolphins are trained to serve as soldiers by US Navy (Welch 2010). Almost one hundred dolphins participate in the War on Terror by patrolling a variety of waters, primarily along California's coast. Approximately thirty sea lions are trained to cuff intruders with leg traps. The marine animals, who are bred in captivity, receive military medical treatment and other benefits. By using whistles and positive reinforcement during daily training, essential bonds are developed between an individual trainer and a specific animal. Positive bonds bring about results. Training that begins in infancy ripens when a dolphin is between three and six years old. Dolphins' duties vary considerably. Using their echolocation, dolphins may track objects better than mechanical sonar devices do. Some are trained to hunt for mines and place acoustic transponders near the mines, and other dolphins may deliver messages. Unsubstantiated reports have circulated that some dolphins were trained to fire guns.

Like sea lions, some dolphins are routinely trained to detect intruders. A dolphin will swim to a handler's boat, where a strobe will be affixed to a dolphin's snout. The dolphin will then swim to an intruder, bump the intruder's torso, and release the strobe light to the surface. Sea lions or human soldiers will respond to the location of the strobe light. If a sea lion responds, then a cuff, which is attached to a line, will be placed on the intruder's leg. Sea lions, whose vision is 500 percent better than humans' vision, exceptionally detect intruders, and dolphins share this strength.

Allegations of abuse surround marine-life military training. US Navy was criticized for placing warm-water dolphins in very cool waters. US Navy brought dolphins to Alaska and South Korea during the winter to test their tolerance for cold. They claimed that the cool waters do not affect dolphins' resting metabolic rates. Dolphins only patrol cool waters for two hours at a time before returning to heated pens. Abuse allegations have been investigated by Marine Mammal Commission, but remain unproven. Some activists believe that all captivity is cruel. In one case, some dolphins, who were being prepared to be released into the wild by US Navy and a special park, were prematurely liberated into the wild by an activist. The activist was fined, but not incarcerated.

Like sea lions, pigeons have exceptional vision (USCG 2012; Welch 2010). The US Coast Guard trained pigeons to occupy an observation dome situated on the underside of a helicopter (USCG 2012). Three birds scoped out a three-hundred-sixty-degree circumference, with a one-hundred-twenty-degree range assigned to each bird. When birds detected floating objects, they were trained to peck a key to guide pilots to the object. Pigeons' accuracy was greater than 90 percent in comparison to humans, who were accurate only 38 percent percent of the time. Pigeons are no longer used by the Coast Guard, though their training and skills could still be useful to homeland security.

Pigeon couriers have been used in criminal justice environments in several nations. More than two hundred thousand pigeons served with the Allies during World War II. Mercury, Princess, and All Alone were three of the thirty-two pigeons awarded Dickin Medals by the People's Dispensary for Sick Animals (PDSA) ("PDSA Dickin Medal Pigeons" 2013). Pigeons, who delivered messages during World War II, demonstrated bravery and took life-saving actions during conflict. Many saved hundreds of lives by delivering messages in the nick of time and under adverse weather or safety conditions. In India pigeons were used by police departments until e-mail and electronic communication made their work redundant (BBC 2002). India's Police Pigeon Service required pigeons to fly vast areas, sometimes during cyclones or floods. Originally trained by the army, India's police began relying on pigeons in 1946. But, the program costs about $10,260 a year, which became impractical.

Cats Helping Cops

Cats have worked outside or inside police stations around the world (Roberts 2013). Sometimes they have been outfitted with photo identification cards or badges. A feral cat in Moscow was naturally skilled at detecting hidden caviar, so police trained the cat to search vehicles, people, and containers for illegal caviar. One cat who normally worked as pest control inside a police station went undercover in a sting. After helping to catch an untrained college student who offered to butcher animals under the pretense of providing licensed veterinary services, the undercover cat was featured on news reports and honored in a ceremony.

Cats aiding police with pest control is not uncommon. In Los Angeles, Voice for the Animals's Working Cats program relocated feral cats to police stations throughout the city (Hall 2007). Feral cats live outside stations, sometimes sleeping under or upon squad cars. Cats catch mice and also deter infestations with their markings and scent. Faithful rat-killing once earned a navy cat a Dickin Medal, which honors war animals (Lawless 2012). Aboard the *Amethyst*, a Royal Navy ship, the cat was wounded during an attack but continued to fulfill duties to the utmost while the *Amethyst* was trapped for months at sea. The cat died shortly before a Dickin Medal could be awarded.

Conclusion

Training or relationship building between government agents and animals demonstrates animals' value to society and the criminal justice system. It also suggests that additional animals could become more deeply involved in society in exchange for increased respect and protection. Contribution of natural or developed skills could strengthen a number of governmental entities and criminal justice efforts. Animals' work in government may never replace human efforts, but their work often surpasses and enhances human abilities.

References

Aratani, L. 2013. "Belvoir Veterinarians Keep Law Enforcement's Dogs Ready for Action." *Washington Post*, July 9. http://articles.washingtonpost.com/2013-07-09/local/40458817_1_dogs-labrador-retrievers-malinois.

BBC. 2002. "Indian Pigeons Lose out to E-Mail." May 26. http://news.bbc.co.uk/2/hi/south_asia/1892085.stm.

Briggs, K. 2006. "Toronto police horse killed on duty." *The Horse*, April 1. http://www.thehorse.com/articles/16076/toronto-police-horse-killed-on-duty.

Cooper, M. 2011. "Police Departments Downsize, from 4 Legs to 2." *New York Times*, February 14. http://www.nytimes.com/2011/02/15/us/15horses.html?pagewanted=all&_r=0.

Cusack, C. M. 2015. *Criminal Justice Handbook on Masculinity, Male Aggression, and Sexuality*. Charles C Thomas: Springfield.

Dunn, C. 2005. "Balancing the Right to Protest in the Aftermath of September 11. *Harvard Civil Rights-Civil Liberties Law Review* 40:327.

Guelpa, P. 2011. "Occupy Albany Encampment Brutally Attacked by Police." *World Socialist Website*, December 24. http://www.wsws.org/en/articles/2011/12/alba-d24.html.

Hall, C. 2007. "LAPD Puts Cats on Patrol." *Los Angeles Times*, December 24. http://articles.latimes.com/2007/dec/29/local/me-feralcats29.

Hodgin, M. D. 2013. "Police Chase after Wild Horses Loose in Watchung, Report Says." *NewJersey.com*, May 31. http://www.nj.com/somerset/index.ssf/2013/05/police_chase_after_wild_horses.html.

Houston Police Department. 2013. "Houston Police Department: Mounted Patrol—Our Horses." http://www.houstontx.gov/police/mounted/horses.htm.

Huddleston, S. 2012. "TSA Dog Breeding Facility to Close." *My SA: San Antonio's Homepage*, November 18. http://www.mysanantonio.com/news/local_news/article/TSA-dog-training-facility-to-close-4048762.php.

Inquirer. 1995. "Cincinnati Player Arrested after Slugging Police Horse." May 4. http://articles.philly.com/1995-05-04/sports/25675892_1_police-horse-athletes-security-breach.

In re Dorwarth. 258 B.R. 293 (Bankr. S.D. Fla. 2001).

Jennings, D. 2008. "Texas Prison Inmates Train Dogs for TSA, Adoption Organizations." *Dallas News*, September 2. http://crimeblog.dallasnews.com/2008/09/pups-in-prison.html/.

Lawless, J. 2012. "British Army Dog Joins List of Animal War Heroes." *Desert News*, October 25. http://www.deseretnews.com/article/765613737/British-army-dog-joins-list-of-animal-war-heroes.html.

Lovitt, R. 2013. "TSA Dog Bites Passenger at Atlanta's Hartsfield-Jackson Airport." *NBC News*, May 13. http://www.nbcnews.com/travel/tsa-dog-bites-passenger-atlantas-hartsfield-jackson-airport-1C9904739.

Millstone, K. 2013. "TSA tests dogs as new airport screening method." *MSN News*, July 2. http://news.msn.com/us/tsa-tests-dogs-as-new-airport-screening-method.

Moran, R. 2013. "Police Horse Rear-Ended; Officer Injured." *Inquirer*, August 31. http://articles.philly.com/2013-08-31/news/41622065_1_police-horse-minor-injuries-44-year-old-officer.

Morton, B. C. 2001. "Bringing Skeletons out of the Closet and into the Light: 'Scarlet Letter' Sentencing Can Meet the Goals of Probation in Modern America Because It Deprives Offenders of Privacy." *Suffolk University Law Review* 35:97.

People's Dispensary for Sick Animals (PDSA). 2013. "PDSA Dickin Medal Pigeons." http://www.pdsa.org.uk/about-us/animal-bravery-awards/dickin-medal-pigeons.

Reimer, L. 2012. "Chicago Police Horses Attacked in Their Stables." *WREX*, September 18. http://www.wrex.com/story/19573975/chicago-police-horses-attacked-in-their-stables.

Roberts, P. 2013. "Working Felines: Police Cats 1." *Featuring Felines.* http://www.purr-n-fur.org.uk/featuring/wk-police01.html.

Robol, M. 2012. "Two Marshall Police Horses Injured during Break-In." *Marshall Tribune*, September 18. http://www.jmls.edu/criminal-justice-comp/pdf/news-articles.pdf.

Rotstein, A. H. 2005. "Border Patrol Horses Get Special Feed That Helps Protect Desert Ecosystem." *Environmental News Network (ENN)*, June 9. http://www.enn.com/top_stories/article/1731.

Sigal, J. F. 2007. "Out of Step: When the California Street Terrorism Enforcement and Prevention Act Stumbles into Penal Code Limits." *Golden Gate University Law Review* 38:1.

Strunsky, S. 2013. "Dual-Purpose Dogs: TSA Canines Are Bomb Sniffers by Day, Family Pets by Night." *NJ.com*, April 25. http://www.nj.com/news/index.ssf/2013/04/dual-purpose_dogs_tsa_canines.html.

Tierney, M. 2007. "Retired Police Horses Move to Greener Pastures: Park Police Looking for Potential Homes for Future Equine Retirees." *Gazette*, December 19. http://ww2.gazette.net/stories/121907/olnenew205956_32360.shtml.

Transportation Security Administration. 2007. "TSA Sends Future Bomb Dogs to Jail." December 6. http://www.tsa.gov/press/releases/2007/12/06/tsa-sends-future-bomb-dogs-jail.

Transportation Security Administration. 2012. "TSA's Puppy Program: TSA's National Explosives Detection Canine Team."December 16. http://www.tsa.gov/about-tsa/tsas-puppy-program.

United States Government Accountability Office. 2013. "TSA Explosives Detection Canine Program Actions Needed to Analyze Data and Ensure Canine Teams Are Effectively Utilized." http://www.gao.gov/assets/660/651725.pdf.

US Coast Guard (USCG). 2012. "Pigeon Search and Rescue Project (Project Sea Hunt)." http://www.uscg.mil/history/articles/pigeonsarproject.asp.

Waac, L. 2010. "Program Gives Military Working Dogs New Homes in Retirement Years." *MyGuidon.com*, May 20. http://www.myguidon.com/index.php?option=com_content&task=view&id=12128k.

Welch, C. 2010. "Smart and Fast, Marine Mammals Are Guarding Our Military Bases." *Seattle Times*, August 28. http://seattletimes.com/html/pacificnw/2012662209_pacificpdolphins29.html.

6

Animals in Corrections and Rehabilitation

Introduction

Under retributive justice models brutality and deprivation experienced in prison are justified. In contrast, the therapeutic justice models call for treatment and development that address underlying behavioral, social, and psychological issues to prepare offenders for successful reentry into society. Animals' presence in rehabilitative and correctional environments offers offenders companionship and emotional warmth. The animals also provide opportunities to learn responsibility, commit to projects, practice ethical behavior, and learn new skills. Offenders may contribute to society by training animals. Pet programs allow offenders to demonstrate that they are capable of behaving appropriately with vulnerable populations and prove that they want to improve to society, others, and themselves. Some members of the criminal justice system have been unaccepting of animals in corrective environments, yet the popularity of these programs and funding for them increase annually.

The Premise behind Allowing Pets on the Premises

European prisoners have kept dogs for pest control, companionship, and message delivery for at least several hundreds of years (MacDonogh 1996). Today, some European prisoners continue to buy and maintain pets legally, including canaries and parrots whose well-being is enforced by prison behavior rules (Bond 2012). US prisoners generally have no such privileges. American inmates are usually forbidden from owning or possessing pets in prison. However, many prisoners in more than half of states are given opportunities to live with animals who belong to other people or organizations. Prison pet programs, which exist in North America, Africa, Asia, Europe, and Oceania, house animals with prisoners because the animals are said to rehabilitate, educate, and comfort prisoners (Britton and Button 2006; *Nine Lives around the Word* 2011; Robbins 2009; Tenna 2013). Programs reportedly rely on animals for therapeutic benefits similarly to other rehabilitative institutions' use of animals, for example, senior centers and hospitals. Prison pet programs can help build character and responsibility (Jones and McDougall, 2007). In many programs pets accompany inmates to most activities, including meals, sleeping, and exercise. This requires inmates' full discipline, attention, and commitment.

Reported benefits of prison pet programs are mainly anecdotal (Achen 2012). Based on observation, self-reporting, and studies of pets in noncorrectional institutions, it is widely believed that prison pet programs lower recidivism, violence, and reliance on medication in prison. This is not surprising since many inmates volunteer for prison pet programs because they love dogs (Britton and Button 2006). Love and affection can provide these benefits for some inmates. Another reason that inmates volunteer is that they have increased opportunity for liberty, socialization, and activity (Britton and Button 2006; Gremillion 2009). Incentives help train prisoners to behave responsibly. Inmates may volunteer to participate in programs that benefit animals or society (Britton and Button 2006). Altruism reflects well on prisoners' demeanor and attracts volunteers. Thus, prison pet programs may provide a variety of motivations.

Participation in the program increases pressure on prisoners because they are monitored more closely by prison staff and are more visible to other inmates. Pressure and attention can contribute to reform. However, it should not be taken for granted that pressure is positive because occasionally, nonparticipating inmates behave hostilely toward pets or attempt to corrupt their training. Inmates who positively respond to and overcome these challenges certainly may build positive character traits. Yet, additional tension could possibly negatively affect prisoners. However, this pessimistic view is not supported by empirical or much anecdotal evidence. Some negative anecdotal evidence suggests that handlers have mistreated animals. Other inmates may respond violently toward irresponsible or cruel handlers. Inmates have responded violently when handlers follow protocol that seems cruel, like jerking dogs using leash correction. Negative emotions may also be associated with having to give up pets at the end of training. However, these emotions are to be expected from the outset and have not been reported to impact prisoners' behavior negatively.

Prison Pets and Policies

Fish, birds, dogs, chickens, cows, pigs, cats, horses, injured wildlife, and other animals have legally resided in prisons (Carpentieri 2001; Greene 2014). Pet training is increasingly being offered by prisons as a service to the community. Animals may be trained as companions, as therapy or service animals, or as domesticated farm animals. Prisoners might only share a cell with some animals or may train certain animals over the course of several months. Depending on the species and the program, inmates, animals, and facilities must satisfy certain qualifications.

Maximum security prisons, medium security corrections facilities, and minimum security houses of correction all participate in pet programs when animals' well-being can be ensured (NBC 2006). In general, prison pet programs screen inmates prior to accepting volunteers. A record of violent crimes could preclude inmates from participation in some programs (Achen 2012). However, other programs will permit inmates with histories of violence to participate as long as violence was not perpetrated against vulnerable populations, for example, animals, children, seniors, or disabled individuals (NBC 2006).

Prisoners may adopt rules among themselves about how to protect pets (Korten 2007). In addition to program screening, pets are protected by informal agreements and enforcement among prisoners. Prison pets are rarely harmed because harm to a prison pet would be met with severe sanctions by other prisoners. For example, in one maximum security prison, nearly three-quarters of inmates were murderers. Some of these inmates were allowed to bunk with cats. One inmate spit soda on another inmate's cat. The offending inmate was killed. In another case a cat was killed, and the killer could not be identified by the prison authories, so inmates contracted for the responsible party's assassination.

Many programs may require inmates to have been well-behaved while incarcerated (Achen 2012). Programs might only investigate inmates' recent prison records and cap time limits for exclusionary infractions, for example, infractions within the past six months. Many programs require inmates to serve sufficiently long sentences, which permit inmates to bond with pets or allow adequate time to complete pet-training modules. This would exclude many jails or institutions that hold pretrial populations who could be transferred or released. Programs sometimes require inmates to have served a certain amount of time at a particular location, for example, one year. Animals may benefit from training with inmates who are stable and accustomed to their environments.

Departments of corrections must allot sufficient budgets to programs (Achen 2012). One reason that programs are so well-liked is that they can be relatively inexpensive. Facilities that train horses, dogs, or other animals that require exercise must have courtyards and necessary space to train animals. Most participating facilities have required space; and few opt to modify recreational areas. Dogs may require crates, but this expense is minimal in comparison to the cost of maintaining stables for horses (O'Brien 2005). Cats require even less money for boarding (Achen 2012), though at least one facility spent around a thousand dollars on an outdoor enclosure area for cats and volunteers. Food, collars, toys, and other supplies are usually donated by the public or participating inmates, and animals are generally adopted, donated, caught, or rescued from pounds' "death row." Thus, acquiring animals may be inexpensive or free.

Structural limitations can impede prison pet programs. Many programs require pets to become accustomed to a single inmate who takes full responsibility for the animal. Buildings must have enough cells available so that some inmates can reside without roommates (Achen 2012). Many prisons are overcrowded and cannot house single occupants. Some facilities opt against prison pets because they lack accommodations, for example, air conditioning. However, facilities without air conditioning have successfully partnered with pet programs (O'Brien 2005). Inmates have used their personal fans to cool pups' beds. In certain facilities cats are prohibited from roaming. Thus, prison cells with bars may be challenging. Some corrections facilities require cats to be leashed at all times so that they do not exit through cell bars (Korten 2007). However, prison guards can be quite lax about these rules. If participating inmate's neighbors are allergic to animals, then they can transfer cells. Facilities that lack this sort of flexibility are not well-suited for programs.

Institutional limitations have led to innovations in prison pet programs. In one example, a prison could not alter their policies, so they developed a program called "Pups on Parole." As in many prisons, regulations forbid decorations like framed paintings or pottery (O'Brien 2005). Animals trained as companions at one prison became extremely comfortable with people, but were evidently skittish around home furnishings once they were adopted to families. Dogs had not been exposed to furnishings while in prison. Prior to being adopted to the public, puppies were signed out to acclimate the dogs to volunteers who would take the puppies into public areas and private homes. Those dogs who were taught special tasks would learn to perform those tasks in public places, for example, malls and sporting events. These outings also helped dogs adjust to noise since they had not been exposed to loud voices in prison. Dogs exposed to a variety of environments are highly desirable, and observing "paroled" animal companions could motivate inmates to earn parole.

Prison Pet Programs

In the majority of prison pet programs, inmates train or socialize animals for adoption. Many varieties of partnerships have evolved in facilities throughout the country. While some programs may pay for animals' needs through sponsorship or adoption fees, other programs may rely on prisoners' donations, grants, or state funding. Each program has varying budgetary considerations and resources. All programs require supervision and accommodation by correctional facilities.

Some prison pet programs foster dogs from shelters, train them, and then return them for adoption. Many of the animals who are selected would likely be euthanized without intervention by the programs. Programs that house-break animals make them more desirable and likely to be adopted. Trained animals are easier to love and care for, and the history of their training also attracts attention from families. The Colorado Correctional Industries (CCI) Prison Trained K-9 Companion Program (PTKCP) is an example (CCI 2013). PTKCP is one of a few dozen similar programs within the CCI. Young and mature animals may be trained, but all animals are hand-picked based on their dispositions. The program provides rescued dogs with veterinary care, including vaccines, nourishment, attention to injuries, and spay or neuter surgery. PTKCP charges a five hundred dollar fee for each animal. Collected fees fund the entire program. PTKCP distinguishes itself from other pet programs by providing boarding and training services to local dog owners. One-month training is five hundred dollars. The program only charges owners fifty dollars per week for additional boarding or socialization with inmates. Many correctional facilities take in cats as well as dogs, or solely focus on socializing cats for adoption (DCWS 2012).

Pet programs have become so successful that several state prison systems operate expansive partnerships. For example, in Washington State all correctional facilities operate some sort of adoption or training program (DCWS 2012). In the State of Florida hundreds of correctional facilities and greyhound adoption programs partner in prison pet programs (National Greyhound Foundation 2007). Florida racetracks retire greyhounds who would otherwise be destroyed, but who are adoptable. More than one hundred correctional facilities socialize and train greyhounds. The program, which saves thousands of greyhound lives each year, is not restricted to Florida prisons.

A few of these programs offer highly specialized training. Service animals may be trained to assist and accompany people with disabilities. Dogs may learn to use specialized skills to assist disabled people with daily tasks, or they may provide companionship for traumatized war veterans. 4 Paws for Ability is a service dog–training program that places dogs in Warren Correctional Institution (Greene 2014). Dogs receive five hundred hours of training to serve children with autism, post-traumatic stress disorder, fetal alcohol syndrome, brain damage, pervasive developmental delays, deafness, physical disabilities, bipolar disorder, wheelchair confinement, seizure disorders, cerebral palsy, spina bifida, Down syndrome, and diabetes. Inmates attend classes and read books about training in their spare time. Dogs may receive specialized training to detect seizures, perform tasks like switching on lights, aid mobility, and do numerous other tasks in varied environments. Gifted trainers may become employed in the field after release. Yet, murders and others facing life terms may participate in the program as long as they have not been convicted of sex offenses or domestic violence; thus, some stigmatized inmates will likely never train or work outside prison.

Horses, in addition to other species of animals, are trained by inmates. Program structure may vary widely, but for the most part, horse-training prison programs are very successful (Office of the Deputy Commissioner for Women 2012). For example, a prison program in Canada reported a 1 percent return rate of horses given basic training by inmates. In Nevada the government has organized a multitier program. Northern Nevada Correctional Center (NNCC)/Stewart Conservation Camp Saddle Horse Training Program partnered with Bureau of Land Management (BLM), Nevada Department of Corrections (NDOC), and Nevada Department of Agriculture (NDOA) to accommodate several state and community needs at once (NNCC 2013). When wild horse and burro populations expand too rapidly, BLM calculates how many animals must be culled to sustain biodiversity and reduce starvation among wild populations. Culling is discussed in chapter 17. Rather than cull, the government rounds up a calculated number of animals into captivity. Hundreds of animals might be gathered each year. Animals are enrolled in the Adopt-a-Horse or Adopt-a-Burro Programs. Horses and burros who are frequently malnourished receive care and training from inmates. Since the program began in the 1970s, hundreds of thousands of animals have been adopted. Adopted animals may become employed on farms or live as family pets. All adopters are vetted through the program. Private owners may also apply for horses to be trained in the same fashion as captured horses. Training uses a least-resistance method that relies on behaviors that come most naturally to each animal. This training method lasts up to one year and costs adopters about five hundred dollars per month. Prison programs that train equine species present unique challenges due to increased risks that inmates will become injured during training (Office of the Deputy Commissioner for Women 2012). These concerns are minimized by the establishment of trust between inmates and animals. The trust factor also contributes to the program's rehabilitative goals.

Therapeutic Pets Programs

A study of a prison pet program examined differences between inmates living in a control ward who did not have pets, and those living with pets (Carpentieri 2001). After one year inmates in the experimental ward were less dependent on medication, less violent, and less suicidal. Other studies have indicated that inmates involved in prison pet programs have lower recidivism rates. These results are so promising that institutions, outpatient programs, juvenile incarceration programs, and other alternative forms of justice have adopted prison pet program strategies.

When offenders are declared incompetent to stand trial, are found to be legally insane, or suffer from severe mental illness, then they may be committed to an institution for a specific or indefinite period of time. Institutions can resemble prisons and be heavily secured. When prison pet programs cannot permit animals to live with mentally ill offenders, therapeutic animals may still visit offenders (Kuchta 2011). Adults and juvenile offenders can be institutionalized. Animals have been used successfully in inpatient and outpatient psychotherapeutic treatment of adults who may be involved in the criminal justice system (Jackson 2012). Juvenile offenders or delinquents who are institutionalized usually have committed serious and violent crimes (Kuchta 2011). Visits reward deserving children and allow doctors to observe children with animals.

MacLaren Youth Correctional Facility incarcerates youth between the ages of thirteen and twenty-five (Project POOCH 2013). These youth have committed serious crimes but find reprieve and rehabilitation through Project POOCH. Inside a new K-9 building, Project POOCH maintains a kennel where unadopted dogs are groomed and trained by juveniles, which helps dogs become adoptable. Youth sell merchandise and collect adoption fees so that revenue can be used for victim restitution and local charities. Studies conducted on Project POOCH found behavior improvements, increased respect for authority, improved sociality, and increased leadership among incarcerated youth. Youth self-reported becoming more honest, empathetic, understanding, confident, accomplished, and nurturing. Respondents reported no recidivism.

Therapeutic programs can prepare inmates for reentry by giving them marketable, specialized job skills (InGov 2013). The Indiana Canine Assistant (ICAN) program provides inmates with a year of curriculum centering on physical and developmental diseases. Offenders learn about cognitive and physical aspects of disability assisted by dogs. ICAN educates offenders far beyond other prison pet programs and emphasizes job readiness. Dog training lasts two years while inmates teach dogs more than fifty commands. Upon reentry, offenders can work as handlers, trainers, or in other related positions because they become certified through the US Department of Labor Apprenticeship Program.

Conclusion

Delinquent, inpatient, outpatient, and incarcerated populations reportedly benefit from pet programs. Pets in need of homes and training benefit from programs also. Communities benefit from services provided, reasonable service fees, and rehabilitative effects on offenders. However, little quantitative data demonstrates reduced rates of recidivism, though anecdotal and qualitative evidence is overwhelmingly positive. However, facility and policy concerns may weigh against the benefits of pet programs, and may sometimes impede implementation. Generally, these programs seem promising and are quite popular.

References

Achen, P. 2012. "Some Yacolt prison inmates given pet cats." *Seattle Times*, April 10. http://seattletimes.com/html/localnews/2017950824_apwacatsintheclink2ndldwritethru.html.

Bond, A. 2012. "The Prisoners Who Have Their Very Own Jailbirds: Convicts Buying Budgies, Canaries and Parrots to Keep Them Company in Cells." *UK Online*, January 24. http://www.dailymail.co.uk/news/article-2091160/

The-prisoners-jailbirds-Convicts-buying-budgies-canaries-parrots-company-cells.html#ixzz2fP5gXOwD.

Britton, D. M., and A. Button. 2006. "Prison Pups: Assessing the Effects of Dog Training Programs in Correctional Facilities." *Journal of Family Social Work* 9, no. 4:79–95.

"The Cats of the Prison." 2011. *Nine Lives around the World*, May 31. http://theninelives.blogspot.com/2011/05/cats-of-prison.html

Carpentieri, J. D. 2001. "Jail House Flock." *Guardian*, August 24. http://www.theguardian.com/theguardian/2001/aug/25/weekend7.weekend3.

Colorado Correctional Industries (CCI). 2013. "Prison Trained Dog Program." https://www.cijvp.com/serviceproviders/puppy/index.html?intro.

Department of Corrections Washington State (DCWS). 2012. "Dog Training and Adoption Programs." http://doc.wa.gov/facilities/prison/animaltrainingprograms.asp.

Greene, M. F. 2014. "The Prisoner's Gift." *Reader's Digest*, March.

Gremillion, G. 2009. "Carrots, Sticks and Corrections." *Corrections Today* 71, no. 1: 58.

Indiana Government (InGov). 2013. "Programs." http://www.in.gov/idoc/2799.htm.

Jackson, J. 2012. "Animal-Assisted Therapy: The Human-Animal Bond in Relation to Human Health and Wellness." *Winona State University*. http://www.winona.edu/counseloreducation/images/justine_jackson_capstone.pdf.

Jones, C., and T. McDougall. 2007. "Dialectical Behaviour Therapy for Young Offenders: Lessons from the USA," pt. 2. *Mental Health Practice* 11, no. 2 (October):20.

Korten, D. 2007. "Indiana State Prison, Michigan City, Indiana: A Better Place for Everyone." *Cat Odyssey*, May 31. http://catodyssey.blogspot.com/2007/05/indiana-state-prison-michigan-city.html.

Kuchta, L. 2011. "Note from the President." *Dogs on Call*, September 1. http://www.dogsoncall.org/wp-content/uploads/2011/09/Newsletter_9-1-11.pdf.

MacDonogh, K. 1996. "Prison Pets in the French Revolution." *History Today* 46, no. 8: 36.

National Greyhound Foundation. 2007. "Second Chance at Life Greyhound Prison Partnership." http://www.giveasecondchance.com/prisons.html

NBC News. 2006. "Prisoners Rehabilitate Death Row Dogs." October 3. http://www.nbcnews.com/id/15014860/ns/health-pet_health/t/prisoners-rehabilitate-death-row-dogs/#.UjVEEMasim4.

Northern Nevada Correctional Center (NNCC)/Stewart Conservation Camp Saddle Horse Training Program. 2013. "Saddle Horse Training Program." May 20. http://www.blm.gov/nv/st/en/prog/wh_b/warm_springs_correctional.html.

O'Brien, S. 2005. "Partnering with Correctional Facilities to Raise and Train Assistance Dogs." *New Horizons*. http://www.neads.org/document.doc?id=27.

Office of the Deputy Commissioner for Women. 2012. "Women Offender Programs and Issues: Pet Facilitated Therapy in Correctional Institutions." December 18. http://www.csc-scc.gc.ca/text/prgrm/fsw/pet/pet-13-eng.shtml.

Project POOCH. 2013. http://www.pooch.org/.

Robbins, S. 2009. "The cats of Pollsmoor Prison." *Cat Channel.* http://www.catchannel.com/magazines/catfancy/february-2009/pollsmoor-prison.aspx.

Tenna, A. 2013. "The Taming of the Shrewd." *Slippery Rock Gazette.* http://slipperyrockgazette.net/index.cfm/pageId/542/.

7

Animal Mistreatment

Introduction

Numerous governmental and private organizations attempt to oversee animal-human interactions and rely on a mosaic of laws to eliminate mistreatment. Defining and prosecuting animal mistreatment is difficult for many reasons. Different industries are obligated to treat animals in a certain way under standard practices, policies, duties, and laws depending on the activities and animals involved. Animals living on farms, in laboratories, as companions in homes, in the wild, or in captivity are typically considered under discrete and overlapping policies. Degrees or types of mistreatment may be difficult to prove or may not equally apply to all nonhumans or activities. Some animals receive heightened protection due to their status. However, heighted attention or protection may have little or no affect.

Abuse, Neglect, and Abandonment

Animal abuse, neglect, and abandonment are the most common criminal charges against animal owners. These categories are not necessarily discrete, theoretically, but distinct laws define each harm and correlative remedies. Jurisdictional and definitional variations influence the application of law to specific cases. What constitutes a crime in one jurisdiction might not constitute the same crime in another jurisdiction. Nevertheless, descriptions of "abuse," "neglect," and "abandonment" are relatively generalizable.

Animal abuse is cruelty. Cruelty usually includes intentional acts or acts that wantonly cause animals to suffer. For example, cruelty might include locking a cat in a hot car, punching a bird, breeching experimental protocol by torturing a primate, or taunting a caged animal. Cruelty laws often apply to many laboratory, exotic, domesticated, game, companion, and wild animals (Burke 2005; LaFrance 2007).

Overlap between abuse and neglect is not uncommon (Otto 2005). For example, overworking a domesticated animal and keeping an unsheltered animal outside in freezing temperatures could be abuse or neglect depending on a statute's wording and the exact circumstances involved (LaFrance 2007). Whereas cruelty describes affirmative acts of abuse, neglect typically occurs due to omissions. Neglect reflects an owner's failure to perform a duty. Thus, neglect charges can only be filed against animal owners or caretakers, whereas cruelty charges could potentially be filed against anyone.

In neglect cases animal owners usually fail to feed animals and provide proper veterinary care. Neglect charges are commonly brought against horse owners or other livestock owners (LaFrance 2007; Satterberg 2003). Horses consume copious amounts of food. Often, neglectful owners fail to feed them. Dirty or sparse water is another common form of neglect. However, lack of resources may only be one reason that people neglect animals. Like abuse, neglect can relate to deeper problems. Abused and neglected domesticated animals often belong to homes that suffer from domestic violence or instability (Nelson 2011). When authorities discover neglect, they are more likely to issue a warning than if they uncover abuse. At first neglectful owners may be warned to provide adequate care. They may be required to provide evidence to the state of compliance within a certain time limit or during a follow-up visit. Additional warnings may follow, but persistent neglect is likely to result in criminal charges, animal seizure, and perhaps fines.

Neglect and cruelty can overlap quite easily when numerous animals are involved because some animals might be in more advanced stages of neglect than others. Carcasses, fully emaciated animals, or lame animals might evidence such callous neglect that the state charges an owner with some counts of cruelty and neglect. Neglect is frequently charged when hoarders or breeders amass dozens, hundreds, or thousands of animals (Berry, Patronek, and Lockwood 2005). Normally, these owners do not wish to harm animals, but they fall far below the standard of care by failing to provide animals with requisite or even basic care.

Neglect at some point can constructively become abandonment. If animals are left completely neglected for long periods of time, then they may be abandoned in the eyes of the government. A common example of animal abandonment occurs when exotic pet owners tire of caring for novelty pets (Burke 2005). They may dump animals, especially reptiles like gators and boa constrictors, into canals or wooded areas. Sometimes abandoned animals are captured and transported to wildlife sanctuaries, but at other times they are killed. They may find their way into nature or survive as feral animals within society. Owners who abandon exotic pets are rarely discovered. However, if they are caught, then owners may be charged in violation of state or federal laws prohibiting the introduction of nonnative species into the environment or possessing unlicensed or endangered animals. In response to rampant animal mistreatment, numerous states have attempted to ramp up prosecution and penalties as well as stratify alternative responses. One example is court orders requiring people who mistreat animals to attend psychological counseling or pet ownership courses, or to abstain from owning or working with animals in the future (Graves, Mosman, and Rogers 2012).

Species-Specific Protection

Particular animals are protected against certain forms of abuse. Protections offered to all or some animals vary widely by state. For example, in Utah, anticruelty statutes apply to any vertebrates, but protection is not extended to agricultural animals or wildlife (UT ST § 76-9-301 – 307, 2012). Texas does not protect crustaceans and some other invertebrates (Ravenscroft 2012). As opposed to the majority of states that exclude livestock from cruelty statutes, some states, like Illinois, Mississippi, and Nevada, protect to any living creature, but enforcement of protection may be scant or dubious for many species, for example, ants (510 I.L.C.S. 70/1 – 18, 2012; Hirsch 2003; MS Stat. § 97-41-1; NV Stat. § 574.010, 2013).

Federal legislation, for example, the Animal Welfare Act (AWA), also offers species-specific protection (Favre 2002). Under the AWA the definition of "animal" is limited to living or deceased dogs, cats, nonhuman primates, bunnies, hamsters, guinea pigs, birds, and other similar warm-blooded animals typically used for lab research, companionship, exhibition, or testing. Any livestock used for these purposes are included, but livestock, including horses and poultry, which are used for food, breeding, and other related purposes, are excluded. Nonmammalian, cold-blooded animals, including fish, reptiles, and amphibians, receive no protection under the AWA. Licenses may permit infliction of regulated types of harm on specific species for sanctioned purposes.

Farm Animals

Lawful treatment of domesticated farm animals varies according to the kinds of farming jurisdiction and the species. One nearly unregulated farming industry is fur. The United States is one of the largest producers of farmed fur in the world next to China, the Baltic states, and

Scandinavia. The US federal government does not regulate fur farms. The majority of states contain several hundred licensed fur farms, but most states do not specifically regulate fur farming (Born Free USA 2013). States may only require licensing. For example, in New York beaver, skunk, otter, bobcat, muskrat, raccoon, sable, and other similar animals can be bred and kept in captivity as long as a twenty-five-dollar licensing fee is paid (NY CLS ECL § 11-1907, 2013). Animals can be killed and pelted using any method at any time. Carcass trade, pelt trade, and pelt possession are unregulated. By comparison, in Canada fur-farmed animals may require vaccinations, must be cared for, and must be given clean food and water (R.S.B.C., 2010). In the United States dogs and cats are the only unthreatened, fur-bearing animals to receive federal protection. Dogs and cats cannot be slaughtered in any state under the Dog and Cat Fur Protection Act 19 U.S.C. § 1308, 2013). State laws also prohibit such slaughter, but may only require violators to pay civil fines for dealing in dog or cat fur, skin, hair, or meat (NY CLS Agr and M § 96-h, 2013).

In China and Southeast Asia, millions of dogs and cats are killed for fur annually. Some dogs are farmed, while others are rounded up. Video exposés demonstrate that animals are packed so tightly into crates that their bones break. They are tossed like objects, wounded, electrocuted, butchered while alive, and hung. A national scandal involving Sean John clothing at Macy's department store raised public awareness about dog fur. Some coats were alleged to be made of dog fur; however, tests revealed that garments were made of raccoon-dog fur. Raccoon-dogs are not canines. Public and governmental concerns about Chinese dog fur illegally entering the United States remain valid because of the volume of dog fur produced in China and the difficulty of regulating unmarked fur on the free market. The Fur Products Labeling Act attempts to address this problem by requiring fur to be labeled with the species's name, manufacturer's name, country of origin, and chemical treatment; and by requiring labels to indicate whether fur was obtained from certain parts of an animal (15 U.S.C. § 69, 2013). Yet, small items, like collars or trim, do not require labels. Falsely guaranteeing the truthfulness of labels is a misdemeanor that carries a five-thousand-dollar fine. It is an affirmative defense that a merchant relied on a false guarantee. Since mislabeled fur often enters the country, responsible parties can easily evade responsibility.

Wild fur is mostly trapped in North America and Russia. Individual state laws vary widely regarding which and how animal hides can be hunted and sold. Yet, enforcement in any jurisdiction may be challenging. It may be difficult to detect where an animal was hunted or whether the animal was farm raised. Thus, illegal hunting, trapping, and fur trade can go undetected, especially on the open market. The Lacey Act, which is federal legislation prohibiting illegal transportation of fur between states, may serve as an additional deterrent (16 U.S.C. §§ 3371–3378, 2013). Countless seals are legally clubbed to death in Greenland and Canada. In the United States the Fur Seal Act prohibits any seal taking unless it is authorized governmental taking for education, science, or certain Native American groups for subsistence. The Marine Mammal Protection Act regulates taking of certain species from the wild for fur and leather, but like the Fur Seal Act, it does not criminalize fur or leather farms.

Captive-bred animals normally receive only the most basic protection under anticruelty statutes. Farmers typically consider industry-standard treatment of animals rather than cruelty laws. Industry standards may be lower, higher, or equal with anticruelty standards. Legal protection for livestock animals is relatively minimal. Cruelty statutes and humane slaughter laws generally may apply to livestock, but additional state or municipal laws may further regulate the treatment of livestock (7 U.S.C. § 1901–1907, 2012; Texas Penal Code 42.09, 2007). For example, in Texas, the treatment of cattle is supposed to be better regulated than in other states. The State of Texas contains the most livestock, and animal agriculture is one of the state's top exports. Intentional or knowing cruelty, neglect, and abandonment are prohibited. Causing livestock to fight, using livestock to race or train dogs, tripping horses, and seriously overworking livestock are a few of the prohibited activities under Texas's statutes. Cows, pigs, sheep, goats, emus, chickens, horses, donkeys, and other farm animals are covered under the Texas statute that requires animals to maintain good health. Some first-time and second-time offenses can be misdemeanors, but repeat offenses are felonies.

Protection of farmed birds varies. For example, chickens, rabbits, ducks, and other Easter-related animals usually receive little protection, but in Florida it is a misdemeanor to dye or color any animal or fowl (FL Stat. § 828.161, 2011). Artificially colored animals cannot be transported into the state. It is also a misdemeanor to sell or give away any juvenile bird for commercial purposes. A few jurisdictions have attempted to extend some other special protection to birds. California was a leader in banning force-feeding of any birds within the state

(Cal Health and Safety Code § 121910, 2013). However, a Humane Society officer can only issue a civil citation for each violation every day that it continues. Accumulation of several civil fines could directly result in separate but related criminal charges.

Lab Animals

The Animal Welfare Act (AWA) protects many kinds of animals, but not all animals; for example, fish are not protected (Galanes 2010). Animals protected by the AWA are regulated according to certain principles. Animal and human welfare must be considered in the light of knowledge, health, and a good society (NIH 2002). Only the minimum number of an appropriately chosen species may be used for experimentation when other research methods are unavailable. Whenever possible, mathematical models and computer simulations should be used rather than animal experimentation. Animals' distress, discomfort, and pain must be minimized by researchers unless those effects are necessary for the experiment. Sedation or anesthesia should be provided prior to all surgeries, and humane euthanasia is required (NIH 2002; Leary 2013).

Animals must be transported, housed, and cared for in conditions that are comfortable for their species (NIH 2002). Municipal, state, federal, and international regulations can govern transportation of research and educational animals (National Research Council 2006). One example of a condition that applies to transport and care conditions is AWA Section 2143, which requires additional space for brachiating species. These are any primates who ambulate using any appendages while an animal's trunk is suspended (Policy #7, 2011). Monkeys, gibbons, orangutans, chimpanzees, gorillas, and bonobos are brachiating species.

Experimenters and lab technicians must be adequately and properly trained to work in the experiment and with particular species. Any deviation from these principles must only occur under the direction of an institutional review board (IRB) or animal care committee, who cannot relegate decision making to the researcher or allow infringements of the rules merely for teaching.

The US Department of Agriculture (USDA) enforces the AWA, including animal laboratory use (NEAVS 2013). The Animal and Plant Health Inspection Service (APHIS) Animal Care Program annually inspects facilities and regulated animals. Federal research facilities are not subject to inspection. Around one hundred inspectors inspect thousands of research facilities annually, which often results in lax oversight of the nearly eighty thousand animals that are reported to experience pain and distress annually. An absence of serious penalties has also contributed to numerous violations of the AWA. The penalty for a single violation may be between a couple of hundred dollars and several thousand dollars, but fines barely affect well-funded research facilities (Cambridge Municipal Code, 6.12.090, 2013; NEAVS 2013).

In 2012 the USDA proposed a change to the AWA to include birds, mice, and other animals bred for research (NEAVS 2013). Changes affect about five million captive-bred birds because they were bred for purposes other than research. However, not all research animals are bred. Animals used for experimentation may be bred or come from zoos, pounds, or other facilities. Dogs and cats are frequently used in animal testing (Policy # 18, 2011). Animals may be strays that are collected from streets or animal control. Under federal regulations, animals' health certificates must accompany them if they are in interstate commerce, for example, in a commercial vehicle or travelling between states. Research animals and breeding stock used for educational purposes must be identified with a microchip, and possibly a tattooed code as well (Policy # 13, 2011). Puppies less than sixteen weeks of age must be maintained in their litters and transported as a unit. After sixteen weeks they may be individually identified. However, animals who are transported intrastate within private vehicles do not require health certificates. Thus, these laws facilitate somewhat controversial business relationships between corporations, universities, and animal control.

Pound seizure by labs is required upon laboratories' requests for animals in a few states and municipalities (PETA 2013). This means that labs can require pounds to give them stray animals. However, more than a third of states prohibit pound seizure. Cats and dogs whose owners cannot be located after one to five days may sell for around fifteen dollars each to labs in most states. Wholesale licensure for animal sales is not required unless more than twenty-four cats or dogs are sold to labs annually. The USDA will license individuals to sell fewer than twenty-four animals annually. Many people do not solely obtain animals through the pound. They will illegally "rescue" free animals from classified ads, trap or sedate strays, and sometimes imitate animal control to steal unleashed or outdoor pets. In 2004 an entire family was the subject of a 108-page complaint filed by the USDA. The family committed hundreds of such violations over the years, and yet the father only paid $262,700 in fines. This was the most significant fine

107

imposed by APHIS at the time. Only a handful of such crimes have ever been pursued by the USDA.

International standards are quite similar to US standards (International Guiding Principles 2012). Knowledge is prioritized, but experimentation is considered to be a privilege. Moral responsibility must guide researchers' consciences and institutional ethic. Humane treatment of animals must be ensured through strict compliance with all regulations. Respect for animals and accountability must be demonstrated in animal use and welfare. Experimentation must be necessary and justifiable, and only the minimum number of suitable animals can be used. "Replacement, reduction, and refinement" of animal use for scientific and educational purposes is the benchmark of sound scientific practice. Neither cost nor convenience alone justifies experimentation. In every aspect animal welfare must be of the utmost concern. Researchers must assume that any activity that would cause pain to a human would have the same effect on an animal unless evidence supports the contrary, and animals should not experience discomfort unless it is necessary.

These principles may take distinct shapes between nations and cultures due to religious, social, and economic factors (AAALAC International 2013). Yet, welfarists' arguments against experimentation are quite generalizable (Galanes 2010). In addition to arguments about suffering and cruelty, welfarists argue that animal models are not fully compatible with human models and thus, are unnecessary, fallible, or unsafe. Furthermore, thousands of animal experiments already attest to the majority of knowledge that is merely being reproduced by researchers. What has not yet been discovered can be modeled mathematically. Welfarists often cite the European ban on animal testing in cosmetics as a prime example that a large industry or nations can function properly and safely without animal testing (European Commission 2013).

Companion Animals

Companion animals are better protected under the law than most animals. Other well-protected animals include police animals and service animals. Of these three, companion animals are the only animals who do not have to fulfill professional duties. Companion animals are not solely protected because of their status as property. Cattle are property and they receive far less protection. Companion animals are not better protected because they are loveable. For example, pet skunks may be loveable, but they are usually not protected to the same extent as traditional companion animals. Companion animals probably receive increased protection because of their role as quasi-family members and their species. For example, in Utah, Nevada, Mississippi, Pennsylvania, and numerous other states, regulation of companion animals is heightened by imposition of stiffer sentences (18 Pa.C.S.A. § 5511, 2013). These heightened protections are typically reserved for owned cats and dogs. The Mississippi Dog and Cat Pet Protection Law of 2011 specifically criminalizes negligent deprivation of adequate shelter, food, or water; or cruel carrying or confinement of any owned dog or cat (MS Stat. § 97-41-16, 2011). Alabama also enforces dog-specific and cat-specific legislation. Protective legislation in Mississippi aggravates charges if an offender maliciously disfigures, burns, maims, or mutilates an owned dog or cat. Mississippi's laws preclude anyone from permanently marking dogs or cats for any reasons. This law is quite distinguishable from treatment of other owned animals, for example, bulls and cows, who are often required to be maimed with identifying markings. Owned animals who are not companion animals might only receive protection if markings are needless or wanton.

Nevada provides protection for any cat or dog, whether owned or feral, from being unjustifiably killed (NV Stat. § 574.010, 2013). Nevada also prohibits dog owners from placing companion dogs in any situation where they could accidentally hang themselves with leashes. North Carolina prohibits any cruel restraint, and California greatly broadens this protection by prohibiting all tethering of dogs unless it is temporarily necessary to complete a task (CA Health and Safety § 122335, 2012). Dogs who participate in dog shows or competitions receive greater protection than all other companion dogs in Nevada. Nevada requires that any dogs and cats who are kept outside must have sufficient shelter to remain dry and properly heated or cooled. This treatment of outdoor cats seems to exceed conventional treatment of outdoor cats who may receive little or no protection. In South Carolina ownership of outdoor cats is not permitted since cats are not permitted to run free (SC Stat. § 47-3-50, 2012). Whether this is for cats' protection or due to perceived undesirability of outdoor cats, South Carolina's laws are somewhat unique and stand in contrast to Nevada's laws. However, it should be noted that any animal control agencies that actively pick up strays effectively enforce codified or uncodified prohibitions against keeping outdoor cats. Outdoor cats are virtually indistinguishable from feral cats without the presence of updated microchips or tags and collars. Even if animals are not prohibited from living outdoors by statute, the fact that unidentified cats will be picked up and killed promptly evidences an unarticulated prohibition against allowing companion cats to roam freely (CA Penal § 597f, 2012).

Wild Animals

Almost all wildlife is protected to some extent (DEC 2013). Only a few unprotected species can be taken indiscriminately. Hunting mainly becomes criminalized because of safety regulations, land use regulations, and ecological regulation, though regulations institutionalizing sportsmanlike conduct may serve to reduce cruelty. Hunting licenses grant limited privilege and allow authorities to regulate the sport (Burns2012). Illegal hunting may occur if licensed hunters violate any laws or ordinances, including killing animals in prohibited areas; killing prohibited animals; hunting during a prohibited time of day; using prohibited weapons; or hunting during the wrong season. State constitutions, private landowners, state natural resource departments, the US Bureau of Land Management, and other authorities may oversee hunting on specific lands or overlapping jurisdictions (ADFG 2013). Animals that are accidentally killed—for example, road kill—or are hunted on certain lands may subject hunters to various regulations. Hunters may be required to obtain one, a few, or no permits, or mix state and federal licenses and stamps before killing or entering certain lands to hunt. Municipal or local laws will likely prohibit use of weapons within a certain distance from public roadways or other unsafe areas. Youth, seniors, veterans, low-income persons, persons with disabilities, residents, nonresidents, and other groups may be subject to distinct regulations, including fee differences or weapon limitations. Though leniencies tend to provide animals with less protection, licensing exceptions apply to only a small percentage of hunters. Thus, animals typically retain the majority of whatever incidental protection is available to them through licensing regulations.

Generally, animal hunting is delimited by species' abundance or scarcity. The government determines the amount of hunting that a local species population can endure. When species are numerous, regulators may increase bag limits (ADFG 2013). Authorities may also permit hunting by proxy, which allows individuals to hunt other peoples' bag limits. Bag limits can range from a few animals per person each season to a single animal per license holder every few years. Certain parts of animals may be illegal to trade, transport, sell, or buy. Sometimes, these regulations relate to market-driven concerns about overhunting. Rather than risk overhunting, the government may attempt to eliminate the market entirely. At other times these regulations may relate to wasteful hunting practices. While hunters are usually required to salvage carcasses, body part–specific regulations deter hunters from killing animals exclusively for their horns and other trophy parts. Wantonly wasting big game can be severely fined and punished with prison terms.

Hunting methods and tactics may be regulated, but they are more likely to be strictly regulated for hunting scarce animals than abundant animals (ADFG 2013). When animal populations are excessive, hunters may have to compete against state sponsored trappers if the state elects to cull. Culling is discussed in chapter 17. Though competitive tactics are legal, it may be illegal to hinder another hunter. Hindering could include using one's body, smells, sounds, or other stimulus to interrupt a hunter's view or animals' natural behavior. This applies to birds, fish, predators, big game, and all other lawfully hunted animals. These laws are generally meant to deter animal welfarists from obstructing or harassing hunters. Many jurisdictions take these crimes seriously. For example, in Alaska violators face up to thirty days in jail and a five-hundred-dollar fine. Hunters may not harass animals either. Using motorboats, snowmobiles, aircraft, or other vehicles to herd, molest, or chase down fleeing game is often prohibited. Though motorized vehicles can be used to position hunters, drive-by or fly-by shootings are often illegal. Killing certain small game with bows or firearms could be illegal (DEC 2013). Weapons like machine guns, double arrow crossbows, spears, tasers, pits, smoke, lasers, and gas arrows are frequently illegal because they are dangerous, cruel, or unsportsman-like (ADFG 2013). Other unfair advantages could include hunting an animal while the animal is swimming, hunting a sow while she is with her cubs, using electronic calls, or using lights or scopes on crossbows. Lawful advantages, like the use of falcons or dogs, may require special licensing (DEC 2013). Hunting with animals may also limit the kinds of animals that can be hunted and the types of firearms that can be used. Training hunting animals is also likely to be regulated according to season, location, and the animal species used for training.

Entertainment

The Animal Welfare Act (AWA), Endangered Species Act (ESA), state cruelty laws, and the American Humane Association's (AHA) industry guidelines regulate treatment of animal actors during Screen Actors

Guild (SAG) productions (Rizzo 2012). Any regulating entity can and will flag criminal abuse.

The AHA is a welfare agency that works on behalf of children and animals (AHA 2013). The agency is exclusively authorized to monitor movie, television, commercial, video, and other SAG productions. SAG also requires compliance by films produced by US companies that are filmed overseas. Production could be subject to the Convention on International Trade in Endangered Species of Wild Fauna and Flora (CITES), federal law, and foreign laws. Prior to production certain animals must be properly permitted by the government (AHA 2013). Animal injury, illness, or death must promptly be reported to the AHA and law enforcement. Any person who abuses an animal may be dismissed from the remainder of a production.

The AHA protects animals by following guidelines that exceed state cruelty laws in terms of compassion and respect for animals as living beings not property. Guidelines also exceed most states' definitions of "animal" by including all insects, fish, and other animals who are not typically protected by the government. Guidelines prohibit infliction of any pain or loss on an animal; and guidelines require kindness and mercy. Because of AHA's inclusive definition of "animal" and its high standards for compassion, actions that constitute abuse on-set may not be criminal acts, and thus, they will not be reported to the government for prosecution. For example, torturing numerous actor spiders on-set would be flagged by the AHA, but may not constitute cruelty under state statutes. Another example is that on-set, birds cannot be stacked in cages that permit them to defecate on one another. In some jurisdictions birdcages can be stacked in a manner that permits them to defecate on one another.

In addition to federal and state laws, the AHA enforces variations in local laws. For example, guidelines focus heavily on nonharmful rodeo activities and equipment because local rodeo laws vary greatly between jurisdictions. AHA equalizes all state or local hunting and trapping laws by forbidding all such activities on-set. Animals are not permitted to prey on other animals either. Unauthorized transportation, relocation, or release of animals is strictly prohibited by the AHA. Instead, it encourages local animal control or animal welfare agencies to oversee permanent placement or adoption of animals when necessary. The AHA will require reporting to local animal control of primate bites that break the skin, but not necessarily dog bites. Dog bites will only be reported in compliance with local laws or if they require medical or veterinary attention, though the AHA states that dog bites that break the skin should receive medical or veterinary attention.

Compliant productions are certified by animal safety representatives who verify adherence to the AHA's Guidelines for Safe Use of Animals in Filmed Media (AHA 2013). Certified productions may post a disclaimer at the end of a production's credits stating that no animals were harmed. Separate from certification, the AHA also rates films for the public's benefit. Ratings for monitored films are "outstanding," "acceptable," "special circumstances," and "unacceptable." The AHA can elect to rate films that were not monitored as "production compliant."

The AHA monitors postproduction to ensure that final cuts of footage are the same scenes that were monitored by the AHA during production (AHA 2013). One reason for this is that animals used in one-time events, for example, morning talk show appearances, do not require compensation. The USDA will exempt these appearances from AWA regulations that would require owners of repeat performers to be licensed exhibitors. Licensing requirements are strict, and even animals who make an appearance following the taping of a live show will require licensing. If an exempted animal is reused during production or in postproduction in any way, then the AWA will have been violated.

Because the AHA receives its authority to monitor animal actors from the SAG, it is not authorized to monitor treatment of animals in training compounds that supply animals for productions (AHA Blog 2011). Training of animal actors is not regulated by the government beyond cruelty and welfare laws, and no private certification ensures proper treatment. Only trainers' mistreatment of animals on-set can lead to criminal consequences through the AHA. Thus, the AHA prompts productions to consider US Department of Agriculture (USDA) inspection reports. Reports flag abuse and neglect. Productions may avoid dealing with animal suppliers or trainers who have either recently or repeatedly violated USDA regulations (AHA 2013). Exposés demonstrating abusive training methods have prompted the AHA to express interest in extending its jurisdiction to include certification of training and housing facilities (Cieply 2013).

Conclusion

Numerous governmental and private organizations are willing to protect animals. Typically, protections are species-specific and can vary substantially between species. Some species-specific protections, usually affecting domesticated animals, may be similar to protections for children insofar animals may not be abused, abandoned, or neglected. Yet, industry-standard slaughter practices are generally legal. Generally, protections are lacking for all animals. One reason that animals lack protection is that there is no single law or authority defining "mistreatment" for all animals that protects all animals equally in every circumstance. Another reason that animals may lack protection is that animal mistreatment may be relatively difficult to prosecute. A final reason relates to traditional industry practices and commercial interests.

References

7 U.S.C. § 1901–1907 (2012).

Alaska Department of Fish and Game. 2013. "2013-2014 Alaska Hunting Regulations." http://www.adfg.alaska.gov/static/regulations/wildliferegulations/pdfs/general.pdf.

American Humane Association Blog (AHA). 2011. "A Message on the Safety of Animal Actors." May 14. http://americanhumaneblog.org/2011/05/a-message-on-the-safety-of-animal-actors/.

American Humane Association (AHA). 2013. *Humane Hollywood.* http://www.humanehollywood.org/index.php/film-makers.

Association for Assessment and Accreditation of Laboratory Animal Care International (AAALAC International). 2013. "International Regulations and Resources." http://www.aaalac.org/resources/internationalregs.cfm.

Berry, C., G. Patronek, and R. Lockwood. 2005. "Long-Term Outcomes in Animal Hoarding Cases." *Animal Law* 11:167.

Born Free USA. 2013. "The Fur Farm Fallacy." http://www.bornfreeusa.org/facts.php?p=372andmore=1.

Burke, K. A. 2005. "Looking for a Nexus between Trust, Compassion, and Regulation: Colorado's Search for Standards of Care for Private, Non-Profit Wildlife Sanctuaries." *Animal Law* 12:39.

Burns, G. 2012. "Bow Hunters Face Prison, Charged with Animal Cruelty for Allegedly Hunting Deer in Warren." *MLive*, December 26. http://www.mlive.com/news/detroit/index.ssf/2012/12/bow_hunters_face_prison_charge.html.

Cal Health and Safety Code § 121910 (2013).

Cambridge Municipal Code § 6.12.090 (2013).

Cieply, M. 2013. "Flaws Seen in Protection of Animals on the Set." *New York Times,* April 14. http://www.nytimes.com/2013/04/15/business/media/guidelines-for-animal-safety-on-film-sets-questioned.html?pagewanted=all&_r=0.

Committee on Guidelines for the Humane Transportation of Laboratory Animals, National Research Council. 2006. "Guidelines for the Humane Transportation of Research Animals." *National Academies Press.* http://www.nap.edu/catalog.php?record_id=11557.

Department of Environmental Conservation (DEC), New York. 2013. "Small Game Hunting." http://www.dec.ny.gov/outdoor/27801.html.

Dog and Cat Fur Protection Act, 19 U.S.C. § 1308 (2013).

European Commission. 2013. "Health and Consumers." September 12. http://ec.europa.eu/consumers/sectors/cosmetics/animal-testing/.

Favre, D. 2002. "Overview of U.S. Animal Welfare Act." *Animal Legal and Historical Center.* http://www.animallaw.info/articles/ovusawa.htm.

Fur Farm Act, R.S.B.C. (2010).

Fur Products Labeling Act, 15 U.S.C. § 69 (2013).

Fur Seal Act, 16 U.S.C. §§ 1151–1187 (2013).

Galanes, K. C. 2010. "Quick Summary of Animal Testing in Commercial Products." *Animal Legal and Historical Center.* http://www.animallaw.info/topics/tabbed%20topic%20page/spusanimaltesting.htm.

Graves, P., K. Mosman, and S. Rogers. 2012. "2011 Legislative and Administrative Review." *Animal Law* 18:361.

Hirsch, V. 2003. "Overview of the Legal Protections of the Domestic Chicken in the United States and Europe." *Animal Legal and Historical Center.* http://www.animallaw.info/articles/ovuschick.htm.

Lacey Act, 16 U.S.C. §§ 3371–3378 (2013).

LaFrance, A. B. 2007. "Animal Experimentation: Lessons from Human Experimentation." *Animal Law* 14:29.

Leary, S., et al. 2013. "Guidelines for the Euthanasia of Animals." *American Veterinary Medical Association (AVMA).* https://www.avma.org/KB/Policies/Documents/euthanasia.pdf.

Marine Mammal Protection Act (MMPA), 16 U.S.C. §§ 1361–1407 (2013).

National Institute of Health. 2002. "Office of Laboratory Animal Welfare." August 1. http://grants.nih.gov/grants/olaw/references/phspol.htm#USGovPrinciples.

National Institute for Health (NIH). 2012. "International Guiding Principles for Biomedical Research Involving Animals." http://grants.nih.gov/grants/olaw/Guiding_Principles_2012.pdf.

Nelson, S. 2011. "Bibliography: The Connection between Animal Abuse and Family Violence: A Selected Annotated Bibliography." *Animal Law* 17:369.

New England Anti-Vivisection Society (NEAVS). 2013. "Laws and Regulations." http://www.neavs.org/research/laws.

NY CLS Agr and M § 96-h (2013).

NY CLS ECL § 11-1907 (2013).

Otto, S. K. 2005. "State Animal Protection Laws: The Next Generation." *Animal Law* 11:131.

People for the Ethical Treatment of Animals (PETA). 2013. "How Animals End up in Laboratories." http://www.peta.org/issues/animals-used-for-experimentation/how-animals-end-up-in-labs.aspx.

"Policy #7: Brachiating Species of Nonhuman Primates." 2011. 9 CFR 3 § 3.80. http://www.aphis.usda.gov/animal_welfare/policy.php?policy=7.

"Policy #13: Animal Identification." 2011. 9 CFR 2 §§ 2.38(g), 2.35(b), 2.50, 2.75(a). http://www.aphis.usda.gov/animal_welfare/policy.php?policy=13.

"Policy #18: Health Certificate for Dogs, Cats, and Nonhuman Primates." 2011. 9 CFR 2 § 2.78. http://www.aphis.usda.gov/animal_welfare/policy.php?policy=18.

Ravenscroft, G. M. 2002. "Overview of Texas Animal Cruelty Laws." *Animal Legal and Historical Center.* http://www.animallaw.info/articles/ovustx-cruelty.htm.

Rizzo, V. 2012. "Quick Summary of Laws concerning Animals in Film Media." *Animal Legal and Historical Center.* http://www.animallaw.info/topics/tabbed%20topic%20page/spusfilmanimals.htm.

Satterberg, W. 2003. "Tales from the Interior: Dog Bite Cases." *Alaska Bar Rag* 27:20.

Texas Penal Code 42.09 (2007).

UT Stat. § 76-9-301–307 (2012).

8

Service Animals in the Criminal Justice System

Introduction

Use of service animals in public and private places is federally protected. The definition of "service animal" is narrow, and the types of animals who may act as service animals is very limited. Some animals may qualify as service animals but serve in therapeutic capacities similar to service animals. Businesses and public places are not required to permit entrance to therapeutic animals; however, businesses often welcome them. In courts therapeutic animals have offered comfort and calm to defendants, victims, and witnesses, but some members of the criminal justice system contest their presences in the courthouse.

Service Animals

The term "service animal" is used to describe animals who work with disabled individuals and accompany disabled individuals. Service animals are protected and regulated under federal and state legislation. It is illegal to prohibit service animals from entry into public places that normally prohibit pets, for example, courthouses or domestic violence shelters (Gonzales 2011). "Service animals" may also describe animals who serve a therapeutic purpose. Therapy animals may receive consideration from private organizations, like airlines that permit therapy animals to fly outside of kennels with passengers. However, it is not unlawful to deny entry or access to therapy animals.

Service animals are almost always dogs; however, training for and employment of therapy animals has caused the field to expand rapidly in recent years. Under the Americans with Disabilities Act (ADA), only dogs can qualify as service animals (ADA 2011). The only exception contemplated by the ADA is miniature horses. Yet, miniature horses are only permitted to serve in certain appropriate situations, and they are not an official substitution. Miniature horses can serve as therapy animals, along with an array of animals, including rabbits, llamas, rats, cockatoos, macaws, and other medium or large birds, but wild or exotic animals would normally not serve in a therapeutic capacity (Hilario 2011; Panchak 2008; Pet Partners 2012). Therapeutic relationships with animals can serve as an early intervention in the lives of troubled or high-risk youth, or can help to rehabilitate offenders.

Service Animals in Court

Under the American with Disabilities Act (ADA), federal law permits service dogs entry into courthouses. Service dogs assist disabled individuals by providing services directly related to an individual's disabilities, for example, blindness or paraplegia. Denial of admittance would likely result in a civil rights violation (Wakefield 2000; Guide Dogs 2011). Alabama, Illinois, Minnesota, Missouri, New Hampshire, and Oregon are just a few of the many states to pass state legislation permitting service animals in public places (Colker and Milani 2002). States' definitions of "service animals" and their requirements for how service animals are to appear and behave may vary (Colker and Milani 2002). For example, some states may require service animals to dress in orange, or they may permit enforcement of noise ordinances against barking service animals (Guide Dogs 2011). In many jurisdictions trainers and companions are liable for damage caused by dogs.

Nonservice animals are not usually permitted inside of courthouses, but exceptions to the rule do occur. Support dogs may accompany specific individuals, or they may serve as courthouse dogs, whereby they work for the court or an individual trainer who works in court. Many judges support the growing trend of allowing support dogs in court (Maraghy 2009). For example, in Pittsburg Judge Gene Ricciardi has allowed Lucy, his rescued Chihuahua-mix dog, to perch on the bench during trial (Miklas 2011). Witnesses are reportedly put at ease by Lucy. Some people hold and stroke Lucy to soothe their nerves. Thus, she expresses and facilitates sensitivity toward youth, victims, and other vulnerable parties. Lucy also serves Judge Ricciardi therapeutically by allowing him to gather his thoughts and remain focused during difficult cases.

One drawback is that a courthouse dog likely requires a million-dollar insurance policy. Another drawback is that if dogs respond to heated outbursts in the courtroom, then their barking could be grounds for an appeal (Appellate Cases 2012; Maraghy 2009). A third drawback is that people may be allergic to dogs or feel uncomfortable around dogs (Bice 2010). A fourth drawback is that the presence of any dog in a courthouse bucks the traditional adversarial model (Wakefield 2000). For example, Judge Linda Van De Water kept her elderly dog in chambers, but the city's attorney in her district asked her to desist because people were allergic and the dog's presence was unconventional.

Service animals may be trained to accommodate physical or psychiatric disabilities. Concerns, like allergic reactions, do not limit access for ADA service dogs because disabled individuals have civil rights under the ADA (Appellate Cases 2012; DOJ 2011). Some courts would rely on a doctor's note or training certificate, while others may require evidence that the dog performs a specific task related to the psychiatric disability. Individuals who are disabled but are not classified as disabled under the ADA may use emotional support animals, and nondisabled individuals may own dogs who provide them with therapeutic benefits. Yet, neither of these roles is that of "service animals" (ESA 2011). Nondisabled people are not entitled to civil rights under ADA. Therefore, service dogs that accommodate people with psychiatric disabilities cannot be barred from court, but individual's supportive therapy dogs or emotional support animals might likely be, and courthouse dogs might also be susceptible to complaints and criticism (DOJ 2011; ESA 2011). The manner in which a person may prove that an animal is a psychiatric service dog remains varied (Disability Rights California 2011).

Around the United States dozens of dogs provide support and comfort in more than one-third of states (Clarridge 2012). Because courthouse dogs have been so effective, legal challenges have been raised about whether defendants can receive fair trials. For example, a support dog may nudge a victim who is too terrified to speak, and some may view this as creating a bias in the jury's mind (Clarridge 2012; Holder 2013). Some critics might argue that a jury may place greater weight on the victim's testimony because a dog is so likeable. However, the use of courthouse dogs has been upheld on appeal since dogs are neutrally supportive. The support of a dog assigned to a courthouse does not create unfair bias in the minds of the jury because dogs can soothe and support defendants, victims, or other witnesses. Dogs will support anyone in need within the courtroom. Some critics have suggested that perhaps judges should instruct juries about the fact that dogs are trained to be neutrally supportive. Currently, there are no national requirements for courthouse dog training, though most training programs cost taxpayers little to nothing. Use of taxes to support training programs may ensure that training remains neutral and based on emotional need or unconditional love. Standardized training practices could also increase accountability and might better ensure justice.

Service Animals in Prisons

The Americans with Disabilities Act (ADA) requires accommodations for inmates with disabilities. The ADA also requires that all public spaces permit Seeing Eye dogs. However, prisons cannot typically accommodate prisoners who require Seeing Eye dogs (CBC 2013). Blind inmates are not numerous; yet, accommodations have been generally deficient in many prisons. Though many corrections facilities train Seeing Eye dogs and allow some inmates to share cells with dogs, blind prisoners are routinely denied access to Seeing Eye dogs. Blind prisoners illegally have been denied other accommodations, for example, talking books and watches, walking canes, bottom bunks, and braille (AELE 2013; Walter 2012). Perhaps as Seeing Eye dog training programs expand, prison policies will accommodate visually impaired inmates with Seeing Eye dogs. Sparse accommodations for blind inmates might require inmates to be accompanied to the toilet and showers or to remain under protective custody. Protective custody requires near constant confinement and has the effect of increasing a prisoner's overall discomfort while incarcerated. To avoid this aggravation, a Canadian court sentenced a blind offender to eighteen months of house arrest where he would be accommodated by a guide dog (CBC 2013). The court explained that denying accommodations to an offender would amount to a human rights violation. House arrest may be impracticable for long terms or for dangerous offenders. Parolees living at home or participating in halfway programs may be permitted to live with Seeing Eye dogs or enroll in Seeing Eye dog programs (Taylor and Murphy-Taylor 2007). In one case a prisoner lost both eyes from a gunshot wound he received while he was incarcerated (*Evening Independent* 1944). About fifty fellow inmates donated to send the inmate to a seeing institute so that he could be trained to use a Seeing Eye dog. Friends donated the dog, which he received when he was paroled.

Service animals are permitted to enter correctional facilities with disabled visitors (CDCR 2013). Documentation, identifying harnesses, or prior arrangements may be required. Service animals could be required to pass through metal detectors with a disabled visitor, or they may be subject to searches by detection dogs. Many correctional facilities work with detection dogs. Their many responsibilities include cell phone detection and tracking escaped prisoners (Frazier 2009). Injuring or killing one of these working dogs could carry serious penalties. For example, in Kentucky it is a felony to assault law enforcement or corrections service animals (KRS § 525.200, 2013; KRS § 525.215, 2013). The penalty could also require an offender to pay veterinary bills, handlers' lost wages, and other costs.

Conclusion

Each jurisdiction may set forth requirements for proving disabilities and identifying service animals. These restrictions influence affairs in courts, correctional facilities, and other public and private establishments. People traveling between jurisdictions may encounter difficulties due to misunderstanding and documentation. Therapeutic animals are frequently rejected in public places. Nevertheless, animals aiding people physically and emotionally play important roles and cannot be mistreated. The presence of therapeutic animals in the criminal justice system may strengthen the democratic process or may be compromised in some cases.

References

Americans for Effective Law Enforcement (AELE). 2013. "Disability Discrimination: Prisoners." http://www.aele.org/law/Digests/jail29a.html.

American with Disabilities Act (ADA). 2011. "Highlights of the Final Rule to Amend the Department of Justice's Regulation Implementing Title II of the ADA." May 26. http://www.ada.gov/regs2010/factsheets/title2_factsheet.html.

Bice, D. 2010. "Bringing Dog to Work Comes Back to Bite Judge." *Journal Sentinel*, March 21. http://www.jsonline.com/watchdog/noquarter/88785992.html.

"Blind Prisoner to Get Seeing Eye Dog upon Parole." 1944 October 14.

California Department of Corrections and Rehabilitation (CDCR). 2013. "Visiting a Friend or Loved One in Prison." http://www.cdcr.ca.gov/visitors/docs/InmateVisitingGuidelines.pdf.

Clarridge, C. 2012. "Courthouse Dogs Calm Victims' Fears about Testifying." *Seattle Times*, September 22. http://seattletimes.com/html/local-news/2019235703_courthousedogs23m.html.

Colker, R., and A. Milani. 2002. "Garrett, Disability Policy, and Federalism: A Symposium on Board of Trustees of the University of Alabama v. Garrett; The Post-Garrett World: Insufficient State Protection Against Disability Discrimination." *Alabama Law Review* 53:1075.

Courthouse Dogs. 2012. "Appellate Cases." http://www.courthousedogs.com/legal_appellate_cases.html.

Disability Rights California. 2011. "Psychiatric Service and Emotional Support Animals." http://www.disabilityrightsca.org/pubs/548301.pdf.

Frazier, I. 2009. "Scratch and Sniff." *New Yorker*, October 19. http://www.newyorker.com/talk/2009/10/19/091019ta_talk_frazier.

Gonzales, A.R. 2011. "Access for All: Five Years of Progress." *US Department of Justice*. http://www.ada.gov/5yearadarpt/fiveyearada.pdf.

Guide Dogs for the Blind, Inc. 2011. "Individual State and Province Access Laws." http://www.guidedogs.com/site/PageServer?pagename=resources_access_statelaw.

Hilario, F. 2011. "Pet Therapy Birds." *Frandelhi's Flyers*. http://frandelhisflyers.com/pettherapybirds.

Holder, C. 2013. All Dogs Go to Court: The Impact of Court Facility Dogs as Comfort for Child Witnesses on a Defendant's Right to a Fair Trial." *Houston Law Review* 50:1155.

"Jail Violates Blind Sex Offender's Rights, Judge Rules." 2013. CBC, April 9. http://ca.news.yahoo.com/blind-man-gets-house-arrest-sexual-assault-011923697.html.

KRS § 525.200 (2013).

Maraghy, M. 2009. "Jacksonville Judge Wants Dogs Used in Justice System." *Jacksonville.com*, August 24. http://jacksonville.com/news/metro/2009-08-24/story/jacksonville_judge_wants_dogs_used_in_justice_system#ixzz2ayJaNyRQ.

Miklas, J. 2011. "Lucy on the Bench: A Chihuahua Mix Brings Order and Understanding to the Courtroom." *Animal Friends, Inc.*, March 1. http://animalfriendsinc.blogspot.com/2011/03/lucy-on-bench-chihuahua-mix-brings.html.

Panchak, P. 2008. "Rat Therapy for Autism?" *Post-Gazette*, June 14. http://autisminnb.blogspot.com/2008/06/rat-therapy-for-autism.html.

Pet Partners. 2012. "Pet Partners Therapy Animal Program: Frequently Asked Questions." http://www.petpartners.org/page.aspx?pid=267.

Service Dogs of Florida, Inc. 2011. "Emotional Support Animals (ESA), Therapy Dogs & Rights." September 7. http://2012.servicedogsfl.org/?p=22.

Taylor, J. P., and K. Murphy-Taylor. 2007. *Willow in a Storm: A Memoir*. Minneapolis, MN: Scarletta Press.

US Department of Justice (DOJ). 2011. "Service Animals." *ADA 2010 Revised: Requirements*. http://www.ada.gov/service_animals_2010.htm.

Wakefield, V. 2000. "Suing for civic access." *Jacksonville.com*, August 9. http://jacksonville.com/tu-online/stories/080900/met_3752700.html.

Walter, Shoshana. 2012. "Disabled Prisoners' Rights Scrutinized in California County Jails." *Huffington Post*, October 8. http://www.huffingtonpost.com/2012/10/08/disabled-prisoners-rights_n_1948542.html.

9

Animal Control

Introduction

Animals are subject to the law. Animals neither obey nor disobey law, but their behavior is subject to legal authority; their status makes them subject to legal recourse. A variety of circumstances could cause an animal, as property or as an actor, to come before the court. In the majority of cases, the law treats animals differently from people. Private and public organizations may be responsible for controlling animals; however, organizational intervention may result in dramatically different outcomes for animals depending on which organization intervenes and jurisdictional policy requirements.

Seizure, Courts, and Animal Control

Animals might come before the court for reasons ranging from housing violations to dangerousness. Animals also may be classified as contraband if they are owned illegally by prisoners or convicted offenders who have been forbidden from owning animals by court order (Graves, Mosman, and Rogers 2012). Contraband animals could be confiscated by authorities, seized, or surrendered to animal control. Illegal owners may not be entitled to a hearing, but if they were to have standing, then they would not likely prevail on any due process challenges.

Animals may be seized or voluntarily surrendered if they are thought to be dangerous, or they may be seized or voluntarily surrendered if they have been abused, abandoned, or neglected. Animal hearings most often occur when animals are seized from owners due to the animal's dangerousness or the owner's abuse. Anyone who believes that a domestic animal is dangerous may file a formal complaint with local police or animal control (Girgen 2003). Usually complaints are filed against dogs. If allegations are substantiated, then an initial hearing will be held to evaluate the evidence. Owners are entitled to hearings under due process, and are also entitled to be notified that they might appear to defend their pets. Public health officials or judges can hear the evidence and declare that a dog is dangerous or vicious. Judges may order owners of dangerous dogs to keep dogs confined and take other measures. These dogs will not be destroyed. Vicious dogs could be declared vicious after biting several people or behaving particularly egregiously, for example, killing a child, though some dogs have been sentenced to death for behavior as minor as chasing a horse. Vicious dogs might be euthanized or ordered to vacate the jurisdiction. Owners could be ordered to transfer ownership of a dog to a more responsible party.

Numerous dog bite cases filter through the justice system annually. Dog bite incidents arise millions of times each year throughout the United States (Huss 2005). More than half of all children will be bitten by dogs before the age of twelve. Many of these bites, which occur inside homes, will require medical attention. Usually owners are responsible for damages. Homeowners claim hundreds of millions of dollars under insurance policies annually because of dog bites occurring in their homes. If a renter owns a dog, then a landlord may be sued by a bite victim, especially if the bite occurs in a common area, for example, a community pool or parking lot. In response to a civil claim, a landlord may report the bite to animal control as evidence of his or her guilt-lessness—even when a landlord does not truly believe that an animal presents further threat. A renter may no longer be able to reside in a rental property even if a dog is not found to be dangerous by the court.

Owners who abuse animals are entitled to the same rights as owners of dangerous dogs. Each owner is entitled to be heard. Special masters could potentially be appointed by the court to animal seizure cases involving abuse (Fox 2008). A special master might likely be appointed by a judge when a large number of animals have been seized, for example, in the case of puppy mills. The court may appoint a special master if abused animals are highly valuable, publicly visible, or controversial, for example, chimpanzees at a university laboratory. Special masters can facilitate cases by suggesting specialized remedies, encouraging those with legally cognizable interests in animals to voluntarily relinquish their rights, and asking the court for increased protection for animals. Special masters can also oversee rehabilitation of rescued animals. Many animals who are abused must be humanely euthanized to prevent prolonged suffering. However, many can be rehabilitated. When numerous or high-profile animals are involved, increased coordination may be required to ensure that appropriate care is provided. When special masters are involved, courts can operate under a "best interest" of the animal standard, rather than solely under

124

a property paradigm. The court may ask special masters to determine whether seized or surrendered animals are dangerous (Huss 2008). For example, when pit bulls were seized from football player Michael Vick (see chapter 2), many had been trained to fight. A special master was appointed as a guardian. The special master was responsible for determining whether animals were too dangerous to be adopted and ought to be euthanized. Special masters may not be appointed to all high profile cases. Thus, vicious animals who receive sympathetic media coverage may benefit from public interest in the case (Girgen 2003).

Animal Control and Criminal Justice

Potentially dangerous animals may be seized. Jurisdictional variations will determine whether owners were required to know of animals' dangerous propensities prior to seizure (Fugate 2006; Phillips 2013; Texas Health and Safety Code § 822.044, 2013). Once the state determines that an animal can legally be seized, an owner's due process rights will be put into motion. Sometimes civil hearings will require owners to present evidence on behalf of an animal, but other times criminal charges will be filed against owners.

Sometimes dogs elect to or are ordered to attack police or civilians. In the eyes of the law, outcomes for dangerous dogs may be the same irrespective of whether dogs are uncontrollable or obedient. Yet, owners who unjustifiably order dogs to attack will certainly be subject to charges, for example, aggravated battery, attempted murder, or murder. Animals who are uncontrollable may subject their owners to criminal recklessness charges. Dogs who are declared to be vicious may be euthanized, or their owners can be ordered to permanently remove a dog from a jurisdiction (Girgen 2003). If an owner violates a court's order by failing to remove a dog or returning to a jurisdiction with a dog, then a court may issue a fine or sentence an owner to jail. Subsequent incidents increase the likelihood of the owner being fined or jailed and of an animal being euthanized.

Criminals often use dogs as weapons or shield with very little regard for a dog's well-being. Such "weaponization" is discussed in chapter 18. Offenders may hide drugs or weapons inside a dog's kennel or collar in an attempt to discourage police from discovering the illegal items (Ortiz 2010). This strategy always fails. If animals cannot be controlled, then they are destroyed so that police can search them. The government's treatment of animals who are ordered to attack has been criticized because of the three parties involved, that is, a victim, an owner, and a dog. A dog following orders may be the most severely punished, yet the least culpable (Schwartzberg 2008).

When officers shoot animals, owners may sue. Municipalities will not be held legally responsible for animals who are shot by police officers (Roudebush 2002). Thus, municipalities are immunized by the state. However, people may sue police departments and individual officers. If police departments have failed to properly train officers, then they will be liable. The state will immunize officers who acted under the color of law. The color of law is usually interpreted to be behavior that is within proximity to law, not strict adherence to the law. If rights are not clearly established or the reasonable officer would not have acted differently, then the state will immunize officers even when they behave incongruously with the law. Immunized officers may be held liable in court, but the department will pay any awards on their behalves. Immunization has been said to lower officers' incentives to comply with the law. Yet, without it officers might be too hesitant to perform their duties, and few people would take such risky civic work. If officers act outside the color of law, then they will not be immunized (Roudebush 2002).

Fourth Amendment rights guarantee that the government will not seize personal property unless seizure is warranted. Warrants must be based on probable cause. When police shoot animals, they seize animals. If officers are threatened, then they may defend themselves. However, if an animal does not pose a threat, but a police officer shoots and kills that animal, then it amounts to an illegal seizure. Police will usually be immunized from lawsuits even when seizures are illegal. The totality of the circumstances may determine when officers will qualify as immunized.

Officers are trained to wound threatening animals; thus, killing an animal almost always triggers lawsuits. Oddly, even if police may not be held civilly liable in one case, the same case may result in police suspension or discipline if employers believe that officers' actions were reckless. Thus, courts' responses and departments' responses may differ in unexpected ways. Usually police discipline in these cases results from public pressure. For example, police have shot animals who are being held by children or passively standing next to children (Abbott 2013). These cases tend to rouse public ire. On more than one occasion, police have aimed poorly and accidentally shot people instead of their intended animal targets (MSN 2013). These cases tend to raise community awareness, forcing departments to respond with disciplinary measures. In some cases police have hunted down annoying animals onto their owners' property or maliciously killed animals. In these cases officers can be held liable for other civil damages like intentional infliction of emotional distress on owners. Police may not be immunized for malicious killing and could be criminally charged. However, these cases are somewhat uncommon.

Animal Control and Private Organizations

"Animal control" may describe an agency, governmental authority, or a role within the criminal justice system (Huss 2007). Not every jurisdiction has a government-sponsored animal control agency. Thus, animal control duties are often entrusted to and regulated by private organizations, for example, the Humane Society or the American Society for the Prevention of Cruelty to Animals (ASPCA). These organizations may work with the state, or they may serve as an official animal control authority. Relationships between the government and private organizations began with the animal welfare movement in the late 1800s. The government contracted with private organizations to enforce anticruelty statutes for many years. This relationship is also discussed in chapter 1. Depending on the agreement struck and the role played by the private organizations, prosecutors may presently have the authority to supervise any enforcement of cruelty laws conducted by private animal control organizations. The role of private animal control agencies later expanded to include advocacy for humane euthanasia (also discussed in chapter 1). To some extent, advocacy has led to policy changes and new criminal laws to reduce animal suffering. Eventually alternatives to euthanasia became a mainstream ambition of rescue organizations. Finally, agencies included animal adoption, veterinary service, and lost pet location assistance.

However, some critics view no-kill policies as one major problem resulting from collaborative strategies between government and private organizations (Huss 2007). Whereas government agencies euthanize animals rapidly, animal control rescue organizations attempt to adopt as many pets as possible. Thus, they sometimes adopt animals to hoarders and dogfighters rather than euthanize animals. Animal control organizations do willfully adopt animals to abusers—not intentionally, but because many organizations have few, if any, barriers in place to prevent it. For example, most hoarders are single females. Without a home check, these seemingly kind and stable people, who likely require psychiatric or psychological treatment, can adopt dozens of animals locally without detection as long as they avoid adopting from the same agency too frequently and they pay adoption fees.

The government and private organizations may employ a variety of means for funding programs. One benefit of relying on private rescue organizations is that they may be self-sustaining or accept minimal government aid. Organization may provide veterinary services for a fee, charge adoption fees, collect donations and grants, and receive tax-exemption status (Huss 2007). Fees collected by the government from pet food sales may be applied toward animal programs and animal database maintenance (Mass. H.R. 1335, 2014). Fines generated from cruelty or neglect cases can often go directly to shelters or animal agencies (Local Memphis 2013; Graves, Mosman, and Rogers 2012). For example, in one case where one hundred animals were illegally living in a single home, the owners were placed on probation, banned from future ownership, and ordered to pay fifty thousand dollars in fines, eighteen thousand of which went to local animal shelters (Local Memphis 2013).

Not every private rescue organization that works with the government takes control of animals in an animal control capacity. Many serve rehabilitative functions. For example, the Witness Protection Program for dogs protects dogs from abusers (Ciampanelli 2013). Abused dogs can be evidence, witnesses, and victims in abuse and neglect cases. While cruelty cases are being investigated, dogs are taken to secure locations and given new identities. These dogs are usually not returned, but instead, they are adopted.

Animal Control Officers

Animal control officers play an important role within the criminal justice system. Animal control can be an independent agency, a department, or a unit within a police department that works to control and manage animals in society. It usually deals with stray animals, animals in emergency situations, dangerous animals, and mistreatment. Wildlife that enters society is often managed by specialized organizations. Thus, animal control usually handles dogs, birds, cats, and other animals commonly found in society. However, animal control can handle other exotic, wild, and domesticated animals as well.

Animal control is subject to and enforces animal welfare laws. For example, animal control is prohibited from trapping or destroying animals in an inhumane manner, and it can investigate anyone who does, including other animal control officers. Animal control's power, organization, and capability vary widely between jurisdictions. Animal control may operate with police or other organizations, and it might rely on community tips and reports to locate animals or investigate allegations of mistreatment. Its authority and procedures are dependent on budget, and sometimes on local political disposition regarding the importance of animal control, animal mistreatment, or animal suffering. For example, animal control in one jurisdiction might routinely search for strays and post their photos online, or it may have no such capability (Humane Society 2013). Animal control may proactively capture animals, may only collect animals who are dropped off on-site, or may be obligated to ignore all animals other than those who must be euthanized by court order. Some agencies may only accept animals who it believes will be adopted. Animal control could be comprised of untrained shelter employees but very frequently relies on at least some trained officers who have attended animal control academies or have been formally trained (New England Animal Control 2013).

Interagency cooperation may involve animal control and local police working together when owners file police reports for missing animals. Cooperation provides the public with greater informational resources. If local animal control does not operate a lost-and-found pet website, people may check the status of their lost pet reports with local police. Police may aid attempts to search for and capture lost animals. Outside of animal control units, police are usually not trained to capture lost animals, and their techniques may be rudimentary or crude, albeit well-intended or well-equipped. Police may carry dog leads in the trunks of their cars to aid animal control. Sometimes their best option may be to attempt to drive at, wrangle, or herd animals, or they may direct traffic around animals until animal control arrives, for example, when animals have strayed onto expressways. However, using vehicles to herd animals may be illegal under certain circumstances in some jurisdictions. Thus, police may not be authorized to use this technique.

Animal control usually becomes involved after someone complains about an animal for whatever reason. Foul odors give rise to complaints quite frequently when hoarding occurs (Avery 2005). Neighbors may witness abused or neglected animals and file complaints. Animal control will often attempt first to investigate using plain-view tactics: animal control officers may walk up to yards, curtilage, and front doors, and may peer into windows. They will look for signs of abuse and neglect and attempt to interview property occupants or neighbors.

If animal control officers view evidence within a property, then they may petition a magistrate for a search warrant or report evidence to the police, who can legally search. Sometimes only animals specifically enumerated by a warrant can be seized, but other times all animals on a property might be seized. Animal control officers may be required to bring animals to in-house or affiliate veterinarians who will clean, treat, or possibly euthanize animals. Animals' environments and conditions will be documented and used as evidence at trial. Animal control officers may work with prosecutors and testify at trial. Animals may be adopted, returned, placed with a previous owner's relatives, auctioned, or otherwise disposed of at the conclusion of a trial.

Conclusion

Animals are vulnerable to humans, homelessness, other animals, society, and the criminal justice system. Animal control organizations and courts may become involved to assist animals. Though their roles are varied, usually courts and animal control become involved to control scenarios that are undesirable to humans or are adverse to animals' well-being. Outcomes may include adoption or death. Animal control is a widely varying and imperfect system. However, compassionate responses to animals are likely to continue evolving.

References

Abbott, R. 2013. "Killing of Dog May Leave Florida Cop Liable." *Courthouse News Service*, July 3. http://www.courthousenews.com/2013/07/03/59083. htm.

Avery, L. 2005. "From Helping to Hoarding to Hurting: When the Acts Of 'Good Samaritans' Become Felony Animal Cruelty." *Valparaiso University Law Review* 39:815.

Ciampanelli, P. 2013. "Witness Protection Program for Dogs?" *PawNation*, August 22. http://www.pawnation.com/2013/08/22/witness-protection-program-for-dogs/?icid=maing-grid7%7Cmain5%7Cdl27%7Csec1_lnk2%26pLid%3D362094.

Fox, A. C. 2008. "Using Special Masters to Advance the Goals of Animal Protection Laws." *Animal Law* 15:87.

Graves, P., K. Mosman, and S. Rogers. 2012. "2011 Legislative and Administrative Review." *Animal Law* 18:361.

Humane Society. 2013. "What to Do If You Lose Your Pet." August 2. http://www.humanesociety.org/animals/resources/tips/what_to_do_lost_pets.html.

Huss, R. J. 2005. "No Pets Allowed: Housing Issues and Companion Animals." *Animal Law* 11:69.

———. 2007. "Rescue Me: Legislating Cooperation between Animal Control Authorities and Rescue Organizations." *Connecticut Law Review* 39:2059.

————. 2008. "Lessons Learned: Acting as Guardian/Special Master in the Bad Newz Kennels Case." *Animal Law* 15:69.

"Incoming Police Chief Tries to Shoot Dog, Shoots Woman." 2013. MSN, June 27. http://now.msn.com/barry-rountree-incoming-winston-salem-nc-police-chief-shoots-at-a-dog-hits-owner-and-is-placed-on-administrative-duty.

Mass. H.R. 1335, 188th Cong (2014).

"Moscow Couple Sentenced to Probation, Pet Ban for Animal Cruelty." 2013. *Local Memphis*, July 23. http://www.localmemphis.com/news/local/story/Moscow-Couple-Sentenced-to-Probation-Pet-Ban-for/sO6vQ_tQl-0G33qTeBKoUzA.cspx.

"New England Animal Control/Humane Academy." 2013. *University of New Hampshire*, August 9. http://www.unh.edu/neacha/index.html.

Phillips, K. M. 2013. "Dog Bite Law." http://dogbitelaw.com/.

Roudebush, P. L. 2002. "Detailed Discussion of Police Shooting Pets." *Animal Legal and Historical Center.* http://www.animallaw.info/articles/dduspo-liceshootingpets.htm#id-3.

Schwartzberg, H. M. 2008. "Tort Law in Action and Dog Bite Liability: How the American Legal System Blocks Plaintiffs from Compensation." *Connecticut Law Review* 40:845.

Texas Health and Safety Code § 822.044 (2013).

10

Animal Welfarists

Introduction

Society's relationship with the animal welfare movement is multidimensional. Some welfare organizations are loathed; yet, some animal lovers may appreciate certain welfarist groups' stances on particular animal issues. Many members of society may be unaware of how instrumental welfarists have been in improving treatment of animals. If they are aware, then people may differentiate between nonprofit organizations, animal rights activists, and extremist organizations to some degree. Distinct political positions may define various groups, but essentially, groups are deeply focused on institutionalizing greater compassion for animals, abstention from cruelty, and improved treatment for animals in society and in the wild. Mainstream organizations and radical organizations sometimes work together to accomplish similar goals. Overall, the criminal justice system protects lawful political activism.

Animal Welfare Movement

Animal welfare involves feelings, politics, ideas, activism, morality, and policies. The concept of animal welfare may be as old as humanity, but criminalization of cruelty in contemporary society is relatively recent. The term "animal welfare" identifies the fact that animals can be the victims of cruelty, neglect, or other undesirable conditions, and that humans can take animals' well-being under consideration by behaving in ways that reduce animal suffering. From this simple idea, numerous ideologies, philosophies, political factions, and organizations have arisen. Some people concern themselves with animal welfare because they believe that cruelty is useless; others may help animals for compassion's sake; still others may believe that animals ought to be legal persons or possess certain rights; and finally, some groups may only want to protect and help attractive, cute, or majestic animals, but not all animals.

Animal Welfare Organizations

In general, there is an overarching animal welfare movement and agenda. Animal welfarists attempt to eliminate or reduce harm and increase animal well-being. The movement began slowly around the beginning of the twentieth century, when altruistic philanthropists supported humane legislation and established animal shelters. The movement at large has been extremely successful and productive over the past century.

The Humane Society of the United States (Humane Society) is a nonprofit organization that has deeply embedded itself into US legal frameworks since its inception (HSUS 2013). The Humane Society distinguishes itself from other animal welfare organizations in a few respects. First, the organization promotes a completely cruelty-free, vegan lifestyle. It discourages dairy, beef, poultry, fish farming, leather, fur, or any other similar enterprises. It rejects the premise that humans may harm animals in any way. Thus, the Humane Society very popularly rejects euthanasia of healthy animals. Many people donate to the Humane Society because they support no-kill shelters that house some animals indefinitely rather than destroy animals who have not been adopted. The Humane Society has become very powerful in part because of copious public support for their no-kill position.

The Humane Society may work in conjunction with animal control. The Humane Society can serve in an official capacity as animal control in some jurisdictions. Some local humane societies may rescue animals or participate in legal proceedings to the same capacity that any governmental organization would. Their involvement in disasters can be extraordinarily beneficial. For example, they may have proper connections to place numerous hoarded animals into various shelters following a seizure. Hoarding and emergency responses are discussed in chapters 11 and 17. Humane societies are relatively well-funded, politically popular, and highly networked. Though animal welfare organizations are always short-handed, humane societies are better staffed by volunteers and employees, and they may be tightly connected to governmental departments that provide them with information or resources. For example, police who personally believe in animal welfare may take it upon themselves to share tips with the Humane Society, bring animals to shelters, or donate. There are many organizations that model themselves after the Humane Society. Though state and local humane societies are not affiliated with the national Humane Society of the United States, the national Humane Society may support smaller humane societies with resources and training.

Beginning in the 1980s People for the Ethical Treatment of Animals (PETA) developed hardline strategies and politics (PETA 2013). The group's most divisive political position is its practice of painlessly euthanizing healthy animals. This position is rooted in their belief that peaceful death is better than forcing animals to live in crates for the duration of their lives. Previously, PETA supported pit bull bans specifically because pit bulls suffer so greatly. However, it has shifted their position to emphasize elimination of all animal breeding, which leads to animal abandonment.

In the 1980s PETA secretly investigated and uncovered serious abuse of monkeys that occurred in a laboratory in Silver Spring, Maryland. PETA provided evidence to the government, which seized the animals in the first police raid of an animal lab in US history. PETA wanted to take custody of the seized primates. PETA's petition was denied by the US Supreme Court, and the monkeys were killed. Due to the fact that this was the first animal research case to reach the Court, PETA gained national notoriety. The Silver Spring monkeys case solidified PETA's reputation in the movement. Because media coverage resulted from the exposé, financial donors became aware of PETA. Two of PETA's main finance strategies continue to be undercover surveillance exposés and notoriously attention-grabbing demonstrations. Donations allow the organization to provide low-cost services to the community, investigate cruelty, and launch corporate boycotts. PETA may serve as local animal control and respond to emergencies and natural disasters. PETA is able to effectively mobilize operations by relying on trained workers, volunteers, and tipsters. Due to its high-profile demonstrations, PETA may be considered by the public to be more political than some other welfare organizations. Furthermore, in addition to improved animal welfare, it desires some legal rights for animals.

The Animal Liberation Front (ALF) is an underground animal welfare organization that has been labeled a terrorist organization by the Federal Bureau of Investigation (FBI) (ALF 2013). It is not a centrally organized group, *per se*, but rather a collective of like-minded individuals who independently participate in activities that the ALF supports. ALF's *modus operandi* is to illegally rescue animals who are condemned to death, torture, or cruelty. Its main mission is liberation, not destruction of property. However, animals are considered to be property in many cases; thus, liberating or absconding with animals damages property. A few organizations, like Earth Liberation Front, Green Peace, and Stop Huntingdon Animal Cruelty, mirror the ALF; however, the ALF is not affiliated with any other welfare organizations.

Almost every welfare organization is involved in the criminal justice system. However, some organizations, such as the Animal Legal Defense Fund (ALDF), exclusively devote themselves to animals' legal defenses. The ALDF began around same time that the rest of the animal welfare movement gained speed (ADLF 2013a). Beginning in the late 1970s, attorneys for ALDF began to file lawsuits on behalf of animals. The ALDF's use of the justice system was innovative, and many of their arguments have shaped the law. The ALDF continuously wages new and interesting battles on behalf of animals. Sometimes it wins, but other times it loses. Yet, by arguing cases, it paves the way for future claims and animal welfare legislation.

In addition to petitioning courts directly, the ALDF uses other strategies to affect policy. Letter writing has proven to be a cost-effective and powerful tool for ALDF attorneys, who also file amicus briefs with the court. The ALDF has established a huge presence within the legal community by offering free legal advice to state and municipal attorneys on how to prevail on cruelty charges. It educates future members of the justice system by assisting laws students' chapters of the ALDF. Law school chapters, called Student ALDF (SALDF), present symposiums on cutting-edge issues. SADLFs offer the community opportunities to talk with key figures in contemporary US Supreme Court cases or appellate cases. The ADLF is an activist organization that lobbies to strengthen welfare legislation; however, it is adverse to governmental policies. For example, it recently filed suit in Utah, where undercover surveillance of factory farms is criminalized. It claimed violations of the First Amendment and Fourteenth Amendment resulting from criminalization of certain surveillance strategies. Another example is that it once halted US Navy's plan to kill five thousand wild burros. It is very common for animal welfare organizations to work with the government, as well as against the government. Government programs or policies may directly or indirectly compromise animal welfare. Thus, several organizations or law firms following in the ALDF's footsteps may be quick to take those matters before the court.

Animal Welfare and Free Speech

Animal rights activists can be very vocal about welfare issues. Welfare groups, like PETA and Green Peace, routinely canvas areas, distribute literature, and use politically charged symbolism in public (*U.S. v. O'Brien*,

1968). Under the First Amendment free speech is guaranteed. This guarantee includes political speech in public areas. The government cannot restrict the content of speech unless a narrowly tailored restriction is necessary and it can prove that there is a compelling reason for specifically banning certain speech. Thus, some speech is illegal, for example, fighting words and defamation. Illegal speech is not protected even if it is political. Political speech that is truthful and does not incite disorder is usually completely protected even if it is offensive or unpopular.

The government has occasionally succeeded in passing laws that restrict how free speech is exercised in public. Public speech may be regulated according to time, place, and, manner. For example, the government may enforce noise ordinances or require permits for large crowds in a public area. Such laws maintain safety and order. Generally applicable, content-neutral laws are legal. Another legal and common regulation impeding public speech is municipal ordinances requiring public walkways to remain unobstructed. Demonstrators may stand on sidewalks without permits, but they may not obstruct walkways with objects. For example, sidewalks cannot be blocked with literature tables, displays, or signs; protestors must hold the signage. To obstruct a public walkway, permits are likely to be required, so if demonstrators plan to place any object on a sidewalk, then a permit would likely need to be issued first. Violation of such ordinances may lead to warnings, fines, or possibly arrests depending on the extent of the obstruction, police discretion, and demonstrators' behavior.

Animal welfare activists sometimes use visual media to communicate with the public (McGoldrick 2008). For example, activists may dress in costumes, sit inside cages, distribute literature to the public, or march with signs outside animal enterprises. The government will not protect demonstrators who attempt to trespass on private property or block entrances to buildings. Any unpermitted speech acts that block public walkways or private entrances to businesses can be interrupted by police. Subject to time, place, and manner restrictions, demonstrators are free to stand in public spaces, for example, public sidewalks, and manually distribute literature and talk to any pedestrians (*McCullen v. Coakley*, 2014). Activists wearing scanty costumes must first inform themselves about state and local nudity laws, as coverage requirements may vary greatly between jurisdictions. For example, in one municipality men may be required to cover their torsos, while in another municipality women may be permitted to completely uncover their torsos (Cusack, 2012). Nudity may be protected as symbolic speech if it is imbued with elements of communication likely to intimate a particularized message. Politically communicative nudity may be permissible in jurisdictions where clothing is normally required, but a permit could be required. However, nudity may not necessarily be permitted if it incites violence or is otherwise likely to disrupt or impede compelling state interest.

In some cases, free speech has prevailed over antiterrorist animal enterprise laws. Laws designed to prevent "green" terrorism in animal enterprises or threats of terrorism may prevent activists from confronting animal enterprise employees, for example, lab researchers. In California an animal facility's parking lot and walkways were considered by the court to be public forums. A law prohibiting welfarists from using public walkways outside of animal enterprises was stricken (*Kuba v. 1-A Agr. Ass'n.*, 2004). The court held that the content of activists' speech could not be abridged, and that time, place, and manner restrictions could not be applied exclusively to animal welfarists.

Activists may inform local police of their activities even if they do not require permits. This helps police properly vet any public reports about activists, and it also puts police on notice that they may need to protect demonstrators. Law enforcement officers frequently stand by demonstrations to protect demonstrators, enforce ordinances, and maintain order. If activists behave improperly or accidentally break the law, or if miscommunication creates confusion about free speech rights, then undesirable police encounters may result. One example occurs when demonstrators contact the police ahead of time and ask if a permit is required for a specific event. An officer may state that no permit is required, but an officer who arrives at the demonstration may believe that a permit is required. A demonstrator may have to interrupt the demonstration to discuss the law or permitting with an officer, or perhaps an activist may attempt to contact the original officer by phone during the demonstration to clear up the confusion. Officers usually defer to demonstrators and err on the side of upholding free speech. They do so because, on one hand, accidentally shutting down a lawful exercise of free speech can be a serious and costly error, but on another hand, maintaining police presence can maintain requisite safety and order. Nevertheless, confusion occasionally leads to regrettable results. For example, a permit may be required and granted for a demonstration table on a particular street. Then, an activist may set up a demonstration table on the wrong side of the street. The street may be the dividing line between two jurisdictions, which renders the permit useless on the wrong side of the street. Under these circumstances an activist could be arrested, fined, or asked to move. Police would be under no obligation to honor another jurisdiction's permit but may allow the demonstrator to remedy the situation rather than penalize the demonstrator. However, in some rare cases activists will be arrested due to mistakes.

Undercover Surveillance

Many animal welfare organizations conduct undercover surveillance of animal enterprises. Without undercover surveillance routine criminal neglect and cruelty would go undocumented. Animal welfare organizations use a variety of methods to conduct surveillance. Their methods commonly involve staging visits or gaining employment and then videotaping or keeping a log. Staging a visit is one easy and generally legal way to gain entry onto a property. Some farms or plants may allow members of the public to tour a facility or property or make an appointment to visit. After receiving a tip about cruelty, a welfarist will visit and observe animals or conditions while on a property. Some businesses or employees will make no effort to hide cruelty. Undercover investigators may be equipped with miniature cameras or may jot down detailed observations. A single set of data may suffice, or several rounds of observation may be conducted to accumulate sufficient evidence. Visits do not require a high degree of planning, unlike long-term operations.

Long-term operations typically last around six weeks, but could wind up early or last for many years. Investigations usually rely on welfarists gaining employment at a company, for example, a slaughterhouse, factory farm, or puppy mill. To conduct a long-term operation, welfarist organizations will first study the operations. They will discover whether there are vacancies at the company. Activists research animal enterprise surveillance laws. They profile a typical employee and may develop a character. If the first two conditions permit undercover investigation to go forward, then welfare organizations will select an appropriate investigator. To go undetected, an investigator must fit in with other employees. For example, if a farm will be investigated, and the majority of employees on the farm are Mexican migrant workers, then the investigator must pass as a Mexican migrant worker. This would require the investigator to speak Spanish using an appropriate Mexican vernacular and be familiar enough with some Mexican culture and migrant culture to remain in character and avoid discovery. Failure to successfully gain coworkers' trust could endanger the welfarist and compromise the investigation.

In the past welfarists have used false names or information to obtain employment (Graves, Mosman, and Rogers 2012). Several states have attempted to criminalize this to stop animal welfarists' surveillance efforts. In recent years investigators have begun to use their legal names and information to be hired without risking prosecution. Welfare organizations are not responsible for making sure that corporations conduct background checks. There is a risk that employers will conduct a background check and discover an investigator's animal welfare connections. But this may be a risk worth taking so that welfare organizations can truthfully assert that they did not trick employers. Once they are hired, investigators observe premises, employees, and animals. When they are legally allowed to record, they do, but they may be forced to journal their experiences.

Undercover surveillance is necessary and abundant within the animal welfare movement. The Humane Society, PETA, and other organizations rely on it heavily. Much of what has been discovered about animal abuse in every industry has resulted from undercover surveillance. Well-financed animal industry lobbying has spurred some serious attempts to legislatively restrict surveillance. Restrictions have caused welfarists some alarm for three reasons: (1) they want to protect their investigators from committing crimes, (2) they want to protect their charitable status by complying with the law, and (3) they want to be assured that evidence will not be undermined by accusations of illegality. Yet, welfarists are committed to surveillance; thus, they invest a significant amount of time and resources into formulating lawful surveillance strategies.

Most recorded surveillance occurs in places of business where there is no heightened expectation of privacy, but the law still protects businesses' privacy to some extent. Generally, surreptitious audio recording by a third party is prohibited by many state laws (Reporters' Committee for Freedom of the Press 2008). In some states conversation participants must knowingly assent to being recorded, but in other states conversations may be recorded without a participant's permission. In a few states eavesdropping is illegal, and in most states placing an audio recording device, that is, a wire or wiretap, in a room is prohibited. Video recording is less restricted and nuanced, especially when cameras are worn by welfarists. Taping laws are usually general, and not specifically aimed at welfarists.

The federal Animal Enterprise Terrorism Act (AETA) of 2006 was designed to prohibit welfarists from impeding animal enterprise with intent to commit a crime (Graves, Mosman, and Rogers 2012). It does not criminalize visual or audio documentation. Many states have tried to criminalize recording specifically to hamper welfarists through what are called Ag Gag Bills. California, Florida, Illinois, Indiana, Minnesota, Nebraska, New Hampshire, New Mexico, New York, North Carolina, Pennsylvania, Tennessee, Vermont, and Wyoming have introduced legislation that prohibited recording, long-term investigations, providing false information, or other related surveillance techniques (Graves, Mosman, and Rogers 2012; LCA 2013). Currently, Idaho, Iowa, Kansas, Missouri, Montana, and Utah criminalize some aspect of surveillance, and Arkansas only permits law enforcement to investigate cruelty, while North Dakota makes it a crime to record in any animal enterprise without permission (Graves, Mosman, and Rogers 2012; Hodges 2011a; LCA 2013). In many states, however, investigators are free to go undercover, but they will be labeled terrorists if they commit any illegal activities while conducting surveillance.

Animal Welfarists' Crimes

Rather than avoiding crime, some animal welfarists intend to engage in crime. They mainly commit crimes for three reasons. First, they are interrupting or damaging animal enterprises or activities that harm animals. Second, they are making political statements using civil disobedience. Third, they are freeing animals from confinement or aiding their escape. Some crimes are committed spontaneously by individuals, some loosely connected individuals may claim to be part of the same group and work together, or established units may plan highly organized and costly missions. Certain crimes may be designed to attract media attention, while other crimes may be covert.

Early in the animal welfare movement, welfarists were labeled as criminals because of a few public criminal acts of politically motivated protest. The public is familiar with the image of activists throwing red paint on fur coats or chaining themselves to trees to prevent destruction of an animal habitat. Today mainstream animal welfare groups are almost never affiliated with crime. Out of concern for the protection of their 501(c)(3) tax status, mainstream groups avoid any criminal attention-getting in the United States, and they do not destroy property. Groups that are frequently involved with crime, including civil disobedience, are labeled as "domestic terrorists" in the United States and some other countries, and they are not entitled to charitable tax status. Yet, some groups, like PETA, broach the line. For example, rather than dousing fur coats in red paint, which destroys property, PETA activists abroad may "flour bomb" a celebrity who wears fur, and domestic activists distribute disparaging, neon green stickers that activists may adhere to pedestrians' fur coats.

Domestic terrorism of animal enterprises is prohibited federally under the Animal Enterprise Terrorism Act (AETA). Animal terrorism laws have been enacted in the majority of states (Hodges 2011b). At the federal level, crimes—for example, threatening or intimidating employees of animal enterprises—may be considered to be terrorism. Threats are prohibited in many states as well. Under many state animal terrorism laws, entering, remaining, or concealing oneself in an animal facility that is closed to the public with intent to commit a crime is considered to be terrorism (Hodges 2011a). The kinds of crimes considered in this definition include destruction or defacement of property and disruption of operations, research, or experimentation. The definition also includes taking control of or copying facility records, for example, lab reports. Almost any business that uses animals is considered to be an animal enterprise. Livestock operations, research or testing labs, zoos, and dog shows are just a few examples. Normally, activists who lawfully gain entry, that is, who are hired using their actual identities, do not engage in crime and are not considered to be terrorists. In some cases penalties for animal enterprise crimes can be much higher than if the same crimes were committed against other businesses or an individual. For example, in South Carolina misdemeanor animal terrorism can be penalized with a ten-thousand-dollar fine and a three-year prison term (Hodges 2011b). In Pennsylvania the price for a single felony may be a hundred-thousand-dollar fine plus a forty-year prison term. The level of interference or immediacy of the threat may determine, in some cases, whether activism is protected speech, misdemeanor or felony terrorist activity, or civil disobedience.

Civil disobedience occurs when a person intentionally breaks a law to protest the injustice of that law (*U.S. v. O'Brien*, 1968). Depending on the act and the interpretation of the act, civil disobedience may be considered to be terrorism under the AETA. For example, animal welfarists may commit civil disobedience when they openly continue taping cruelty inside a private animal enterprise after being ordered to stop taping (Graef 2013). Failure to obey an order to end taping calls attention to an activist's belief that police power is misused when it aids cruel business practices. The term "civil disobedience" previously only referred to actions that exclusively and directly violated unjust laws or principles for the purpose of protest. But now the term "civil disobedience" is sometimes applied to all peaceful, mainly demonstrative, politically oriented crimes usually involving failure to follow police orders to end an illegal protest. Some animal welfare organizations have now adopted the term to describe harassment activities. For example, Stop Huntingdon Animal Cruelty (SHAC), a "terrorist" organization, describes some of their activities as "electronic civil disobedience" (Grubbs 2010). They effectively shut down businesses temporarily by bombarding websites, e-mail servers, telephone lines, and fax lines. These nuisances are not threatening, so they do not necessarily fit legal description of "terrorism." However, activists are not intending to protest communication; thus, they are not truly committing civil disobedience. Critics may believe that harassment amounts to terrorism when it is not traditional civil disobedience.

Some organizations and activities clearly fall within the purview of the AETA, even when those activities help animals. The Animal Liberation Front (ALF) is a title given to a guerilla mission to liberate animals. The ALF is not a terrorist cell insofar as there is no wide-reaching central leadership commanding missions from an underground headquarters. Rather, the ALF is a collection of like-minded people who take it upon themselves to liberate animals. Sometimes the ALF liberates a few animals at a time, but other missions have liberated thousands of animals at once. People who liberate animals are inspired by and attribute their actions to the ALF mission. ALF members may independently engage in other crimes, like chaining themselves to circus doors or defacing a laboratory, but the ALF's established mission is to liberate animals. For this reason, many ALF activists keep their identities hidden, and the black ski mask has become emblematic of the ALF. A few activists have been arrested dozens of times for a wide variety of crimes, including civil disobedience, and are famous/infamous. Some well-known activists give public speeches about cruelty and the importance of civil disobedience and animal liberation.

Despite some members' candor and public appearances, the FBI closely monitors the ALF since the liberation of animals could involve felony larceny, burglary, or numerous other serious crimes. The ALF is considered to be a terrorist organization, but other slightly more mainstream organizations have been placed on FBI watch lists. For example, Green Peace, which engages in some questionably disobedient activities from time to time, was placed on a watch list, much to the public's surprise (ICR 2013). The group maintained its 501(c)(3) status, which demonstrates that it is not a terrorist organization. Another organization placed on a watch list was Sea Shepherds, whose mission is to investigate and prevent illegal activity involving marine life, such as shark finning. Illegal fishing activity is not considered to be protectable animal enterprise under the AETA. Thus, Sea Shepherds maintains its 501(c)(3) status. Animal activists have claimed FBI harassment, with some being asked to turncoat or have their names placed on a domestic terrorist list (ALDF 2013b).

Aggressive animal welfare activism can fuel a variety of responses. Civil racketeering actions have been waged against the ALF, and other similar groups, like the Animal Defense League of New Jersey, the Coalition to Abolish the Fur Trade, and the Vegan Resistance for Liberation (Beltran 2002). Some mainstream and underground investigators and activists have been brutalized by corporations and the public. Famous retaliatory actions against welfarists include arson, knifing, beating, rape, death threats, fire bombing, shooting, assault, and murder. Welfare activists have at times become strange bedfellows with other groups. For example, a court in Oregon held that an animal interference statute violated the Constitution because it allowed people in labor disputes to interrupt animal enterprise, but not activists (Borowski 2009; Hodges 2011a). Around the world aggressive animal activism receives a variety of responses. Australia, for example, considers animal enterprise terrorism similarly to the United States, while Israel seems to have taken a more lax approach, which fails to preemptively label aggressive activists as terrorists (Goldenberg 2013).

Conclusion

Animal welfarists are involved at every level of the criminal justice system. From street-level protection offered by police to hearings at the US Supreme Court, activists employ the system on behalf of animals. Means and results vary, and sometimes lead to stigmatization of certain groups or the movement as a whole. Nevertheless, some welfare groups' popularity or notoriety brings animal welfare issues to the forefront of social consciousness, which activates change.

References

Animal Enterprise Terrorism Act, 18 U.S.C. § 43 (2013).

Animal Legal Defense Fund (ALDF). 2013a. http://aldf.org/.

Animal League Defense Fund (ALDF). 2013b. "Interview with Will Potter." http://aldf.org/cases-campaigns/features/interview-with-will-potter/.

Animal Liberation Front (ALF). 2013. http://www.animalliberationfront.com/.

Beltran, X. 2002. "Applying RICO to Eco-Activism: Fanning the Radical Flames of Eco-Terror." *Boston College Environmental Affairs Law Review* 29:281.

Cusack, C. M. 2012. "Boob Laws: An Analysis of Social Deviance within Gender, Family, or The Home" (études 2). *Women's Rights Law Reptr.* 33:197.

Goldenberg, T. 2013. "Israelis Brand Selves in Solidarity with Animals." *Yahoo! News*, June 27. http://news.yahoo.com/israelis-brand-selves-solidarity-animals-061447667.html.

Graef, A. 2013. "Man Arrested for Videotaping Rodeo Cruelty in Oregon." *Care2*, May 24. http://www.care2.com/causes/man-arrested-for-video-taping-rodeo-cruelty-in-oregon.html#ixzz2cxb634BG.

Graves, P., K. Mosman, and S. Rogers. 2012. "2011 Legislative and Administrative Review." *Animal Law* 18:361.

Grubbs, K. R. 2010. "Comment: Saving Lives or Spreading Fear; The Terroristic Nature of Eco-Extremism." *Animal Law* 16:351.

Hodges, C. 2011a. "Detailed Discussion of State Animal 'Terrorism'/Animal Enterprise Interference Laws." *Animal Legal and Historical Center.* http://www.animallaw.info/articles/ddusstateecoterrorism.htm.

———. 2011b. "Summary of State Animal Enterprise Interference Laws." *Animal Legal and Historical Center.* http://www.animallaw.info/articles/qvusecoterrorism2011.htm.

Humane Society of the United States (HSUS). 2013. http://www.humanesociety.org/.

Institute of Cetacean Research (ICR). 2013. "Illegal Harassment and Terrorism against ICR Research." http://www.icrwhale.org/gpandsea.html.

Kuba v. 1-A Agr. Ass'n. 387 F.3d 850 (2004).

Last Chance for Animals (LCA). 2013. "States of Disgrace." http://www.lcanimal.org/index.php/campaigns/ag-gag-laws-states-of-disgrace/states-of-disgrace.

McCullen v. Coakley. 573 U.S. ___ (2014).

McGoldrick, J. M. 2008. "Symbolic Speech: A Message from Mind to Mind. *Oklahoma Law Review* 61:1.

People for the Ethical Treatment of Animals (PETA). 2013. http://www.peta.org.

Reporters' Committee for Freedom of the Press. 2008. "Can We Tape." http://www.rcfp.org/rcfp/orders/docs/CANWETAPE.pdf.

State v. Borowski. 231 Or.App. 511 (2009).

U.S. v. O'Brien. 391 U.S. 367 (1968).

11

Animals in Emergencies

Introduction

The government aids humans and animals in need of rescue, in crises, and in emergencies. Preparation for emergencies is the best way to prevent loss of life. A few jurisdictions routinely follow policies that require rescue of animals, but many jurisdictions and individual rescuers elect to aid and rescue animals. Public support for the heroic rescue of animals further enforces society's approval of expenditures and risks associated with rescue operations.

Private Emergencies

Police, first responders, fire fighters, Homeland Security, and other agencies deal with animal rescue. The image of a firefighter attempting to rescue a kitten from a tree is iconic, and it attests to civil servants' willingness to assist animals in emergency situations. The availability of public servants during a crisis is imperative. Rescuing animals may not be required, but it increases goodwill and improves public relations. It also maintains a sense of kindness and humility among members of the civil service. Though the public is aware that authorities will aid animals in crisis, comparatively few citizens contact members of the criminal justice system for help in relation to the number of animals involved in emergencies daily.

The US Coast Guard (USCG) serves as law enforcement on the water and conducts search and rescue (SAR). Boaters may send distress signals after their motors fail, they run out of fuel, they are trapped by a storm, or they become ill at sea. Many times boaters who are on the water with animal companions will require rescue. The USCG may invite rescued animal companions, for example, dogs, onto boats and helicopters. The USCG may dispatch SARs in response to boaters' distress calls when boaters or USCG crews observe that animals are in need of rescue. This was the case with a horse in California who swam several miles out to sea (Taylor 2012). The USCG affixed the horse to the side of a boat and towed the horse to shore. In another example an unaccompanied dog was observed in Honolulu Harbor (*Coast Guard News* 2013). The dog seemed to struggle while swimming. The USCG received the report and rescued the animal. Then the USCG used its media and public relations resources to attempt to reunite the dog with the dog's family.

Police regularly rescue animals. Though officers cannot rescue every animal, they frequently attempt to aid animals who are involved in traffic accidents or who are trapped. Animals involved in traffic accidents may require police to respond to injured domestic animals who were passengers in vehicles or to wild or feral animals who are injured during collisions (CBS 2013). Police must quickly notify appropriate animal agencies, or units may be prepared to provide emergency care. Trapped animals often receive extraordinary attention. For their compassion police are typically rewarded with attention and praise from the public. Public interest tends to increase when police rescue wild animals or when animals are involved in unusual circumstances. Unusual circumstances include a horse falling off a bridge into quicksand, police removing a skunk's head from a glass jar, and police caring for a baby bird found lying on a police cruiser (Cook 2013; UPI 2013; WKMG 2012).

National Emergencies

The fifty thousand domesticated animals that were abandoned during Hurricane Katrina revealed two faces of animal owners in New Orleans (Huss 2007). The first face was of people who would abandon their animals during a natural disaster. Before they evacuated, countless people locked their animals inside their homes, many of which were flooded or inaccessible for weeks. Between 50 and 90 percent of abandoned animals could not be rescued, and many died during the storm or of starvation in weeks after the storm. For example, gang members abandoned thousands of pit bulls and bait dogs without any provisions. Some domestic animals were rescued from homes by helicopters, boats, and volunteers on foot. Others were rescued as they roamed New Orleans following the storm.

The other face shown during Hurricane Katrina was of people who refused to be rescued unless their pets could not be rescued as well. Such persons risked their lives and chose to die rather than abandon four-legged, finned, and feathered members of the family. As a result of this tragic dichotomy, the Federal Emergency Management

Association (FEMA) was ordered to coordinate with states to develop emergency rescue plans (42 U.S.C. § 5196a–d, 2006). The Pets Evacuation and Transportation Standards (PETS) Act requires FEMA to work with other government agencies to develop evacuation and transportation plans for individual animals and service animals. PETS does not require specific preparations or steps. Since Hurricane Katrina most states have adopted emergency preparedness legislation that calls for care; transportation; shelter; and record of guardian location, food and water, or other provisions for animals during emergencies (Hodges 2011).

Several state emergency preparation laws only provide for animal companions, though service animals must be evacuated in every jurisdiction (ADA 2011; NV ST 414.095, 2013). In Colorado lethal flooding required FEMA assistance and evacuation (Hodges 2011). The National Guard chose to evacuate all domestic animal companions, including fish tanks, goats, chickens, and monkeys, because it claimed that it did not want people to have to choose between safety and staying with their companions (CBS2013; Curry 2013). Ground teams airlifted and rescued thousands of pets. Though some cattle and livestock were not rescued, large numbers of horses, longhorn cattle, cows, bulls, calves, goats, pigs, colts, ponies, llamas, and donkeys were rescued. Some states have established emergency plans for all animals. Alabama, Florida, Illinois, Maine, Minnesota, Nevada, North Carolina, Oklahoma, Tennessee, Vermont, Virginia, Washington, and other states have plans that cover animals including zoo animals, exotic animals and wildlife, poultry, sport and exhibition animals, laboratory animals, livestock, educational and research animals, and fish (Hodges 2011).

Animals may also participate in search and rescue (SAR) during emergencies. Urban SARs, wilderness SARs, avalanche SARs, and water SARs may rely on dogs (Mehus-Roe 2002). SAR training may be intense. For example, dogs and their handlers in New Jersey intensely train and bond so that they knowingly communicate with each other during SARs (Bush 2013). In California National Disaster SAR dog training lasts six months (Mehus-Roe 2002). Dogs are trained to locate living victims who are trapped in collapsed or damaged building rubble following explosions and natural disasters. Bomb detection dogs, urban SAR dogs, and dogs trained to locate suspects could all work during single act of terrorism, though detecting different objects or people may require individually trained dogs.

Local Crises

Local crises may be subject to different regulations, and municipalities may prosecute cruelty differently in crises scenarios. Local crises may include any man-made or natural destabilization to the community. Animal mistreatment can destabilize a community, or mistreatment may result from destabilization or during destabilization to the community. Prosecutors throughout the country have set up taskforces to join with local agencies in responding to disasters created by animal abuse, neglect, and abandonment (Lockwood 2006). Cruelty that reaches a crisis level may potentially be met with much greater adversity by the criminal justice system. For example, seizure of hundreds or thousands of animals from a hoarder or breeder may trigger emergency responses. In these situations an offender would be charged criminally, and a court may place a lien on commercial animals so that the government can care for and shelter animals until they can be sold. Money recovered may be used to offset a municipality's or state's expenses.

Local crises may involve the criminal justice system in unexpected ways. For example, an insect plague may lead a citizen to illegally use poisons that threaten or torture animals, or animals' corpses may be handled or disposed of in a criminally reckless fashion following a crisis (WI ST 60.23, 2012). Though these actions could rise to state and federal levels of concern, they may also be municipal crimes that result in misdemeanor or felony charges.

Local crises may expose abuse, abandonment, neglect, or ordinance violations when law enforcement personnel are required to unexpectedly enter private property during emergencies. For example, the presence of potentially dangerous domesticated or wild animals—for example, attack dogs or tigers—may need to be reported to local authorities (McKinney's General Municipal Law § 209-cc, 2013). Very often, unreported animals who remain under their owners' control do not present a threat, and failure to report may only result in a civil violation. This is discussed in chapter 18. However, during local crises, for example, spreading house fire, police or other municipal personnel may need to gain emergency access to premises where unreported animals may live or be trapped. If unreported animals obstruct, threaten, or harm first responders, then criminal charges could be brought against owners.

Conclusion

The presence of animals in emergency situations can significantly complicate emergency responses. However, society seems more than willing to include animals in response plans. Many jurisdictions require minimal responses for animals, but others participate in more comprehensive considerations. Society seems to support prosecution of owners who fail to prepare emergency plans in advance for animals. Police or rescuers may be threatened by protective animals or animals who feel threatened by rescuers' presence. Though these scenarios are infrequent, officer safety is paramount, and thus, policies often require owners to report the status of potentially dangerous animals. In cases where people abandon animals during emergencies, the criminal justice system may prosecute.

References

Bush, J. 2013. "Partners, Not Just Pets." *U.S. News*, August 9. http://live.wsj.com/video/partners-not-just-pets-2013-08-09-171153155/1D6D98DB-13C0-4C9E-872F-84842FCD443C.html#!1D6D98DB-13C0-4C9E-872F-84842FCD443C.

"Coast Guard Rescues Dog in Honolulu Harbor." 2013. *Coast Guard News*, August 25. http://coastguardnews.com/coast-guard-rescues-dog-in-honolulu-harbor/2013/08/25/.

"Colorado's Flood Rescue: 'No Pets Left Behind.'" 2013. CBS News, September 20. http://www.cbsnews.com/8301-201_162-57603852/colorados-flood-rescue-no-pets-left-behind/.

Cook, R. 2013. "Police Rescue Baby Bird Found on Cruiser." *Portsmouth Patch*, June 20. http://portsmouth-nh.patch.com/groups/police-and-fire/p/police-rescue-baby-bird-found-on-cruiser.

Curry, C. 2013. "Colorado Pets, Including Fish, Rescued from Flood." *ABC News*, September 20. http://abcnews.go.com/US/colorado-pets-including-fish-rescued-flood/story?id=20319372.

"Highlights of the Final Rule to Amend the Department of Justice's Regulation Implementing Title II of the ADA." 2011. American with Disabilities Act (ADA), May 26. http://www.ada.gov/regs2010/factsheets/title2_factsheet.html.

Hodges, C. 2011a. "Detailed Discussion of State Emergency Planning Laws for Pets and Service Animals." *Animal Legal and Historical Center*. http://www.animallaw.info/articles/ddusstateemergencylaws.htm.

———. 2011b. "Quick Summary of State Emergency Planning Laws for Animals." *Animal Legal and Historical Center*. http://www.animallaw.info/topics/tabbed%20topic%20page/spusdisasterplan.htm.

Lockwood, R. 2006. "Animal Cruelty Prosecution." *American Prosecutors Research Institute*. http://www.ndaa.org/pdf/animal_cruelty_06.pdf.

Mehus-Roe, K. 2002. "Disaster Search and Rescue Dogs." *Petfinders.* http://
www.petfinder.com/helping-pets/animals-and-disaster-relief/disaster-
search-rescue-dogs/.

McKinney's General Municipal Law § 209-cc (2013).

"Police Rescue Skunk with Head in Jar, Remain Unscented." 2013.
United Press International (UPI), August 30. http://www.upi.com/
Odd_News/2013/08/30/Police-rescue-skunk-with-head-in-jar-remain-
unscented/UPI-10531377882242/.

"Rescuers in New Smyrna Beach Save Horse Stuck in Mud." 2012. WKMG,
Local 6, October 24. http://www.clickorlando.com/news/Rescuers-in-
New-Smyrna-Beach-save-horse-stuck-in-mud/-/1637132/17117962/-/
877cmlz/-/index.html.

Taylor, D. 2012. "Coast Guard Rescues Horse at Sea." *WTKR*, May 17. http://
wtkr.com/2012/05/17/coast-guard-rescues-horse-at-sea/.

"Truckee Police, Volunteers Rescue Injured Bear Cub." 2013. CBS San Fransisco
Bay Area, July 20. http://sanfrancisco.cbslocal.com/2013/07/20/truckee-
police-volunteers-rescue-injured-bear-cub/.

WI ST 60.23 (2012).

12

Relationships of Violence

Introduction

Violence may be inflicted on human or animal victims. Victims of abuse may participate in cycles of abuse. They may become chronic victims or inflict violence on others. Animals may become pawns or targets in domestic violence. These situations have prompted specific legislation, for example, animal abuser registries, that protects animal victims from domestic violence (Mass. H.R. 1416, 2014). Legislation may also protect human victims from threat and psychological abuse resulting from abuse inflicted on animal companions during domestic violence. In general, offenders who would harm one class of vulnerable victims, for example, children, may harm others, for example, animals. Thus, understanding and addressing domestic violence is foundational to reducing and preventing animal mistreatment.

The Generalizability of Abuse

Correlations between human abuse and animal abuse pose safety threats. Researchers surveyed twenty-three males who had abused animals (Coxwell 2005). Respondents provided several possible motives for abusing animals. Abusers wanted control over animals, wanted to retaliate against animals or people, acted on speciesism, used animals to relieve aggression or hostility felt toward a human, wanted shock value and amusement, and were sadistic. These reasons demonstrate dangerous crossovers between humans and animals, which can escalate quickly, especially during domestic violence.

Childhood animal cruelty is directly related to childhood sexual and physical abuse, unavailable or alcoholic fathers, and domestic violence (Duncan, Miller, and Thomas 2005). Adolescent delinquency correlates with abuse of peers, substances, and animals (Battjes, Gordon, and Kinlock 2004). The Federal Bureau of Investigation (FBI) has reported that most serious offenders have a history of animal abuse. A ten-year study of children between six and twelve years old found that 83 percent of children who set fires and were cruel to animals became violent offenders (Lockwood 2006). Children with antisocial personality disorder, who often routinely engage in criminal activity, are the most typical abusers of animals. An extremely high percentage of incarcerated offenders have a history of juvenile or adult animal abuse (Muller-Harris 2011). In one study, 100 percent of offenders convicted of sexual homicide had also abused animals (Muller-Harris 2011). Serial killers often practice abusing animals and then progress to humans (Campbell 2002).

In New York relationships between human and animal abuse became clear to the legislature in the late 1990s. The New York legislature passed Buster's Law after a juvenile convicted felon named Chester Williamson set a young cat on fire, then sexually abused a mentally disabled child on a later date (Gavin 2011). Buster's Law calls for felony animal abuse charges. Charging animal abusers with felonies may reduce risk of recidivism. Almost every state prosecutes certain kinds of animal abuse as felonies, especially when abuse is committed against dogs or cats (Lockwood 2006). Felony convictions are kept in interstate records, but misdemeanors are no longer kept in interstate records on file with the FBI (Challener 2010; Gerwin 2005). Thus, records of misdemeanor animal abuse cannot be tracked in other states.

Because of the correlation between human and animal abuse many states have developed interagency communication and responses to animal abuse co-occurring with child abuse (Muller-Harris 2011). Almost one dozen states and the District of Columbia require animal control and social services to cross-report child abuse and animal abuse. Indirect correlation between violence and victimization may be more difficult to track. Witnessing animal abuse in the home may have similar effects as experiencing violence. Witnessing animal abuse in public may correlate with increased tendencies to commit violent crimes. For example, juveniles who attend dogfighting are more prone to commit or witness violence against humans even though they do not directly perpetuate animal abuse (Ortiz 2010).

Domestic Violence

Links between animal abuse and domestic violence are firmly established (Nelson 2011). Pets are nonhuman victims of domestic violence because they are often considered to be part of the family. In fact, an American child is less likely to have a live-at-home father than a pet (AHA 2013). In response to domestic violence between partners or family members, pets may develop trauma disorders. Animal companions may also become victims of domestic violence by being threatened, abused, hidden, taken, or killed. Animal mistreatment may be a method for inflicting psychological abuse on a human companion, or it may occur because an animal is a member of the home. Pets are more likely to be neglected and poorly cared for in violent households (Fielding and Plumridge 2010). Investigations into animal abuse often serve as etiological pathways for authorities to investigate unreported domestic violence. Frequently animal abusers have violent histories, including domestic violence. Investigators may find that pets were routinely abused to gain compliance from relatives or intimate partners. Violence may be inflicted on humans to incite sufficient fear to trap them in violent relationships. Domestic violence against animals is usually witnessed by children. Children who witness abuse in their homes are ten thousand times more likely to inflict domestic violence in the future.

Many state legislators have attempted to include pets in domestic violence protection orders (Graves, Mosman, and Rogers 2012). This means that when threatening parties are ordered to stay away from partners or relatives, a threatening party would also be barred from contacting, threatening, or harming a family's companion animal. Additional protection for pets is important because many states would not otherwise protect animals against threats, concealment, or other acts that do not amount to "cruelty." Furthermore, offenders who violate protective orders by harming animals face additional charges or more severe charges than they would under cruelty statutes. For example, in Puerto Rico it is a felony to make contact with an animal when contact is prohibited by a protective order (Wisch 2013). Many states provide additional protection for victims of domestic violence who are subjected to psychological abuse under domestic violence statutes. Domestic animal abuse can be considered psychological abuse in many circumstances. These orders are also important because many domestic violence victim shelters do not accept pets (AHA 2013). When victims live in their cars or in friends' homes while awaiting an opening in a pet-friendly shelter, their animals may be especially vulnerable to abusers. Nearly three-quarters of victims in abuse shelters report that their animals were abused by a partner, and more than a third report that their children abused their animals. Though these laws do not directly protect animals, they could deter abusers by increasing the number and severity of charges applicable to abusers' actions (NCADV 2013).

In states and territories that have passed laws protecting animals from domestic violence through protective orders, statutory language varies. Arkansas, Arizona, Oklahoma, Puerto Rico, Texas, Minnesota, North Carolina, the District of Columbia, Massachusetts, West Virginia, Vermont, Louisiana, Washington, Maine, and California courts may grant victims exclusive care, control, and possession of any animal belonging to or residing with their children, abuser, or family (Wisch 2013). In Arizona, Puerto Rico, Washington, and New Jersey, protective orders may prohibit the abuser from approaching an animal within a certain distance. Louisiana's and Nevada's orders can prohibit harassment of animals. Domestic violence protective orders can prohibit municipal ordinance violations or abuse of property, which specifically includes animals. Hawaii, Minnesota, Nevada, Oklahoma, and Massachusetts may prohibit either party from taking, abusing, or threatening animals belonging to a household involved in domestic violence. In North Carolina, Connecticut, and Illinois, courts may protect qualifying victims and prohibit injury or threat to a victim's companion animals. New York's domestic violence protective orders only protect animals from unjustified injury or death. Oklahoma and West Virginia specifically prohibit molestation of animals. In addition to causing physical injury, Tennessee prohibits abusers from attempting to cause injury. In Oregon the court may order any necessary measures to prevent neglect and to protect service animals, therapy animals, guard animals, or companion animals. (Oregon's protective orders do not extend to guard animals kept in businesses or for commercial purposes since those animals are not living in homes with domestic violence or victims.) Maryland statutes allow protective orders to grant temporary possession of pets involved in domestic violence, but orders do not require abusers to surrender animals. Thus, some statutes more directly protect pets, while others focus on humans' psychological well-being and property rights.

Conclusion

Criminally and family law may incidentally or directly protect animals involved in domestic violence. Jurisdictions independently define "domestic violence" and respond to it differently. Jurisdictions may differently consider parties' relationships and the types of threats or aggressive actions committed. Variations between jurisdictions and individual cases may affect the degree of protection received by animals. Laws may specify who will gain control of an animal following domestic disputes or violence. In some cases courts may be able to preemptively intervene or respond, but in some jurisdictions courts are limited by weak laws. Additional reforms and expanded application of family law and criminal law could further protect animals, family members, intimate partners, children, and other victims of domestic violence.

References

Battjes, R. J., M. S. Gordon, and T. W. Kinlock. 2004. "Correlates of Early Substance Use and Crime among Adolescents Entering Outpatient Substance Abuse Treatment." *American Journal of Drug and Alcohol Abuse* 30, no. 1: 39.

Campbell, A. 2002. "The Admissibility of Evidence of Animal Abuse in Criminal Trials for Child and Domestic Abuse." *Boston College Law Review* 43:463.

Challener, D. J. 2010. "Protecting Cats and Dogs in Order to Protect Humans: Making the Case for a Felony Companion Animal Statute in Mississippi." *Mississippi College Law Review* 29:499.

Coxwell, W. 2005. "Student Article: The Case for Strengthening Alabama's Animal Cruelty Laws." *Law and Psychology Review* 29:187.

Duncan, A., C. Miller, and J. C. Thomas. 2005. "Significance of Family Risk Factors in Development of Childhood Animal Cruelty in Adolescent Boys with Conduct Problems." *Journal of Family Violence* 20, no. 4:235.

"Facts about Animal Abuse & Domestic Violence." 2013. American Humane Association (AHA). http://www.americanhumane.org/interaction/support-the-bond/fact-sheets/animal-abuse-domestic-violence.html.

Fielding, W. J., and S. Plumridge, S. 2010. "The Association between Pet Care and Deviant Household Behaviors in an Afro-Caribbean, College Student Community in New Providence, the Bahamas." *Anthrozoos* 23, no. 1:69.

Gavin. R. 2011. "Buster's Law Results: All Bark, Little Bite." *Times Union*, January 8. http://www.timesunion.com/local/article/Buster-s-Law-results-All-bark-little-bite-945017.php.

Gerwin, K. 2005. "There's (Almost) No Place Like Home: Kansas Remains in the Minority on Protecting Animals from Cruelty." *Kansas Journal of Law and Public Policy* 15:125.

Graves, P., K. Mosman, and S. Rogers. 2012. "2011 Legislative and Administrative Review." *Animal Law* 18:361.

Huss, R. J. 2007. "Rescue Me: Legislating Cooperation between Animal Control Authorities and Rescue Organizations." *Connecticut Law Review* 39:2059.

Lockwood, R. 2006. "Animal Cruelty Prosecution." *American Prosecutors Research Institute*. http://www.ndaa.org/pdf/animal_cruelty_06.pdf.

Mass. H. R. 1416, 188th Cong. (2014).

Muller-Harris, D. L. 2011. "Animal Violence Court: A Therapeutic Jurisprudence-Based Problem-Solving Court for the Adjudication Of Animal Cruelty Cases Involving Juvenile Offenders and Animal Hoarders." *Animal Law* 17:313.

Nelson, S. 2011. "Bibliography: The Connection between Animal Abuse and Family Violence; A Selected Annotated Bibliography." *Animal Law* 17:369.

Ortiz, F. 2010. "Making the Dogman Heel: Recommendations for Improving the Effectiveness of Dogfighting Laws." *Stanford Journal of Animal Law and Policy* 3:1.

Pets Evacuation and Transportation Standards (PETS) Act, 42 U.S.C. § 5196a–d (2006).

"Psychological Abuse." 2013. Public Policy Office of the National Coalition Against Domestic Violence (NCADV). http://www.ncadv.org/files/PsychologicalAbuse.pdf.

Wisch, R. F. 2013. "Domestic Violence and Pets: List of States That Include Pets in Protection Orders." *Animal Legal and Historical Center*. http://www.animallaw.info/articles/ovusdomesticviolencelaws.htm.

13

Baaaaaaad Animals

Introduction

The treatment of animals is often debated on philosophical grounds. Questions are raised about whether animals have free will, are sentient, understand social constructs, are moral, or should be treated as persons under the Fifth and Fourteenth Amendments. The answers to these questions underlie policy considerations. Whether animals have rights and legal duties may hinge on whether animals are able to choose to follow human law. If animals were able to conscientiously follow human law, then they may be entitled to increased consideration within the criminal justice system. However, irrespective of whether animals wish to participate in human society, animals are often subject to human law. Humans regulate animals' behavior and punish animals for perceived misbehavior or harm.

History of Criminal Animals

In an episode of *Mister Ed*, the classic TV show about Wilbur and his talking horse named Ed, Ed dreams that he is on trial. The jury box is full of animals. The twelve members of the jury are a donkey, skunk, goat, owl, rooster, sheep, duck, young chimpanzee, turkey, chicken, dog, and pig. A mature chimpanzee presides as the judge over Mister Ed's trial. He has been accused of bird-napping a parrot. Mister Ed testifies but refuses to swear under oath. Wilbur, who is serving as the prosecutor, thinks that Mister Ed should be hanged. Mister Ed flagrantly bribes the jury with bananas. For all intents and purposes, the proceeding becomes a veritable circus. The scene raises the question of what would happen if animals had rights and incurred criminal liability for violating the rights of other animals (Niman 2012). Since the inception of human law, humans have subjected animals to law. Over the past millennium animals have repeatedly stood trial and been held responsible for harms.

In many ways law has not evolved much since the Middle Ages (Wise 1996). Between 824 and 1906 CE, two hundred courts within

France, England, Switzerland, Italy, Germany, Spain, Denmark, Austria, Portugal, Scotland, Yugoslavia, Netherlands, Belgium, Luxembourg, Russia, Ethiopia, Turkey, Brazil, and Canada held proceedings against animals (Berman 2000; Girgen 2003; Wise 1996). Typically proceedings considered the fates of animals accused of killing humans, engaging in bestial relations with humans, or plaguing humans (Wise 1996). Pigs, dogs, horses, goats, donkeys, oxen, bulls, cows, beetles, caterpillars, eels, beetles, bloodsuckers, chickens, cocks, cockchafers, field mice, flies, grasshoppers, pigeons, serpents, sheep, slugs, snails, termites, wolves, worms, vermin, rats, leeches, locusts, mice, moles, serpents, weevils, turtledoves, and dolphins were some of the animals tried during this era (Berman 1994; Ewald 1995; Wise 1996). Today dangerous dogs are still the subjects of legal proceedings, and pests are still sentenced to extermination. One major distinction is that animals are no longer considered parties to bestiality, but instead they are considered to be victims. Previously bestiality trials frequently resulted in animals' executions, though there are recorded instances in which animals were found to be innocent (Berman 2000; Girgen 2003). In France during the eighteenth century, a man was sentenced to death for committing crimes against nature with a donkey. Due to evidence of the donkey's virtuousness presented by humans who had known the donkey for four years, the donkey was found to be a victim rather than a criminal (Berman 2000).

Evidence of defendants' demeanor and character was routinely introduced at trials, and courts also noted animals' in-court behavior (Girgen 2003; Ramsland 2013). Animals who appeared before the court were likely imprisoned within cages in the courtroom (Girgen 2003). Defendants were likely to be imprisoned while awaiting trial, and it would not have been unusual for animals to share the same prison with human defendants. Animals could be sentenced to prison for less serious crimes. For example, in 1712 an Austrian court sentenced a dog to a year in prison within a cell in the public square for biting a councilman on the leg. In 1924 the governor of Pennsylvania tried and sentenced a dog to life in state prison for killing his cat. A chimpanzee was fined five dollars for smoking a cigarette in public in Indiana early in the twentieth century. A three-strikes policy was occasionally instituted for certain animals engaged in trespassory crimes. The first trespass resulted in the mutilation of an ear; the second trespass resulted in the loss of the other ear; the next, in the loss of a limb; and the final trespass, in lethal seizure of the animal. Defendants guilty of capital crimes might be burned alive, buried alive, beheaded, or hanged (Ewald 1995; Girgen 2003). Hanging animals by the hindquarters was the most common capital punishment.

Animals have not truly been entitled to due process even though penalties may be serious. Yet, some courts have attempted to give due process to animals. For example, in 1522 French villagers investigated local rats' crime of eating barley crops (Berman 2000). The local court solemnly summoned the rats to trial. A courier cried out the summons in the general direction of the rats' community, thereby serving them with sufficient notice. The rats were represented by a court-appointed advocate. The rats' failure to appear for trial spurred a series of clever arguments made by their advocate, which led the court to summon all of rats throughout the parish. A continuance was granted to allow all of the rats more time to travel to court. After the rats failed to appear, a final argument was made on their behalves. Their advocate asserted that obeying the summons would require the rats to cross paths with hostile cats. The law, he argued, could not reasonably require the rats to risk their lives to comply with the court's order. On one hand, these proceedings demonstrate the courts' willingness to extend due process to animal defendants, but on another hand, the meaningfulness of the rats' participation in the process cannot be determined.

In contrast to due process that the French court offered to rats in 1522, sea lions in the United States were condemned to death without trial for overfishing salmon (Sykes 2011). The US National Marine Fisheries Service (NMFS) decided salmon populations were decreasing and it was sea lions' fault. However, the NMFS was unable to prove that the less than 1 percent variation in salmon populations caused by sea lion consumption equated to a significant negative impact on the environment. Thus, the US Court of Appeals for the Ninth Circuit held that killing the sea lions would be an abuse of discretion.

Domestic animals' owners have often been entitled to the benefit of the law, though their animals have merely been subjected to law even if they receive legal advocacy. In one case in 1906, a father, son, and dog team were tried for robbery and murder. The father and son were sentenced to life in prison, but the dog was held to be the chief actor and was sentenced to death (Girgen 2003). Animals have been acquitted of crimes as serious as accomplices to murder, but only after their owners have been granted mercy by the court. Legal proceedings against animals have resulted in execution, and occasionally, animals found guilty were seized, spiritually exorcised, or banished (Wise 1996).

There is also evidence that jurisdictions attempted to engage in alternative forms of criminal justice with animals (Berman 2000; Girgen 2003). Today seizure and execution of animals remain fairly common, and jurisdictional banishment is still effectuated. In the past lions in Africa were occasionally crucified to deter predation on humans. The belief was that crucifixion signaled what would become of murderers and attempted murderers. Germans relied on a similar strategy: wolves were hanged throughout public areas, and birds of prey were nailed to houses. These practices were meant to deter animals from committing harms against humans, but may not have been carried out with the same motives as animal trials.

Rights and Responsibilities

Under the law, all humans have rights, most have duties, and certain classes of humans have additional duties. For example, children have a duty to obey the law, but parents have an additional duty to care for their children. Minors have been obligated to follow the law long before they received any rights. Children have some constitutional rights under criminal law, and they are obligated to follow criminal law; yet, they generally are adjudicated by the juvenile justice system. Within the juvenile justice system, children have fewer rights than adult offenders would within the criminal justice system. However, children often receive greater consideration and lenience, too. For example, juveniles cannot be executed (*Roper v. Simmons*, 2005).

Incongruities between rights and duties serve as an excellent starting point for discussions about animal rights, duties, and consideration. Unanswered philosophical and practical questions surround animal rights and animal personhood. For example, if animals were to receive legal rights, then would those rights be accompanied by legal duties? Would animals be responsible for following the law? Would animals be punished directly for biting? Would dogs be held partially responsible for intentionally exiting yards and threatening pedestrians? Would rights and duties change depending on animals' status as domesticated or wild? Animals do not have rights, and can be privately owned as property. If animals had rights, then would all animals have rights? Would animals that possessed rights continue to be quasi-property? If animals had rights, could wild animals continue to be hunted for sport? Could wild animals who attack humans be punished with death or incapacitated and rehabilitated? What degree of certainty would be required that an accused animal committed the harm in question?

Would all animals have rights against cruel and unusual punishment? In some ways, many animals already do have rights against cruel and unusual punishment under cruelty statutes and hunting regulations.

Practical questions should be posed to determine to what extent law could govern animals if rights were granted and duties were required. For example, would animals be held at different levels of culpability and seriousness associated with particular crimes? For example, some animals steal, but they are not dangerous. In Cedar Park Cemetery police conducted surveillance after forty American flags were stolen (Gardinier 2012). The officers discovered that at least one large woodchuck was stealing flags to line underground nests. The eradication of area woodchucks was considered, but it seemed impractical since other woodchucks could continue to steal. Police could not prosecute individual woodchucks, so the cemetery decided to reposition the flags beyond the woodchucks' reach. If animals had legal duties, then could thieving animals be arrested? Could they be required to appear in court? Would jail be similar to living in a shelter, or would conditions need to be worse to deter other animals? Is deterrence possible? Could the state have executed or relocated all woodchucks in the area? Could other woodchucks be culpable as accessories after the fact for failing to report the stolen flags?

Would it be possible to establish an animal court that relies on animal behavior specialists and a special form of animal due process? Answering these questions sheds no light on the current criminal justice system but explores possible innovations in the system's response and society's attitude toward animals who harm humans or become involved with the justice system.

Conclusion

Governments have punished disobedience, depravity, mistakes, nuisances, infractions, crimes, and wrongdoing for thousands of years. In some eras governments' treatment of humans and animals has been more lenient; but, during other eras it has been more severe. New understandings of vulnerable populations raise questions about whether animals should receive greater consideration under the law. Though the law is unclear in many regards, one aspect is certain: animals are not yet entitled to the equal protection or due process guaranteed to humans. However, minors are not entitled to full due process either. Perhaps notions of justice will evolve to protect vulnerable populations.

References

Berman, P. S. 1994. "Rats, Pigs, and Statues on Trial: The Creation of Cultural Narratives in the Prosecution of Animals and Inanimate Objects." *New York University Law Review* 69:288.

Berman, P. S. 2000. "An Observation and a Strange but True 'Tale': What Might the Historical Trials of Animals Tell Us about the Transformative Potential of Law in American Culture?" *Hastings Law Journal* 52:123.

Ewald, W. 1995. "Comparative Jurisprudence (I): What Was It Like to Try a Rat?" *University of Pennsylvania Law Review* 143:1889.

Gardinier, B. 2012. "Thieving Woodchucks Bedevil Cemetery." *Times Union*, September 18. http://www.timesunion.com/local/article/Banners-yet-wave-but-out-of-rodents-reach-3872673.php.

Girgen, J. 2003. "The Historical and Contemporary Prosecution and Punishment of Animals." *Animal Law* 9:97.

Mister Ed. 1965. Season 5, episode 7, "Animal Jury." January 13. http://www.imdb.com/title/tt0649763/.

Niman, J. 2012. "In Support of Creating a Legal Definition of Personhood." *Journal of Law and Social Deviance* 3:142.

Ramsland, K. 2013. "Murder and a Movie: The Jeffrey Lamb Case." *TruTV.* http://www.trutv.com/library/crime/criminal_mind/forensics/ff312_jeffrey_lamb/1_index.html.

Roper v. Simmons. 543 U.S. 551 (2005).

Sykes, K. 2011. "Human Drama, Animal Trials: What the Medieval Animal Trials Can Teach Us about Justice for Animals." *Animal Law* 17:273.

Wise, S. M. 1996. "The Legal Thinghood of Nonhuman Animals." *Boston College Environmental Affairs Law Review* 23:471.

14

Illegal Companionship between People and Animals

Introduction

For better or for worse, the state can intervene in human-animal relationships. Generally, the state attempts to protect people, property, and animals from harm. Law must be clearly set forth and uniformly applied; yet, government intervention into animal-human relationships may sometimes seem counterintuitive, irrational, or unfair. Nevertheless, consistency is imperative to achieve justice.

Contraband in Prison

Animals may be used to ferry contraband into prisons, or they may impermissibly reside in the prison as animal companions. Contraband is just as prolific in prisons as it is in free society. In-demand contraband includes toiletries; written notes, that is, "kites"; cell phones; alcohol; cash; and drugs. Clandestine animal companions are contraband in prison.

Drug dealers throughout the world, for example, in Columbia and Argentina, have used animals as drug couriers. When drug dealers are incarcerated or want to deal drugs in prisons, they may send messages and drugs into prisons using pigeons (Rueda 2013). Pigeons have been caught with messages and drugs, for example, marijuana and cocaine, tied to their legs or necks (*Huffington Post* 2011). This phenomenon ought to raise new possibilities about training pigeons or falcons to serve as corrections officers who are capable of intercepting pigeons carrying contraband. However, this might only be partially effective, since offenders have also used cats and other small land animals to usher in contraband like cell phones, SIM cards, drugs, weapons, or tools for breakout (*Guardian* 2009). Feral or wild animals may be captured and starved to ensure compliance based on a food-reward system (Chew 2013). Birds, for example, pigeons, may be bred inside of prisons and smuggled out. Once the contraband is attached outside the prison, then birds fly home to the prison cell instinctively. Though drugs in prison may carry the heaviest penalties, they may not cause the most destruction. In Brazil prisoners smuggled cell phones to coordinate a series of assaults that killed approximately two hundred people, including police officers as well as civilians in banks and on buses. In addition to arranging drug deals and assaults, gang leaders will use smuggled cell phones to arrange kidnappings and bank robberies.

The seriousness of these problems justifies prison policies prohibiting all wild animals in prison. Though animals may comfort prisoners, they will be removed if they are detected, even if they are not being used as couriers. Sometimes wild animals around prisons may be removed as well. In 2013 the Humane Society began petitioning the California Rehabilitation Center to stop withholding food and water from scores of feral cats living outside the prison. Following a complaint about cat allergies, the prison warden opted against placing the prison's feral cat population in an animal shelter to be adopted, or more likely, euthanized. Instead, the warden prohibited all staff from caring for or feeding the cats (HSUS 2013). Unfortunately, the cats, who lived outdoors on the ninety-acre property, had become companions to the prisoners. Over the years a committee formed by prisoners and volunteers had overseen the cats' medical care, spaying, neutering, nourishment, and humane treatment (*Examiner* 2013). The dilemma between comforting some prisoners or accommodating others highlights one of the numerous variables surrounding the presence of animals in prison. Another consideration is whether that outdoor cat population, or any wild population, eliminates local pests. Some prisons are infested with roaches or mice. Such infestations may violate prisoners' constitutional right to be free of cruel and unusual punishment if infestations affect prisoners psychologically (Stempel 2012). Keeping feral cats on the grounds may be an extraordinarily cost-effective way for prisons to reduce pest populations and uphold the Eighth Amendment.

Unauthorized Interactions

After inflicting animal cruelty, offenders may be forbidden from possessing animals or working with animals temporarily or permanently. Famously, NFL football star Michael Vick was banned from owning dogs for three years after he was caught operating dogfights (ALDF 2010). Shortly after his ban expired, he announced that he would adopt a dog. Pet bans are not restricted to the United States. In New Zealand, it was discovered that an international dog show judge operated an illegal and cruel commercial breeding facility containing 161 cats and 87 dogs (*Life with Dogs* 2012). He and his wife were convicted and fined twenty-five thousand dollars, to be paid to the Society of the Prevention of Cruelty to Animals (SPCA). In addition to the fine, the couple was banned from owning any animal companions for twenty years. Lengthy bans are typically imposed upon those who inflict torture on numerous animals.

Sometimes bans are imposed for less serious crimes. In the United Kingdom a puppy treated himself to a vodka and Coke that he discovered in a cup on the floor after his owner exited their apartment momentarily (NBC News 2012; Rabiner 2012). The owner returned inside and found the puppy drunk, but failed to seek medical treatment and proceeded to leave the puppy alone. Authorities found the puppy stumbling drunk and charged the owner for failing to ensure animal welfare. The puppy was given to another home, and the owner was banned from pet ownership for three years. Hefty bans on working with animals may be imposed for accidental neglect. In England a dog-sitter who had one hundred clients and forty years of experience agreed to sit for a total of five dogs and two cats in two different homes for one week (*Courier* 2013). Unfortunately, she forgot to mark that week's sitting jobs in her calendar even after she collected house keys and specific details for each job. Some of the animals were left without care for between two and five days. She was charged with animal neglect and fined approximately a thousand dollars. She was also banned from running her sitting business or working with animals for more than three years.

Loopholes in these punishments may grant offenders legal access to animals despite the imposition of bans (Gavin 2013). For example, an offender may be sentenced to a ban for the duration of probation. The length of the probation sentence may exceed the length of any prison sentence that would be imposed if the terms of probation were to be violated. If the offender violates probation and serves time, then it might be possible for the offender to have access to animals in a shorter amount of time. Another loophole occurs when an offender must reside with a relative or roommate who owns an animal companion because the animal does not belong to the offender, and the animal is being cared for by the owner. This loophole creates a dissatisfying result.

Dissatisfying prohibitions may emerge from cases in which people technically violate the law in good faith (MSN 2013). For example, caring for a wild animal may be illegal. In Ohio a woman found a deer who had suffered a deep body wound and loss of a hind leg after being run over by a hay cutter. She nursed the fawn back to health on her farm along with another rescued fawn and four raccoons. The Ohio Department of Natural Resources charged her with two counts of possessing wild animals. If she were convicted, then the animals could be destroyed, thereby permanently banning her from caring for them.

Conclusion

When people mistreat animals or inappropriately capitalize on their relationships with animals, the government may intervene. The government may prohibit people from caring for animals under broader considerations about order and health. State power trumps good intentions or exceptional circumstances. At times, leniency or privileges may be granted, but uneven application of the law may create vulnerability in the criminal justice system. Thus, even when unfairness appears to result, lawful governmental intervention may be essential.

References

Animal Legal Defense Fund (ALDF). 2010. "Michael Vick Banned from Dog Ownership—Ask an Attorney." December 22. http://aldf.org/press-room/press-releases/michael-vick-banned-from-dog-ownership-ask-an-attorney/.

"Brazilian Prisoners Use Pigeons to Smuggle in Mobile Phones." 2009. *Guardian UK*, April 1. http://www.theguardian.com/world/2009/apr/01/pigeons-mobile-phones-brazil-prison.

Chew, K. 2013. "Cats Starved and Forced to Smuggle Contraband into Prisons." *Care 2*, June 8. http://www.care2.com/causes/cats-starved-and-forced-to-smuggle-contraband-into-prisons.html.

"Drug-Smuggling Pigeon Captured Carrying Cocaine, Marijuana to Colombia Prisoners." 2011. *Huffington Post*, January 19. http://www.huffingtonpost.com/2011/01/19/drug-smuggling-pigeon_n_811044.html.

"Fife Pet Minder Given 40-Month Ban from Working with Animals." 2013. *Courier*, March 22. http://www.thecourier.co.uk/news/local/fife/fife-pet-minder-given-40-month-ban-from-working-with-animals-1.78888.

"Former Vet Tech Saves Deer and Raccoons, May Go to Jail for It." 2013. MSN, August 13. http://now.msn.com/carol-deyo-saves-deer-and-raccoons-may-go-to-jail-for-it.

Gavin, R. 2013. "Dog Abuser, Banned from Owning Dogs for 5 Years, Lives with Dog." *Times Union*, August 21. http://blog.timesunion.com/crime/dog-abuser-banned-from-owning-dogs-for-5-years-lives-with-dog/13929/.

"No More Dogs for Man Whose Puppy Got Drunk." 2012. NBC News, January 4. http://www.nbcnews.com/id/45875648/ns/world_news-europe/#.UiAl-6Busim6.

"Prisoners Fear 100 Feral Cats at Riverside County Prison Will Be Euthanized." 2013. *Examiner*, June 8. http://www.examiner.com/article/prisoners-fear-100-feral-cats-at-riverside-county-prison-will-be-euthanized.

"Puppy Mill Operators Banned from Owning Pets for 20 Years." 2012. Life with Dogs, July 5. http://www.lifewithdogs.tv/2012/07/puppy-mill-operators-banned-from-owning-pets-for-20-years/.

Rabiner, S. 2012. "Court Bans Man from Owning a Dog after Puppy Got Drunk." *Find Law*, January 11. http://blogs.findlaw.com/legalgrounds/2012/01/court-bans-man-from-owning-a-dog-after-puppy-got-drunk.html.

Rueda, M. 2013. "Police in Argentina Confiscate Drug Ring's Narco-Pigeons." *ABC News*, August 23. http://abcnews.go.com/ABC_Univision/ABC_Univision/argentine-traffickers-pigeons-ship-weed/story?id=20049856.

Stempel, J. 2012. "Mice, Roaches in Prison Cells May Be Unconstitutional: Court." *Chicago Tribune*, September 27. http://articles.chicagotribune.com/2012-09-27/news/sns-rt-us-courts-prison-roaches-bre88q1or-20120927_1_prison-term-cell-unusual-punishment.

US Humane Society. (USHS). 2013. "California Prison Urged to Lift Ban on Feeding Cats." June 21. http://www.humanesociety.org/news/press_releases/2013/06/california-prison-urged-to-lift-cat-feeding-ban-062113.html.

15

Exotic Animals

Introduction

The majority of animals are not domesticated. Wild animals do not become domesticated in captivity; yet, domestication of exotic animals in captivity is attempted millions of times each year. Exotic animals may be transported across national or regional boarders for personal possession, commerce, or entertainment. Illegally transporting wild animals may be mistreatment because wild animals may be fragile and endangered. Transportation often subjects animals to injury, psychological damage, and death. Exotic animals must receive specialized attention and government oversight to ensure their safety and well-being.

Exotic Animals

The term "exotic animals" may include any nondomesticated species. Exotic animals may be bought, adopted, bred, traded, or captured legally. However, exotic animal trade is one of the largest black markets in the world. Exotic animals are ferried using a wide range of sneaky or dangerous tactics that in many cases amount to cruelty. Exotic animals, which may be obtained legally or illegally, may be desirable because they are endangered or rare.

The Convention on International Trade in Endangered Species of Wild Fauna and Flora (CITES) binds signatory nations to international trade regulations for endangered and protected species (ADI 2013). Since 1973, 177 countries have become parties to the treaty. Nations agree to enforce terms using national law and designated management authorities and to regulate animal trade and populations using scientific authorities. Signatory parties meet every three years. In the United States the US Fish and Wildlife Service (FWS) is entrusted with enforcement of regulations of animals as wide-ranging as marsupials, birds of prey, and tusked mammals. The FWS must properly regulate endangered animals that perform in circuses, are held captive in zoos, or are exported as companion animals.

Due to dwindling populations of animals and increasingly strict standards, many nations have fully banned employment of exotic animals in circuses or tightened regulation of wildlife refuges. Tighter regulations may evenly affect good faith operations and cruel operations. For example, in Bangkok, a ten-year-old, award-winning, nonprofit refuge has rehabilitated hundreds of abused and abandoned animals, and the refuge has trained international volunteers without incident (Associated Press 2013). Despite operators' good intentions, they were charged with illegal possession of endangered species.

The Lacey Act is federal legislation that criminalizes illegal taking, transporting, and selling of wildlife and fish (16 U.S.C. §§ 3371–3378, 2013). It is one of the most powerfully broad tools for fighting wildlife crime internationally and domestically (Wisch 2003). It is enforced by the FWS. An example of the Lacey Act enforcement occurred in Idaho recently (*Idaho Press-Tribune* 2013). Aquarium operators allegedly conspired and committed three counts of illegally purchasing and selling fish or wildlife when they bought four spotted eagle rays and two lemon sharks. The animals had been taken from the wild without permits. The aquarium paid approximately sixty-three hundred dollars for the animals; and yet, the maximum fine for each count is two hundred fifty thousand dollars. Each count also carries a maximum prison term of five years and forfeiture.

In the United States restaurants serve lions, rhinos, zebras, alpacas, and countless other exotic species (Ferretti 2013). Some of the exotic meat is farm-raised and processed in USDA-approved slaughterhouses. However, legal vendors sometimes have criminal histories of obtaining exotic animals illegally. Legal and illegal exotic animal markets are often closely knit, which is commonly the case with zoos, pet dealers, and restaurants that fabricate details to make animals appear to be captive-born in order to circumnavigate laws. Other times dealers and restaurateurs will legally and illegally sell exotic animals in the same establishment. In California, a sushi chef was arrested for selling endangered whale sushi (Tepper 2013). Whale meat was purchased from a Japanese dealer who broke Japanese whale-hunting laws. The National Oceanic and Atmospheric Administration (NOAA), not the FWS, first investigated tips about endangered whale sushi. The chef was charged by the US Department of Justice under the Marine Mammal Protection Act (16 U.S.C. § 1361–1421h, 2013). Maximum fines for the crimes are greater than a million dollars and accompanied by around sixty years in prison.

Stories of illegal transportation of exotic animals have been sensationally bizarre (PETA 2013). Baby turtles have been taped inside their shells and stacked into an airline passenger's tube socks, or transported by the thousands on a single flight (PETA 2013; Rosner 2013). Monkeys have been found in passengers' underwear, and birds have been discovered sedated and taped by the dozens to passengers' bodies (PETA 2013). One passenger smuggled hundreds of poisonous snakes onto an international flight (Petersen 2011). There are innumerable other examples of unbelievable attempts to illegally traffic animals. Unfortunately, almost all smuggled animals die while in transit, and most of the survivors die within a year of transport (PETA 2013). Thus, a very slim percentage of animals taken from the wild illegally will survive in captivity. Smuggling in itself carries heavy penalties, as does illegal dealing in exotic animals (18 U.S.C. § 545, 2013).

Exotic Pets

Exotic pets are widely banned throughout the United States and the world. By and large, legal possession of exotic pets requires licensure. Proper permits and the fulfillment of specific enclosure requirements cause the otherwise criminal possession of exotic animals to become lawful. Under federal law, that is, the Endangered Species Act, there is an implied right to own exotic pets, but each state regulates which animals, if any, may be possessed (U.S.C. § 1531–1544, 2013; Liebman 2004).

A large number of exotic and endangered animals worldwide are privately owned. For example, for every large cat in the wild, experts estimate that there may be as many as ten privately owned large cats (PETA 2013). In the United States approximately 5,000 to 7,000 tigers, 8.8 million reptiles, 17.3 million birds, 10,000 to 20,000 large cats, and at least 3,000 nonhuman great apes are being privately kept as pets (CWAPC 2013). Despite these staggering numbers, the government attempts to make exotic pets illegal or difficult to obtain under federal and state laws for several legitimate reasons. The first of many reasons for government intervention is that dealers mistreat exotic animals. Mistreatment during transportation is heavily regulated. US Global Exotics, for example, was investigated by People for the Ethical Treatment of Animals (PETA). PETA's investigation prompted the government to raid the dealer's warehouse. Animals inside were stacked, missing food and water, deprived of ventilation, and without basic care. The government seized approximately twenty-seven thousand animals. In addition to several hundred dead animals, around two hundred dead iguanas had been left to starve inside crates because an order had been canceled. Several thousand varying species of animals died after the raid. Pets may also be obtained illegally from zoos. Zoos will intentionally breed excess animals then pretend to be forced to sell the animals. Exotic animal dealers will forge records to make animals seem captive-born and therefore not subject to international treaties that would prevent animals from being imported or licensed (Grech 2004). A large percentage of these animals die during transport or in private care.

Additionally, animals may be hidden when they are not licensed. Their clandestine existences usually deprive them of exercise, space, and other necessary accommodations. An example occurred in New York City, where dangerous wildlife pets are banned in general and specifically banned from public housing (ECL 3-0301, 11-0325, 11-0511, 2013; 6 NYCRR 175, 180, 2013). Animal Care and Control was called by police to a low-income housing unit to seize animals living in fish tanks (Yakas 2012). Animals included a boa constrictor, five pythons, a couple of bearded dragons, a couple of alligators, a gecko, a tarantula, and a scorpion. New York apartments are cramped. A large number of any animals would be undesirable, but to contain so many reptiles, who can grow to be quite large, is cruel especially when these animals require specific habitats. The absence of licensing opportunities in New York is intended to eliminate this sort of cruelty.

Legal ownership and enclosure regulations may require the bare minimum. Licensure requires the bare minimum to protect the public. The government must balance its interests with property interests and rights (Hessler and Balaban 2009). The state's interest in public protection is legitimate, but laws designed to enforce that interest may do little to accommodate animals. For example, Nevada permits private ownership of mountain lions as long as enclosures are bordered by eight-foot fences with twelve-inch Y-recurves on top (*BigCatRescue.com* 2013). Enclosure gates must have two locks, one of which must be self-locking. Some states require more than minimal accommodation and safety requirements. For example, North Carolina's license requirements consider animals' well-being more than other states, which makes licensing much more selective. North Carolina requires one acre of landscaped and vegetative land enclosed by a twelve-foot fence with a forty-five-degree recurve. It also requires a pool and a den. Even with these perks, North Carolina licenses would not necessarily protect animals from loud noise, for example, exposure to fireworks or other unnatural nuisances.

The supremacy of federal laws on exotic animals preempt state laws; however, some state regulations seem to ignore federal law. For example, the US Department of Agriculture (USDA) prohibits anyone from handling a large cat cub before eight weeks or a juvenile after twelve weeks (*BigCatRescue.com* 2013). The younger age limit protects the animals, while the older age limit protects the public. Yet in Florida, the upper limit is not regulated by age, it is limited by weight, which is twenty-five pounds. Large cats heavier than twenty-five pounds cannot be handled by the public. Florida is very tolerant of private ownership of exotic pets overall. The state spends millions of dollars annually to employ dozens of inspectors who regulate in excess of four thousand permitted exotic animals, which represents a fraction of the total exotic pets living in Florida. Exotic pet ownership in Florida has resulted in severe ecological consequences. People have dumped nonnative exotic pets into the wild and damaged the Everglades in the process (CNN 2013). For example, after numerous people released pet pythons into the wild, the animals bred rapidly and grew to gargantuan sizes. The animals quickly became top predators, swallowing alligators whole and threatening the environment, local domesticated animals, and people to some extent. Now the government is attempting to cull the estimated hundred thousand snakes.

Exotic pet markets are perpetuated by use of exotic pets as status symbols. For example, celebrities often appear in public with large cats, snakes, primates, and other animals to demonstrate their prestige and cool. Eccentrics, socialites, and wealthy homeowners may also tote or display wildlife, for example, rats, skunks, cockatiels, or spiders. The image of animals representing prestige stands in stark contrast to the fact that exotic animals usually carry diseases that are not glamorous. Their propensity for zoonotic disease transmission is one reason why health codes often regulate private ownership of wildlife. For example, the Center for Disease Control (CDC) estimates that seventy thousand people annually contract salmonella from pet reptiles. The status associated with exotic pet ownership is an international phenomenon. Wildlife displays may involve passive or risky activities, for example, elephants playing polo or other strange displays. For example, the trendiness of exotic animals in Columbia reportedly contributed to annual trafficking of sixty thousand animals, for example, in-vogue sloths and birds (Schriffen and Waterfield 2013). The wildlife trade accounts for the third-largest black market in Columbia next to drugs and weapons.

Systemic corruption contributes to the wildlife black market. In addition to corruption among zoo and veterinary officials, animal control officers sometimes become involved in the black market trade. In a particularly egregious example, a Long Island animal control officer was discovered with nearly one thousand illegally owned snakes in his garage, along with tarantulas, turtles, and alligator carcasses (Mallonee 2013; Pfeiffer 2013). He was selling the snakes illegally to customers over the Internet. In addition to losing his job and being charged with running an unlicensed business from his home, the officer faces fines from the Department of Environmental Conservation for unlicensed ownership of certain exotic animals and carcasses. In response to growing illegal possession of exotic animals, Long Island has encouraged a policy that is announced annually. Owners of illegal reptiles to are encouraged to surrender reptiles voluntarily in exchange for amnesty; the policy is announced on Reptile Amnesty Day.

Circuses and Zoos

Exotic animals are obtained by circuses and zoos through a number of means. They may be bred, purchased, or adopted. Each of these activities could result in criminal entanglement. Some zoos have been involved in the practice of breeding surplus animals to sell the animals to taxidermists, exotic animal collectors, or to people who will use animals' bodies as ingredients in food or medicinal products. For example, at the Berlin Zoo, which is Berlin's premier tourist attraction, allegations of criminal conduct were filed against the director for overbreeding and illegally selling animals for the past thirty years (*Telegraph* 2008). Animals, including a hippopotamus, a panther-leopard hybrid, tigers, jaguars, and a family of bears, were sold for slaughter in a Belgium slaughterhouse; they were intended to become Chinese medicines used to cure impotency and other ailments. The Berlin Zoo claims that many of the animals were legally sold to zoos, but records and undercover footage show that animals were relocated to slaughterhouses and then sold abroad. The zoo was also alleged to have bred surplus rhinos and giraffes for sale to circuses. The director claimed that the Berlin Zoo complied with the regulations of Germany's Federal Agency for Nature Conservation. In Germany the crime of selling zoo animals without sufficient reason violates animal protection laws that carry a fine or imprisonment of up to three years. The same Berlin Zoo director also defended his decision to kill feral kittens with his bare hands to prevent disease transmission to zoo animals or patrons (Spiegel 2008).

Though only around a hundred tigers remain in Vietnam's forests, they are overbred by zoos and slaughtered so that their carcasses can be sold on the black market, particularly in China (Chris 2008). Tigers' bodies, which may be frozen, boiled, or otherwise transformed into Chinese medicine, sell for approximately a hundred dollars per gram. Individual tigers sell for tens of thousands of dollars. Vietnamese officials have claimed in the past that animals died naturally or were sold legally, but Hanoi Forestry Management Agency has not approved these operations, and they violate the Convention on International Trade in Endangered Species of Wild Fauna and Flora (CITES).

Under some circumstances, people who trade in the remains of exotic zoo animals will claim that the trade is legal, but undercover investigations reveal that trades are likely criminal (Foggo and Jaber 2013). Thus, the issue may not be how these zoos obtain animals, but how they fail to place them with other facilities. Some accredited European zoos claim to attempt to find suitable homes for animals, but many protected animals—for example, tigers—are killed under the pretense that the zoos cannot afford to care for them. Then their carcasses are immediately sold to taxidermists. This practice violates the law in many nations and CITES.

Endangered animals living at zoos require special consideration when zoos are permanently closed. For example, when facing bankruptcy, the City of Detroit contemplated selling zoo animals to other accredited zoos to alleviate its debt (Stryker and Gallagher 2013). The Detroit Zoo houses around thirty-three hundred animals. A zebra, one of the more easily sold animals, could be legally sold for a few thousand dollars, and a fertile female giraffe can be worth around one hundred thousand dollars if sold to one of the two hundred accredited zoos in the country. If the Detroit Zoo were to sell animals to an unaccredited zoo, then it would violate federal law. Many animals living in the Detroit Zoo are endangered, which requires that animals be placed in suitable and carefully regulated environments. Not infrequently, surplus animals not under national scrutiny (like those in Detroit Zoo were) will be traded or sold to circuses, where they experience a high mortality rate, early death, and cruelty (PAWS 2013). Circuses will claim that they can maintain an animal, but they will fail to do so. Directors of circuses may be fined as a result. Each year zoos receive countless donations of exotic pets from individuals who fail to care for animals (Jacksonville Zoo 2009). Exotic pets may have been bred illegally or captured illegally from the wild and are subsequently donated or seized (Israel 2009; PAWS 2013). Small mammals, reptiles, and birds are some creatures commonly accepted through donation; however, zoos and conservations often accept bears, cats, and other large animals (Jacksonville Zoo 2009). In many cases conservation groups will make efforts to return animals to the wild rather than house them in zoos. In every case zoos are required to comply with the CITES and other endangered species, wild life, environmental, and species-specific legislation.

For a number of reasons, several jurisdictions around the world ban wild animals in zoos or circuses. Bans may include total or partial breeding; trading; or adoption of wild, endangered, or captive animals used for entertainment. Within at least some jurisdictions or in every jurisdiction, bans on the use of wild animals are in effect in the following countries: Austria, Bosnia and Herzegovina, Croatia, the Czech Republic, Cyprus, Denmark, Estonia, Finland, Greece, Hungary, Ireland, Poland, Portugal, Slovenia, Spain, Sweden, the United Kingdom, the United States, Canada, Argentina, Bolivia, Brazil, Chile, Colombia, Costa Rica, Ecuador, Paraguay, Peru, Australia, India, Israel, Singapore, and Taiwan (ADI 2013).

The presence of animals in zoos and circuses also attracts crime. Poaching and cruelty are two common crimes. Poaching from conservation lands is not uncommon; however, poachers are now poaching from zoos (Davies 2012). Poachers brazenly trespass, shoot animals with tranquilizer guns, and then hack animals' tusks and horns with chainsaws. The bloodied animals often die. Zoo poaching poses a threat in Asia and Africa, where numerous species of horned and tusked animals are rapidly becoming extinct, but it also poses a great threat to European zoos, which have ramped up security for this reason.

Anytime the public is exposed to animals, a possibility exists that people will mistreat animals by feeding them garbage, poking them, harassing them, invading their enclosures, and so forth. These actions can result in cruelty charges as well as a number of property charges, for example, trespass or burglary. In one attack a circus elephant enclosed in an outdoor area in Mississippi was shot in the shoulder by a passing motorist using a BB gun (*Huffington Post* 2013). In addition to state laws, the motorist's crime violated federal law since elephants are endangered.

Conclusion

Species-specific legislation, federal laws, international treaties, state laws, and governmental policies attempt to regulate exotic animal trade and protect animals, but the feat is daunting. Exotic animals do not fare well in transit, commerce, or captivity. Thus, the government often attempts to control animals in the stream of commerce. However, detecting mistreatment or unlawful operations is difficult due to clandestine networks, black markets, animal laundering, and the private nature of owning pets.

References

6 NYCRR 175, 180 (2013).

16 U.S.C. § 1361–1421h (2013).

16 U.S.C. § 1531–1544 (2013).

16 U.S.C. § 3371–3378 (2013).

18 U.S.C.A. § 545 (2013).

Associated Press. 2013. "Thailand Animal Sanctuary Owner Decries Charges." May 11. http://bigstory.ap.org/article/thailand-animal-sanctuary-owner-decries-charges.

"Berlin Zoo Director Accused of Selling Animals for Chinese Medicine." 2008. *Telegraph*, March 21. http://www.telegraph.co.uk/earth/earthnews/3336945/Berlin-Zoo-director-accused-of-selling-animals-for-Chinese-medicine.html. http://www.jacksonvillezoo.org/animals/donations_of_animals/.

Brooke, C. 2008. "Hanoi Zoo Admits Selling Tigers to Animal Traffickers." *Environmental Graffiti*. http://www.environmentalgraffiti.com/offbeat-news/zoo-admits-selling-tigers-to-animal-traffickers/681#ovcpUbI60KjhYq9x.99.

Captive Wild Animal Protection Coalition (CWAPC). 2013. http://cwapc.org/education/download/cwapc_factsheets1.pdf.

"Circus Elephant Shot in Drive-By Attack Leads to $33,000 Reward." 2013. *Huffington Post*, April 11. http://www.huffingtonpost.com/2013/04/11/circus-elephant-shot_n_3064456.html?utm_hp_ref=green&icid=maing-grid7%7Cmain5%7Cdl1%7Csec3_lnk2%26pLid%3D297227.

Davies, L. 2012. "Zoos Tighten Security as Threat of Animal Poaching Grows." *Guardian*, February 3. http://www.theguardian.com/environment/2012/feb/03/zoos-security-animal-poaching-threat.

"Donations of Animals." 2009. Jacksonville Zoo and Gardens.

ECL 3-0301, 11-0325, 11-0511 (2013).

"Encourage CITES to return to a Full Ban on Ivory Trade." 2013. Animal Defenders International (ADI), March 4. http://www.ad-international.org/conservation/go.php?id=2994&ssi=14.

Ferretti, E. 2013. "Meat Scandals Highlight Growing Taste for Exotic Animals." Fox News, March 18. http://www.foxnews.com/leisure/2013/03/18/making-killing-in-game/.

Foggo, D., and H. Jaber. 2013. "European AZA Zoos 'Actively Encouraged' to Kill Animals." http://bigcatrescue.org/european-aza-zoos-actively-encouraged-to-kill-animals/.

Grech, K. S. 2004. "Detailed Discussion of the Laws Affecting Zoos." *Animal Legal and Historical Center*. http://www.animallaw.info/articles/dduszoos.htm#s163.

Hessler, K., and T. Balaban. 2009. "Exotic Animals as Pets." *GPSOLO*. https://www.americanbar.org/newsletter/publications/gp_solo_magazine_home/gp_solo_magazine_index/exoticpets.html.

"Idaho Aquarium Operators Arrested on Federal Charges." 2013. *Idaho Press-Tribune*, February 22. http://www.idahopress.com/news/local/idaho-aquarium-operators-arrested-on-federal-charges/article_c721f39a-7ca0-11e2-83a8-001a4bcf887a.html.

"Inside the Exotic Animal Trade." 2013. People for the Ethical Treatment of Animals (PETA). http://www.peta.org/issues/companion-animals/inside-the-exotic-animal-trade.aspx.

Israel, B. 2009. "Dominant Male Iso Sweet-Natured Female: Dating Service for Endangered Apes." *Discover Magazine*, December 9. http://blogs.discovermagazine.com/discoblog/?p=4570#.UhwrUJK1GSo.

Liebman, M. G. 2004. "Detailed Discussion of Exotic Pet Laws." *Animal Legal and Historical Center*. http://www.animallaw.info/articles/ddusexoticpets.htm.

Mallonee, L. 2013. "'Crooked' Animal Control Officer Caught with 850 Snakes in His Garage." *New York Observer*, September 20. http://observer.com/2013/09/crooked-animal-control-officer-caught-with-850-snakes-in-his-garage/.

Petersen, K. 2011. "Nearly 250 Poisonous and Exotic Snakes Found in Passenger's Suitcase." *Examiner.com*, December 27. http://www.examiner.com/article/nearly-250-poisonous-and-exotic-snakes-found-passengers-suitcase.

"Petting Zoo Horror Story: Berlin Zoo Feeds Goat to Wolves." 2008. *Der Spiegel*, June 6. http://www.spiegel.de/international/zeitgeist/petting-zoo-horror-story-berlin-zoo-feeds-goat-to-wolves-a-558123.html.

Pfeiffer, E. 2013. "Authorities Find 850 Illegal Snakes in Animal Control Officer's Home." *Yahoo! News*, September 19. http://news.yahoo.com/blogs/sideshow/-authorities-find-850-snakes-in-animal-control-officer%E2%80%99s-home-215643442.html.

"Plenty More Where Those Came From—Final Take in Fla. Snake Hunt Is 68 Pythons." 2013. CNN, February 18. http://www.cnn.com/2013/02/16/us/florida-python-hunt/index.html.

Rosner, B. 2013. "Two Indian Men Try to Smuggle 10,000 Live Baby Turtles in Their Luggage." *Hypervocal*, July 22. http://hypervocal.com/news/2013/smuggled-turtles/.

Schriffen, J., and A. Waterfield. 2013. "Hottest-Selling Animal in Colombia's Illegal Pet Trade: Sloths." *ABC News*, May 28. http://abcnews.go.com/International/hottest-selling-animal-colombias-illegal-exotic-pet-trade/story?id=19172620.

"State Laws Exotic Cats." 2013. BigCatRescue.com. http://bigcatrescue.org/state-laws-exotic-cats/.

Stryker, M., and J. Gallagher. 2013. "Detroit Zoo Giraffe? Belle Isle? Detroit's Treasure Trove Could Be Vulnerable to Sale to Settle Debt." *Detroit Free Press*, June 2. http://www.freep.com/article/20130602/NEWS01/306020080/Detroit-bankruptcy-assets-sale-DIA.

"Surplus Animals: The Cycle of Hell; A Study Of Captive Wildlife in the United States." 2013. Performing Animal Welfare Society (PAWS). http://www.pawsweb.org/surplus.pdf.

Tepper, R. 2013. "Whale Sushi Scandal: Chefs Kiyoshiro Yamamoto and Susumu Ueda Face Combined 77 Years in Prison." *Huffington Post*, February 4. http://www.huffingtonpost.com/2013/02/04/whale-sushi-kiyoshiro-yamamoto-susumu-ueda_n_2617088.html.

Wisch, R. F. 2003. "Overview of the Lacey Act." *Animal Legal and Historical Center*. http://www.animallaw.info/articles/ovuslaceyact.htm.

"Worldwide Circus Bans." 2013. Animal Defenders International (ADI). http://www.ad-international.org/animals_in_entertainment/go.php?id=281.

Yakas, B. 2012. "Cops Bust Bizarre Crown Heights Apartment Zoo." *Gothamist*, September 8. http://gothamist.com/2012/09/08/police_bust_crown_heights_man_with.php#photo-1.

16

Sexual Abuse of Animals

Introduction

Taboos against human-animal sexual relationships may seem black and white. Society may believe that law can be used to enforce clear taboos against bestiality. US and worldwide traditions tend to deeply chastise and punish bestiality, that is, crimes against nature. However, policies and laws about physical contact may be very gray. "Penetration," "pleasure," and "pornography" are some of the ambiguous terms that may have multiple meanings that potentially lead to dramatically different legal interpretations. In some cases government discretion, statutory wording, and alleged intentions separate legal and illegal acts. The metaphorization and commercialization of animal sexuality may reflect society's duplicitous or unclear approach to animal sexuality within culture and the criminal justice system.

The Case for Pleasure

For moral reasons or other reasons, for example, animal cruelty and welfare or human health, numerous countries ban bestiality. First Judaism, then Christianity, and finally Islam forbade bestiality early on in their religious traditions. Christians and Muslims form a large percentage of the global population and continue to consider bestiality to be immoral. If domesticated animals were to be involved, then initiation of sex acts could be attributable to pleasing a master. Masters can withhold food, shelter, and care. An animal may find that pleasing a master sexually is useful. Where animals rely on masters for food, power disparity may be too great to consider sexual willingness to be genuine. Animals' survival instincts and their willingness to sustain their own health should not be abused or underestimated.

Philosopher Peter Singer penned a famous essay about bestiality entitled "Heavy Petting." In the essay Singer argues from a utilitarian perspective that bestiality is acceptable when the act maximizes pleasure (Singer 2001). Though quite controversial, Singer's essay raises the idea that animals may receive pleasure from sexual acts that they instigate with humans. Even if they cannot legally consent, their initiation of the activity is evidence of their genuine desire to receive pleasure. Are animal abuse laws useless if animals want to have sexual relationships with humans?

One true test of whether animals would voluntarily engage in sexual behavior with humans might be anecdotal or scientific evidence that wild animals voluntarily and randomly initiate sexual relations with humans that result in animals experiencing pleasure. This test ought to exclude incidents in which animals randomly humped or raped humans for control or power. Some proponents of pleasuring animals may argue that wild animals would not want to engage humans sexually because it is a bond between humans and domesticated animals that stimulates desire or sexual feelings. There is very little anecdotal or scientific support for this reasoning, and most scientific and nonscientific literature tends to show that contact between humans and animals relates to abuse and human-animal relationships are consistently admonished ("Last Taboo" 2006).

Research shows that people who sexually abuse animals also abuse children and the elderly. Any person who would take advantage of a vulnerable animal may be likely to do the same to a vulnerable human. Thus, in addition to animal welfare, morality, ethics, and the preservation of human health, the protection of vulnerable populations is another reason to criminalize bestiality.

Bestiality

Bestiality is addressed by society under a few different laws that have evolved in recent years. Generally speaking, injurious bestiality is prohibited by cruelty statutes. Prior to 2003 bestiality laws were lumped together with sodomy laws in many states that prohibited "deviant" sexual intercourse or "crimes against nature." Following *Lawrence v. Texas*, a case that legalized all consensual, private sodomy between adults, some critics thought that bestiality was also legalized 2003). In his dissenting opinion, Justice Antonin Scalia warned that by legalizing sodomy, legalization of bestiality might be on the horizon (*Lawrence v. Texas*, 2003). It seems that Justice Scalia's idea was likely exaggerated since more states have adopted antibestiality legislation since 2003. However, sodomy and bestiality are no longer lumped together. Thus, while redrafting sodomy laws, some states did away with the category of "crimes against nature" altogether. The public tends to sensational-ize new legislation criminalizing bestiality because it seems to suggest that bestiality had previously been legal in that state.

Bestiality is not legal in any jurisdiction. However, bestiality may only be criminalized under cruelty statutes. Some bestiality statutes and cruelty statutes require harm or limit prosecution to certain kinds of sexual contact. Thus, not all sexual contact may be equally prohibited in varying jurisdictions. Whereas one jurisdiction may criminalize all sexual touching of an animal's genitals, another jurisdiction may only criminalize oral contact or penetrative acts.

Recording actual bestiality is illegal, and some simulations are criminalized under obscenity laws. A sharp distinction exists between actual human-animal sex relations and the simulation of human-animal sexual relationships. Simulation of bestiality could be obscene when humans dress as animals. Furries belong to a subculture in which partners may fetishistically dress as animals. Not far removed from the traditional sexy cat Halloween costume, full animal costumes eroticize the image of animals. Furry culture does not typically involve living animals. Though furries' lifestyles generally are not illegal or linked with crime, *per se*, critics have suggested that this subculture may encour-age bestial fantasies. Anecdotally it has been suggested that a furry fetish could lead to hands-on offenses with animals, just as hardcore fetishes can correlate with hands-on sex offenses (Smith and Bailey 2011). This parallel may be unfair, yet there are examples of furries fetishistically abusing animals. In one case a furry crossed the line from fantasy into reality by dressing as a dog to have sex with a cat several times over a year-long period (*Inquisitr* 2013). The man was charged with six felony counts of crimes against nature and one misdemeanor cruelty charge.

During the earliest years of People for the Ethical Treatment of Animal (PETA), activism did not involve sexual motifs. In recent years PETA has been criticized for sexualizing female activists. Female activ-ists dress as sexy tigers, topless reptiles, and other animals to engage in highly sexualized demonstrations for attention. Though the vast majority of PETA employees view themselves as feminists who are intentionally or ironically exploiting gender roles politically, gray areas could arise whenever animal lovers combine sexuality and animal cos-tumes. The public's latent or explicit interest in bestial fantasies may underlie the success of these demonstrations. However, PETA does not promote bestiality.

PETA tenaciously pursues bestial predators. For example, in 2005 a blind man raped his service dog. At that time Florida did not yet have bestiality statutes (WND 2005). The state was reluctant to charge the man with any serious crimes. Without PETA's intervention at the time, the state would have charged the man with misdemeanor cruelty. PETA advocated on the service animal's behalf, raising evidence that the dog was injured, in order to cause Florida to bring felony cruelty charges. Lack of evidence of injury is common since many people who injure their animals while committing bestiality will forsake veterinary care to hide evidence ("Last Taboo" 2006). They are also likely to kill and dispose of injured animals.

Pornography and Animal Abuse

Theoretically, society is not opposed to the concept of animal sexuality or human-animal sexual hybridity. In zoos animals who may become turgid or aroused, who hump, or who copulate are on display for adults and children alike. Though bestiality is not displayed, animal sexuality that would otherwise have remained unviewed by most humans is foisted into the public view (Howard 2009). Religious literature, Shakespearean texts, and other classics are rife with images of gods or humans who transform into or become involved with animals in sexual situations (Goodfellow 2010). This literature is not considered to be obscenity because of its literary value (*Miller v. California*, 1973). The central narrative of the texts is neither about animal abuse nor designed to appeal to prurient interests.

In the criminal justice system, bestiality and creating pornographic depictions of bestiality are illegal because of the depictions' content and purpose. Bestiality is prohibited as cruelty, and creating depictions of it is unprotected speech (Cusack 2014). Dealing in bestial pornography, which is considered to be hardcore pornography and obscenity, can be described as *per se* illegal. Selling, buying, and trading depictions is prohibited by the federal government and by some states (18 U.S.C. § 2256, 2013; Ohio Rev. Code Ann. § 2907.31, 2010). Americans cannot buy or sell bestial obscenity within or outside the United States on the Internet, but Americans can legally view bestial pornography inside their homes (Gallagher 1995; *Stanley v. Georgia*, 1969).

Sex offenses correlate with viewing bestial pornography and other hardcore pornography (Batista 2005). Offenders may force sexual assault victims to view bestial pornography or create bestial pornography. Some theories suggest that addiction to hardcore pornography can reinforce viewers' desires, and then viewers express their fantasies by committing crimes (Smith and Bailey 2011). When viewers watch bestial pornography repeatedly, it can inform them about how to perform abusive acts on animals. Nondeviant pornography users can progress to becoming deviant pornography users who view bestial images of animal abuse (Seigfried-Spellar and Rogers 2013). Pornography critics believe that pornography is abusive. Interests in one form of pornography may influence violent interests in sex. A correlation between the sexual abuse of women and pornography has been established. Supporting this correlation is a study predating the Internet that showed that the rate of circulation of pornographic magazines correlated with rape rates per state (Scott and Schwalm 1988). Another recent study specifies that young men who are prone to aggression are also prone to pornography use (Malamuth, Hald, and Koss 2012). Young adult females who have been exposed to sexual violence and psychological violence within their families are more likely to view pornography, while a substantial percentage of females have viewed pornography that was violent against women (Romito and Beltramini 2011). Female minors who are exposed to pornography are more likely to fantasize about rape and harbor attitudes that are supportive of sexual violence against women Corne, Briere, and Esses 1992). The likelihood of rape increases among young men who use hardcore pornography and are accepting of violence against women (Demare, Briere, and Lips 1988). When looking at the relationship between the physical abuse of animals and humans, the correlation between domestic violence and animal abuse, and the relationship between hardcore pornography use and sexual violence, it is easy to see reasons why society criminalizes pornographic depictions of sexual abuse of animals. In a study of 245 self-reporting respondents, more than 20 percent admitted to viewing bestial pornography, while only about 12 percent admitted to using child pornography (the trade, purchase, and sale of child pornography are illegal in every US jurisdiction). In that study those who viewed child pornography had an increased likelihood of using bestial pornography. Viewers who began using pornography at a younger age were more likely to progress from nondeviant pornography use to deviant pornography, including bestial pornography.

Sexual Abuse and Meat

Linguistic and cultural connections between edible animal products, money, and human sexuality are evident. Sexually insinuative or explicit words and phrases that relate human sex parts to animal products are plentiful. Double entendres include, but are not limited to, "fur burger," "taco," "beef cake," "sausage," "*huevos*," and "milk jugs." Words linking money with animal products include "bacon," "cheddar," "cheese," "milking," and many others. These linguistic links may create conceptual links. Language may also directly connect sex with money. For example, a "rack" means both a large quantity of money and "breasts." A "stack" of money shares a similar counterpart; a woman with a voluptuous figure or impressive secondary sex organs is said to be "stacked." A "bone" is a dollar, and "bone" is also refers to sex or a turgid penis. "Cream" means money or refers to the power of money, and "cream" is also a euphemism for ejaculation, discharge, or sexual fluids. "Jack" can reference the act of masturbation or money. "Ends" can refer to the power of money or orifices located on the lower half of a human or animal body. A "knot" may refer to money, the bulbous base of a dog's penis, or human sex organs. There are several other examples. People may use these words because they overtly or latently connect animal products with sex and money.

Metaphoric pornographication of meat may be linked with abuse of animals, sexual abuse of children, and meat. Some sexual abusers eat children. For example, Albert Fish, a well-known serial killer, molested hundreds of children and ate a few after he cooked them like meat dishes. He memorialized his crimes in sexually descriptive writings. His perversities serve as an excellent example of how sexualization, abuse, killing, and consumption can become linked. Monstrous examples are not rare. Offenders may abuse children during ritualized abuse. Ritualized abuse occurs during a ceremony. Some rituals involve rape, molestation, pornography, forcing children to harm animals or witness abuse, or eating human or animal flesh. Several states specifically criminalize ritual child abuse. Idaho forbids anyone from simulating or actually torturing, mutilating, or sacrificing warm-blooded animals or people in front of children (Idaho Code § 18-1506A, 2013). Children may not be forced to ingest or touch any part of a dead animal or human, including blood, bones, and flesh. These laws are designed to spare children psychological and physical abuse. However, they juxtapose the fact that children may be lawfully forced by parents to touch and consume animal body parts for nourishment or participation in nonritualized traditions. For example, parents could lawfully require their children to consume bull bollocks for dinner.

Breeding

Animals are routinely penetrated and masturbated pursuant to legal breeding practices. No legal consideration is given to animals' interest or disinterest in permitting breeders to touch their sex organs. Though the law never recognizes animals' "consent" for sexual contact, these practices are specifically exempted from sex abuse or cruelty laws (IA ST § 717D.3(2)(b-c), 2012). Surprisingly, little regulation of breeding practices exists within the criminal justice system. The federal government does not directly regulate these practices (Wisch 2013). States use licensing to regulate animal breeding and insemination (CO ST § 12-64-101-124, 2012; NM ST § 61-14-1 to 61-14-20, 2013). Typically, veterinary boards oversee veterinary artificial insemination. Unlicensed practitioners of veterinary medicine can be fined several thousands of dollars, or they could face imprisonment. Farmers may be certified in artificial insemination. Industry standards dictate breeding practice requirements and procedures. Often industry standards can be used to show that a crime may have been committed when actions fall below the professional standard of care, but breeding practices are seldom investigated as sexual abuse. When sexual abuse has been exposed on farms, it has normally been unrelated to breeding practices (PETA 2012).

If any animal were to be masturbated or penetrated for pleasure, then a perpetrator could be found guilty of crimes, for example, cruelty and sexually assaulting an animal (Wisch 2013). However, if a farmer, veterinarian, or another licensed breeder engages in procreative activities with animals, then no crime has been committed because an animal is property and certain sexual activity is a means of creating a product. Though breeders intend to gratify male animals to the point of ejaculation, the law presumes that an animal's arousal does not gratify a professional. Yet, even if a breeder was to be aroused, the activity would probably still be lawful if the professional adhered to industry practices (Cusack 2013).

Breeding practices are unsophisticated and have not evolved much over the past centuries (Cusack 2013). For example, on dairy farms every cow will be subjected to manual recto-vaginal penetration. First, farmers insert one extended arm into a cow's anus. The arm is inserted to approximately the farmer's elbow. Next, by fanning his or her fingers, the farmer presses on a cow's anal cavity to contact a cow's cervix. While holding a cow's cervix through the anal wall, a farmer penetrates the cow vaginally with an artificial insemination device. The cow's cervix is plugged with an inseminator, which is filled with bulls' semen. Finally, the inseminator's contents are emptied into the cow's cervix. Few quality bulls are available as sperm donors. Thus, these high-priced specimens can require farmers to repeatedly masturbate the same bulls. Whales, horses, dogs, and almost all other bred animals experience similar objectification and lawful sexual contact (OH Stat. § 2305.321, 2013; *PETA v. Sea World*, 2011). For example, a breeder or veterinarian will masturbate a male dog until ejaculation. The specimen will be collected. A female dog may have her hindquarters held in the air by an assistant. The specimen will be shot into the female dog's reproductive organs using an inseminating device. None of these actions would be legal if the breeder was not licensed. However, in some states it is a crime to photograph sexual contact with animals, and it is prohibited by the federal government (T.C.A. § 39-14-214, 2013; RCWA 16.52.205, 2013). Yet, scientific and educational value of depicting breeding practices may decriminalize images of animal penetration and masturbation.

Conclusion

Breeding, bestiality, and bonding may be conceptually distinct activities separated by thousands of years of tradition. Though these activities exist in gray areas that approach bright lines, the law attempts to preserve their mutual exclusivity. Due to industry practices, jurisdictional variations, cultural norms, legal interpretations, and other factors, some sexual activities are regulated, but others seem not to be. Possible hints about cultural understandings of animal sexuality appear in colloquial references to animal genitals and sexuality. Embodiment and consumption of animal sexuality seems to be latently or overtly normative to an extent, yet hands-on human-animal amorous experiences are likely to be—though are not certain to be—prosecutable.

References

18 U.S.C. § 2256 (2013).

Adams, C. J. 2003. *Pornography of Meat.* Continuum: New York.

Batista, F. 2005. "The Ramifications of the Federal Communications Commission's Failure to Minimize Negative Media Portrayals of Latinas and Black Women." *Cardozo Women's Law Journal* 11:331.

CO Stat. § 12-64-101–124 (2012).

Corne, S., J. Briere, and L. Esses. 1992. "Women's Attitudes and Fantasies about Rape as a Function of Early Exposure to Pornography." *Journal of Interpersonal Violence* 7:454–61.

Cusack, C. M. 2013. "Feminism and Husbandry: Drawing the Fine Line between Mine and Bovine." *Journal for Critical Animal* Studies (JCAS) 11, no. 1:24.

———. 2014. *Pornography and the Criminal Justice System.* CRC Press/Taylor and Francis: Boca Raton.

Demare, D., J. Briere, and H. Lips. 1988. "Violent Pornography and Self-Reported Likelihood of Sexual Aggression." *Journal of Research in Personality* 22:140–53.

Gallagher, D. A. 1995. "Free Speech on the Line: Modern Technology and the First Amendment." *CommLaw Conspectus* 3:197.

Goodfellow, A. 2010. "Introduction: Religion/Sexuality; Politics/Affects." *Borderlands* 9:3.

Howard, J. 2009. "Creature Consciousness: Animal Studies Tests the Boundary between Human and Animal—And Between Academic and Advocate." *Chronicle of Higher Education* 56:9.

IA Stat. § 717D.3(2)(b–c) (2012).

Idaho Code § 18-1506A (2013).

"Idaho Man Who Dressed as Dog Had Sex with Cat: Police Charge Him with Animal Cruelty Not Rape." 2013. *Inquisitr,* August 14. http://www.inquisitr.com/904062/idaho-man-who-dressed-as-dog-had-sex-with-cat-police-charge-him-with-animal-cruelty-not-rape/.

"The Last Taboo." 2006. *New Scientist* 191 (2564):6.

Lawrence v. Texas. 539 U.S. 558 (2003).

Laws, D. R., and W. T. O'Donohue. 2008. *Sexual Deviance.* New York: Guliford Press.

Lockwood, R. 2006. "Animal Cruelty Prosecution." *American Prosecutors Research Institute.* http://www.ndaa.org/pdf/animal_cruelty_06.pdf.

MacKinnon, C. A. 2004. "Of Mice and Men: A Feminist Fragment on Animal Rights." In *Animal Rights: Current Debates and New Directions,* ed. C. R. Sunstein and M. C. Nussbaum. Oxford: Oxford University Press.

Malamuth, N., G. Hald, and M. Koss. 2012. "Pornography, Individual Differences in Risk and Men's Acceptance of Violence against Women in a Representative Sample." *Sex Roles* 66, nos. 7–8:427–39.

Miller v. California. 413 U.S. 15 (1973).

Minnesota Board of Veterinary Medicine. 2013. "Disciplinary Actions, Thomas Koepke." http://www.vetmed.state.mn.us/Default.aspx?tabid=803.

OH Stat. § 2305.321 (2013).

OHIO Rev. Code Ann. § 2907.31 (West 2010).

NM Stat. § 61-14-1 to 61-14-20 (2013).

People for the Ethical Treatment of Animals (PETA). 2012. "Sexual Abuse of Animals: A Recurring Theme on Factory Farms." September 13. http://www.peta.org/b/thepetafiles/archive/2010/09/13/Sexual-Abuse-of-Animals-A-Recurring-Theme-on-Factory-Farms.aspx.

PETA v. Sea World. Case No.: 3:11-cv-02476-JM-WMC (2011).

RCWA 16.52.205 (2013).

Romito, P., and L. Beltramini. 2011). "Watching Pornography: Gender Differences, Violence and Victimization; An Exploratory Study in Italy." *Violence against Women* 17, no. 10:1313–26.

Scott, J., and L. Schwalm. 1988. "Rape Rates and the Circulation Rates of Adult Magazines." *Journal of Sex Research* 24:241–50.

Seigfried-Spellar, K. C., and M. K. Rogers. 2013. "Does Deviant Pornography Use Follow a Guttman-Like Progression?" *Computers in Human Behavior* 29:5.

Singer, P. 2001. "Heavy Petting." *Nerve.* http://www.utilitarianism.net/singer/by/2001----.htm.

Smith, G. P., and G. P. Bailey. 2011. "Regulating Morality through the Common Law and Exclusionary Zoning." *Catholic University Law Review* 60:403.

Stanley v. Georgia. 394 U.S. 557 (1969).

"State Hikes Charge against 'Dog Raper.'" 2005. WND, August 27. http://www.wnd.com/2005/08/32014/.

Szymanski, D. M., L. B. Moffitt, and E. R. Carr. 2011. "Sexual Objectification of Women: Advances to Theory and Research." *Counseling Psychologist* 39, no. 1:6–38. http://www.apa.org/education/ce/sexual-objectification.pdf.

T.C.A. § 39-14-214 (2013).

Wisch, R. F. 2013. "Table of State Animal Sexual Assault Laws." *Animal Legal and Historical Center.* http://www.animallaw.info/articles/State%20Tables/tbusanimalassault.htm.

17

Multiple Animals

Introduction

Society has an interest in protecting human and animal health. Hoarding, puppy mills, and infestations threaten human health. Keeping multiple animals in small spaces requires compliance with strict regulations to ensure safety and avoid health hazards. The government regulates hoarding and puppy mills in favor of animal health and well-being. Humans are permitted to kill groups of animals when they become a nuisance or are excessively abundant. Perhaps speciesist or utilitarian reasoning helps to explain this difference.

Hoarding

Animal hoarders excessively accumulate animals; typically, hoarding occurs inside homes (Muller-Harris 2011). Numbers of animals may range from a few to several hundred. The hallmark of hoarding is an absence of food, water, shelter, or veterinary care for animals. Animals frequently starve, suffocate, suffer untreated injuries or diseases, go blind or lame, die, and decompose without a hoarder providing any care. Hoarded animals usually live in cluttered and dirty environments that are covered with their feces and urine. Toxic ammonia from excrement may cause respiratory infections and skin burns among animals and residents. Animals have been discovered with broken bones and dislodged eyeballs (Campbell 2009). Because hoarding occurs in the home, interagency cooperation creates responses for children living in these conditions with the animals (Muller-Harris 2011).

When hoarders live in normal conditions and only have "a few too many" animals, for example, six dogs and cats, then authorities may constructively seize animals but allow animals to remain on a defendant's property. On-site seizure allows for authorities to avoid the cost of relocating, housing, and feeding animals, and owners have the opportunity to correct the violation and appear before the court (Campbell 2009). If animals are living in complete squalor, then authorities may likely seize the animals and possibly condemn the property (Muller-Harris 2011). Seized animals, who may be ill, injured, or aggressively unsocialized, are frequently destroyed; however, owners may have standing under due process rights to oppose destruction of healthy animals (Muller-Harris 2011; Skyes 2011).

Each case of hoarding is an expensive burden on the system. Cases require seizure and care for animals, prosecution, and municipal responses to disheveled or hazardous properties (Hoffman and McGinnis 2009). Hoarders can be fined several hundred or thousands of dollars (Graves, Mosman, and Rogers 2012). Yet, hoarders are rarely fined, or fined enough, to cover costs associated with their crimes. In a study of fifty-six cases, researchers showed that the most common consequence for animal hoarding was misdemeanor charges (Berry and Patronek 2005). In one case dead animals were found, but no charges were filed.

The majority of animal hoarding can be linked to mental illnesses. Obsessive-compulsive disorder, delusional thinking, dementia, self-neglect, and noncompliance with psychiatric treatment may be involved. These symptoms or illnesses lend themselves to recidivism. Convicted hoarders may be stabilized or ordered to undergo treatment. Critics argue that punishing hoarders may effectively criminalize mental illness. In some jurisdictions, if offenders can negotiate misdemeanor charges and can be referred to mental health court, then the court may supervise treatment and rehabilitation. If not, then treatment may be ordered in conjunction with penalization. In Illinois juvenile hoarders are required to undergo psychological counseling (I.L.C.S. 70/1–18, 2012). In other cases treatment is never discussed by the court, even when the offender is clearly afflicted with some sort of mental illness.

Not every hoarder is mentally ill. Some are caring pet owners who cannot satisfy duties of ownership. Other hoarders rescue animals, perhaps with good intentions, but cannot support animals' care even though they feel driven to continue rescuing new animals (Manning 2013). Sometimes hoarding overlaps with intentional intensive breeding, that is, puppy mills (CNN 2013; Sykes 2011). Three thousand cases of animal hoarding are reported each year (Muller-Harris 2011). At least a quarter of a million hoarded animals become involved with the criminal justice system annually. More than half of the cases are due to recidivism.

Hoarding cases can involve hundreds of victims across a range of jurisdictions involving complex tiered responses from various agencies including police, fire rescue, animal control, social services, and building inspectors (Muller-Harris 2011). In response to persecution, hoarders may flee to other jurisdictions. After animal hoarders flee a jurisdiction, they may begin accumulating animals rapidly in another jurisdiction. Depending on the jurisdiction, certain agencies may choose not to involve themselves with such severe and complex problems. Some government officials could encourage flight. For example, Vicki Kittles roamed the country in a school bus packed with 115 dogs (Fox 2008). In one jurisdiction officials gave her gas money and instructed her to evade further involvement with the system by leaving town. In another case police hesitated to seize herds of emaciated horses because of the cost and logistics of housing herds of horses while the defendant received due process (Campbell 2009). Economic strains are legitimate concerns when preparedness and emergency responses are not mandated by law. Emergency responses are discussed in chapter 11.

Some states, for example, Illinois and Hawaii, have passed hoarding laws (Graves, Mosman, and Rogers 2012). Hoarding statutes usually mention accumulation and neglect. Other states, for example, California, specify the maximum number of domesticated animal companions permitted within a single home. Exceptions would be made for puppy litters who are not yet weaned or licensed breeders. Animal hoarding may be criminalized by cruelty statutes in the absence of specific legislation. Laws that target hoarding are much stronger than cruelty statutes because prosecutors may limit the number of cruelty charges in comparison to the number of animals involved. Since hoarders homes' are squalid, courts may take pity on them by failing to find the requisite intent to harm animals under cruelty statutes. A court may categorize neglect as incident to a hoarder's general failure to habilitate and apparent mental disconnect from reality. Cruelty charges may also be insufficient if they fail to motivate the court to order treatment for an offender. Some states have tried to incorporate hoarders' disconnected thinking into the definition of "hoarding," which could require courts to address a hoarder's mental illness.

Caring animal owners may become entangled with the justice system under statutes limiting ownership of a certain number of animal companions. A city ordinance in South Dakota proscribed more than four dogs total and more than two dogs weighing more than twenty-five pounds each (Huss 2005). A person was cited for violating that ordinance by owing three licensed and vaccinated dogs; when one of her dogs gained weight, it rendered her the owner of too many large dogs. The case went all the way to South Dakota Supreme Court, which held that larger dogs are potentially more dangerous. Thus, the law was rational and could be enforced despite the fact that owner was not a hoarder and her dog only happened to gain weight. Sometimes the definition of hoarding may vary according to the type of housing, for example, an apartment versus a ranch. Thus, people who are not hoarders in one context may incidentally be classified as hoarders in another.

Puppy Mills

"Puppy mill" is a term used to describe a commercial operation in which excessive numbers of animals are quarantined to minimize costs while maximizing breeding and sales (Tushaus 2009). Animals are exhausted by breeders' demands, and frequently animals are neglected. Properties with legal or illegal puppy mills reportedly are appalling. At puppy mills animals with rotting open wounds, broken bones, and prolapsed organs constantly bark chaotically while they are piled in tiny crates on top of one another with no access to grass or fresh air; in some cases animals are caged for the duration of their unnaturally short and miserable lives (Katz 2009). Scores of wire mesh cages contain several puppies covered in excrement. Drip pans lie under the cages, which are not padded or lined for the puppies' bellies or feet (Towsey 2010). In addition to pathogens and infections arising from animals' submersion in excrement, puppy mills produce ecological ramifications. Individual licensed and unlicensed puppy mills may pollute the environment with tens of thousands of pounds of contaminated waste that seeps into the local water supply. When violations are discovered, puppy mill operators may be asked to correct violations, but violations may not rise to the definition of "cruelty" in a particular jurisdiction. In some jurisdictions operators can legally exterminate puppies rather than spend money to rectify violations. In one case a commercial breeder legally killed eighty dogs by shooting them. In most jurisdictions authorities are not prepared to seize hundreds of animals. In 2007 Carroll County in Virginia had to declare a local disaster following a puppy mill raid (Fox 2008). More than one thousand dogs were stuffed into squalid wire cages. Rather than attempt to exterminate the dogs, the commercial breeder voluntarily surrendered dogs. Carroll County had to organize removal and then clean the dogs; provide veterinary care and vaccinations; and socialize, feed, and house the dogs. Because an emergency was declared, the Virginia Department of Emergency Management, American Red

Cross volunteers, and animal rescue and welfare agencies from around the country aided in Carroll County's effort.

The Animal Welfare Act (AWA) regulates commercial pet breeding (Katz 2009). Under the AWA the secretary of agriculture authorizes the US Department of Agriculture (USDA), through the division of the Animal and Plant Inspection Service (APHIS), to enforce humane treatment of animals. The APHIS reaches animals in the stream of commerce and requires records for commercial animal transport. Seventy inspectors work to enforce the AWA in thousands of breeding facilities throughout the country. This shortage of inspectors leaves gaping holes in enforcement of the AWA. Holes also exist in the APHIS's authority because the AWA exempts pet stores from regulation (Kenny 2012). Yet, pet stores' sale of purebred and boutique dogs is inextricably linked to puppy mills.

In addition to cruelty laws in all fifty states, twenty-eight states regulate commercial breeding, and twenty-six states require kennel licensing (Katz 2009). States may rely on the Department of Agriculture, the Department of Health, zoning administrators, or the Department of Natural Resources to regulate commercial breeding (Fumarola 1999; Katz 2009). Some jurisdictions, for example, Missouri, regulate commercial breeding more closely than other jurisdictions. Some jurisdictions evolved regulate sanitation, animal exercise, nutrition, and ventilation requirements. Pennsylvania, which tracks commercial breeders in a statewide database, requires veterinary care and regulates crate stacking, but appalling conditions may persist even though breeders are in compliance with the law (Towsey 2010). Many states' regulations are insufficient (Katz 2009). Some jurisdictions merely require breeders to pay a minimal licensing fee, but they do not otherwise punish breeders for illegal operations. Almost no states require business licenses for commercial breeding.

Many exemplary cities, for example, El Paso, Texas, and South Lake Tahoe, California, have criminalized any sale of puppies within city limits, banned sales of cats and dogs, prohibited puppy mill operation, and prohibited doing business with puppy mills (Kenny 2012). Some jurisdictions incentivize pet stores to work with adoption agencies. Statewide bans of animal sales in pet stores may efficiently curb criminal or unethical commercial breeding, and closing links between pet stores and puppy mills may force the public to visit breeding facilities to purchase boutique dogs (Tushaus 2009). This may allow the public to evaluate breeding facilities, note and expose violations, consider the sources of their purchases, and contemplate adoption alternatives. Pet stores seeking to attract customers with window displays that capitalize on "puppy dog eyes" could house and care for adoptable animals. Half of the eight million dogs and the 70 percent of cats that annually enter shelters are euthanized because they are homeless; yet, animal shelters spend billions of dollars each year (Kenny 2012). Only about 20 percent of dog companions in the United States are adopted. The remaining 80 percent contributed to the annual billion-dollar live-animal market by being purchased, typically, at pet stores. Approximately one-third of all US pet stores sell the millions of dogs born at puppy mills yearly. Exclusively placing adoptable animals in pet stores and criminalizing pet store sales of puppy mill dogs could target unregulated cruelty and assist animal control.

Laws intended to target cruel pet store policies sometimes inadvertently criminalize cruelty-free animal-human interactions. For example, Japan's recent revision of its Animal Protection Law intends to regulate all-night pet stores, in which animals are kept in small cages within brightly lit rooms at all hours of the night. This important goal will incidentally have an arguably negative effect by restricting all commercial display of any cats and dogs after curfew at 8 PM (Villar 2012). The curfew aims to protect animals from exploitation, but it may force some cat cafes to close shop early. Japanese animal lovers who cannot reside with their animal companions or cannot afford to provide for their own animal companion patronize cat cafes, where they may coddle and interact with cats residing temporarily or permanently at the cafes. Cat cafes previously operated late into the night or twenty-four hours per day. They were widely reported to have a therapeutic effect on patrons and cats. However, cats might have been kept up all night without tranquility. When curfew begins cats must be placed in undisturbed and private areas of the establishment.

Infestation

Animal cruelty laws usually do not apply to animals that can be exterminated. For example, mice can be exterminated using a variety of torturous devices in most jurisdictions. However, some jurisdictions limit methods that can be used for reasons other than cruelty, for example, ecology or safety. In other jurisdictions a number of animals living outdoors together can constitute an infestation even if those animals are regarded as neighborhood residents. In many places invasive species are treated as pests. Almost every jurisdiction is plagued by some form of native pest.

Humane killing is required by law except for exempted animals. Exempted animals are those that are specifically exempted by statute, animals exempted for a purpose in a certain context, or those that fall outside a state's legal definition of "animal." Almost half of states specifically exempt animals from cruelty statutes if the animal is a pest (Burdyshaw 2011). The definition of "pest" varies widely; it includes animals that threaten other animals or can spread disease. Animals that can be considered pests to some are pets to others. A famous example is New York City's pigeon problem (Mooallem 2006). Pigeons are like outdoor pets to some residents, and they typify New York City's charm for tourists. However, it is legal to exterminate pigeons in New York City. Plans to import hawks or poison pigeon populations have been concocted, but the pigeon population remains constant because numerous people feed and care for the pigeons. The US Department of Agriculture culls sixty thousand pigeons annually, but only in response to complaints. To keep the peace with pigeon lovers, many people and businesses opt to pigeon-proof their edifices rather than exterminate.

By far the most controversial pest-pets dichotomy occurs with cats. Companion cats may be indoor-outdoor. Many pet owners believe that cats' natures require them to be free-roaming. Some cats with homes may temporarily stray or become lost (Wisch 2005). Thus, at any given time, cats that belong to families may be confused for pests. Almost half of all domesticated companion cats are indoor-outdoor, and many do not wear tags. Adding to the controversy is the fact that cats may kill wildlife, such as birds. Some birds, for example, endangered birds, may be carefully monitored by birdwatchers or the government. When cats attack them, otherwise protected cats may become vulnerable to pest statutes. When domesticated cats freely roam, they may enter other properties, destroy property, attack or disturb other animals, and create noise nuisances. These activities may lead communities or property owners to classify cats as pests. In a number of states, outdoor cats are not listed within the definition of "animal." In some states outdoor cats, which might be considered to be feral, are specifically targeted for extermination. In a few jurisdictions the government actively impounds feral cats and immediately destroys them.

There is a significant amount of legal overlap between the extermination of pets and pests. Most jurisdictions do not heatedly debate pest extermination regulations, for example, the use of mousetraps versus glue trapping. Yet, controversy often arises when cats and dogs are exterminated as pests. Some jurisdictions require that animal companions be euthanized by painless, humane means. In a few jurisdictions an animal's age will determine how an animal must be euthanized. In the United States most jurisdictions deal with homeless dogs and cats distinctly from other pests. However, foreign jurisdictions—for example, Sochi, Russia—have undertaken massive extermination of feral dogs using pest control companies (*Reader's Digest* 2014). Generally, in the United States feral cat populations raise more awareness since they reproduce more rapidly than dogs and are euthanized more routinely. There is often a clearer line between feral dogs and domesticated dogs than there may be for many outdoor cats. Collecting, housing, and humanely euthanizing a single cat can cost around a hundred dollars. However, cumulative costs may be expensive for many jurisdictions. Cats that are pests can be poisoned in carbon monoxide gas chambers or imploded in decompression chambers, which could be less expensive. About half of states and numerous municipalities criminalize one or both of these forms of extermination because they are very gory and cause animals to suffer tremendous pain (AHS 2008). Using a gun to exterminate pests in residential or metropolitan areas is generally illegal either because of cruelty statutes, gun-use regulations, euthanasia regulations, property laws, or pest statutes. For example, in Maine it is lawful to kill a dog or cat with a gun, but the animal must belong to the shooter. Thus, the statute precludes shooters from regulating outdoor cat populations with guns. However, bills have been introduced in Utah and Wisconsin that would have allowed people to hunt feral cats (PETA 2013). In a few jurisdictions federal trappers have been charged with cruelty after recklessly or intentionally causing serious injury and death to neighborhood dogs with steel traps and explosives intended for other animals (Federal Trapper 2012; HSLF 2013). Some federal trappers have retaliated by claiming that some people intentionally poison their pets in order to sue the federal government for compensation (Federal Trapper 2012).

Poisoning pests is common. Yet, poisoning cats and dogs may be controversial and illegal. There have been countless cases of community members illegally poisoning dogs and cats. Antifreeze is commonly used to poison animal companions because it is sweet or undetectable in food. Inevitably, a necropsy will reveal the poison, and the offender will be charged with cruelty. Sometimes feral animals are poisoned, but a municipality will not invest too much attention into the cause of death unless a rash of feral animals dies. Then municipalities or private welfare organizations may collect tips and investigate the source of the poison. Some people poison animals for revenge, amusement, or population control, but other people may kill pests in misguided attempts to defend other local animals. In one case a Smithsonian bird researcher, who was studying the effect of "killer cat" populations on birds, was convicted of attempting to poison neighborhood cats with rat poison (Hall 2011). The researcher, who maintained her innocence, was convicted for misdemeanor cruelty because no cats ate the poison. In some states, like California, it is legal to poison dogs who are killing livestock on an owner's property (CA Penal § 596, 2012). In a few states, like Maryland, it is illegal to poison a dog, but not a cat (MD Crim Law § 10-601-623; MD Crim Law § 3-322, 2013).

Culling

Excessive populations of animals in captivity or in the wild may result in culling. Private and public entities will reduce the number of animals necessary to be able to sustain populations and ecological balance. Often, culling policies are controversial among environmentalists, but welfarists' interventions usually come too late, are tied up in court for years, or fail. In the wild, land and natural resources may not support animals whose breeding practices become unsustainable. Some groups of animals may become hungry and sickly. Large populations may excessively prey upon or threaten other animals, or they may compromise human hunting activities when predators consume too much prey. Animals may become entangled with human civilization as they search for food and roam. The government has no interest in arbitrarily exterminating abundant species. Indeed, extermination policies may be met with great disapproval. Yet, the government does have an interest in preserving biodiversity, human safety, and health. Thus, it often allows hunters to take greater numbers of certain animals, contracts trappers to reduce numbers, or systematically eliminates a certain percentage of animals.

The manner in which animals are culled has been challenged, and in some cases regulated. For example, some welfare organizations have successfully claimed in court that aerial shootings are cruel (*Animal Liberation Ltd. v. National Parks and Wildlife Service*, 2003). During aerial shootings hunters shoot animals from helicopters. Due to aim and distance, some animals are not killed instantly. Because animals languish and bleed to death, aerial shooting has been enjoined in some jurisdictions. In other cases these findings have not been persuasive. Furthermore, fine distinctions have been raised to permit hunting in cases where other forms of animal killing seem unlawful. For example, distinctions between statutory prohibitions on "killing, capturing, or wounding" and hunting to cull have successfully impacted policy and persuaded the court (*Wildearth Guardians v. National Park Service*, 2013).

Protected species are sometimes culled. Often, though not always, culling of protected species occurs after conservation efforts are successful and animals are no longer protected. In Florida in the 1960s, great efforts were made to protect dwindling numbers of alligators from extinction after excessive hunting and environmental damage (Skoloff 2008). For a time alligator killing was met with severe punishment. After twenty years populations rebounded, and the Florida Fish and Wildlife Conservation Commission began a program to cull alligators. Biologists and volunteers collect wild gator eggs for twenty days over the summer. In some circumstances stealing eggs may be considered an infraction or crime, for example, disrupting natural habitats, but these activities are government sponsored. Approximately forty thousand eggs are divided and dispersed to thirty farmers for approximately twelve dollars each. Gators are then raised in captivity. Due to stress, females in captivity do not reproduce, but approximately one-third of captive gators are killed. This process reduces numbers of wild populations because female alligators will produce large numbers of eggs over the course of twenty-five years. Alligators' breeding habits allegedly cannot be sustained in south Florida, where human populations have steadily increased. Lower survival rates allow greater food and territory per wild alligator. Unfortunately, gators raised in captivity do not have any habitat or space, and hundreds of alligators often live on top of each other in small concrete enclosures. More than six hundred thousand eggs have been sold to farmers in the past twenty years. Farmers lawfully earn millions of dollars annually from tourism, hides, leather, and meat. Thus, culling efforts and the program's design are sometimes questioned, especially since animals in captivity live so poorly and farmers each earn more than a hundred thousand dollars annually. Suspicions about culling practices among conservation organizations are common. Captive breeders, for example, reserves or zoos, control breeding of protected animals; and breeding can be difficult, which makes excessive populations somewhat anomalous (*Born Free*

USA v. Norton, 2003). Furthermore, records have been illegally falsified to justify culling covertly that was intended to facilitate exotic animal trade and sale of animal parts.

Conclusion

Animals may reproduce or be bred excessively to their detriment. Human control over animals sometimes results in excessive populations. These operations often relate to greed, mental illness, and mistreatment of animals. Sometimes human interventions into natural breeding patterns attempt to contain populations to protect humans and animals from starvation, harm, and death. Animals that pose a threat or nuisance to humans are likely to be contained by individuals or the government; however, reduction of populations may result to ensure biodiversity or hunting opportunities. Cruelty cannot be inflicted on animals, irrespective of their quantities or threat to humans. Yet, species-specific legislation, definitions of "cruelty," and definitions of "animal" will vary in context and may determine how the government criminalizes or classifies certain human-animal group interactions.

References

"40 Pythons Seized from Ontario Motel Room." 2013. CNN, August 17. http://www.cnn.com/2013/08/16/world/americas/canada-motel-pythons/index.html?hpt=hp_t2.

American Humane Association (AHS). 2008. "State Euthanasia Laws." http://site.americanhumane.org/site/DocServer/Euthanasia_Laws_by_State.pdf?docID=7906

Animal Liberation Ltd. v National Parks and Wildlife Service. NSWSC 457 (2003).

Berry, C., and G. Patronek. 2005. "Long-Term Outcomes in Animal Hoarding Cases. *Animal Law* 167:176.

Born Free USA v. Norton. 278 F. Supp 2d 5 (D.D.C. 2003).

Burdyshaw, C. 2011. "Detailed Discussion of the Laws concerning Invasive Species." *Animal Legal and Historical Center.* http://www.animallaw.info/articles/ddusinvasives.htm.

Campbell, D. M. 2009. "A Call to Action: Concrete Proposals for Reducing Widespread Animal Suffering in the United States. *Animal Law* 15:141.

CA Penal § 596 (2012).

Fox, A. C. 2008. "Using Special Masters to Advance the Goals of Animal Protection Laws." *Animal Law* 15:87.

Fumarola, A. J. 1999. "With Best Friends Like Us Who Needs Enemies? The Phenomenon of the Puppy Mill, the Failure of Legal Regimes to Manage It, and the Positive Prospects of Animal Rights." *Buffalo Environmental Law Journal* 6:253.

Graves, P., K. Mosman, and S. Rogers. 2012. "2011 Legislative and Administrative Review." *Animal Law* 18:361.

Hall, C. 2011. "Smithsonian Bird Researcher Is Convicted of Trying to Poison Cats." *L.A. Times*, November 1. http://opinion.latimes.com/opinionla/2011/11/a-dc-bird-researcher-is-convicted-of-trying-to-poison-cats.html#sthash.RhTwVkjq.dpuf.

Hoffman, N. R., and R. C. McGinnis. 2009. "2007–2008 Legislative Review." *Animal Law* 15:265.

Humane Society Legislative Fund (HSLF). 2013. "Federal Trapper Arrested for Animal Cruelty." February 4. http://hslf.typepad.com/political_animal/2013/02/federal-trapper-arrested-for-animal-cruelty.html.

Huss, R. J. 2005. "No Pets Allowed: Housing Issues and Companion Animals." *Animal Law* 11:69.

Katz, R. F. 2009. "The Importance of Enacting a Texas Commercial Breeder Law to Regulate Loopholes That the Federal Law Creates." *Texas Tech Administrative Law Journal* 11:185.

Kenny, K. 2011/2012. "A Local Approach to a National Problem: Local Ordinances as a Means of Curbing Puppy Mill Production and Pet Overpopulation." *Albany Law Review* 75:379.

Manning, S. 2013. "Hoarded Calif. Dogs Await Rescue Groups." *Yahoo! News*, July 5. http://news.yahoo.com/hoarded-calif-dogs-await-rescue-groups-213526472.html.

MD Crim Law § 3-322 (2013).

MD Crim Law § 10-601–623 (2013).

Mooallem, J. 2006. "Pigeon Wars." *New York Times*, October 15. http://www.nytimes.com/2006/10/15/magazine/15pigeons.html?pagewanted=all&_r=0.

People for the Ethical Treatment of Animals (PETA). 2013. "The Great Outdoors? Not for Cats!" http://www.peta.org/issues/companion-animals/the-great-outdoors-not-for-cats.aspx.

Predator Defense. 2012. "Federal Trapper Targeted and Killed Dog according to Texas Dept. of Ag." June 18. http://www.predatordefense.org/m44s_bella.htm.

Reader's Digest. 2014. "Trending in: Animals." March.

Skoloff, B. 2008. "Fla. Keeps Gator Farms Full by Culling Wild Nest." *USA Today*, July 18. http://usatoday30.usatoday.com/news/nation/2008-07-18-2320390608_x.htm.

Sykes, K. 2011. "Human Drama, Animal Trials: What the Medieval Animal Trials Can Teach Us about Justice for Animals." *Animal Law* 17:273.

Towse, M. 2010. "Something Stinks: The Need for Environmental Regulation of Puppy Mills." *Villanova Environmental Law Journal* 21:159.

Tushaus, K. C. 2009. "Don't Buy the Doggy in the Window: Ending the Cycle That Perpetuates Commercial Breeding with Regulation of the Retail Pet Industry." *Drake Journal of Agricultural Law* 14:501.

Villar, R. 2012. "Japanese Cat Lovers Snarl at New Law." *Reuters*, March 1. http://www.reuters.com/article/2012/03/02/us-japan-cats-idUS-TRE82105G20120302.

Wildearth Guardians vs. National Park Service, 703 F.3d 1178 (10th Cir. Ct. App., 2013).

Wisch, R. F. 2005. "Detailed Discussion of State Cat Laws." *Animal Legal and Historical Center*. http://animallaw.info/articles/dduscats.htm#id-7.

18

Animals as Weapons

Introduction

Animals in the criminal justice system may be used as weapons. From the time of Roman antiquity to the contemporary era, animals have been used to hunt, apprehend, kill, and devour criminals and enemies of the state. Some historical uses of animals as weapons are no longer lawful; however, guard dogs, war dogs, and animals used in other combative roles are still quite popular and legal. Animals may become victims of abuse when people misuse animals as weapons. Overall, one hallmark of proper weaponization is task-oriented or mission-oriented training to accomplish lawful goals.

Historical

Damnatio ad bestias was a form of execution involving animals throughout history. Convicted criminals were pitted against or fed to animals. Sometimes this "condemnation to beasts" was a public spectacle. The Romans are most widely recognized for having implemented this form execution. In ancient Rome the emperor and governors of imperial provinces could condemn criminals to death by animals (Davies 1976). One understanding of the Roman criminal justice system's use of animals comes from the account of Ignatius of Antioch early in the second century of the Common Era. Ignatius, a professed martyr, writes that he was in chains awaiting an opportunity to be executed by wild beasts in Rome. During his wait he feared that the church would intervene and thwart his martyrdom. This may have been possible because he had been interrogated and imprisoned but had not yet received a sentence of capital punishment from the governor. At some point during his detention, he was released from chains once guards learned that he was a citizen of Rome. Although Roman citizens could legally be fed to beasts, they were more likely to be decapitated because it is less painful. Usually only noncitizens, prisoners of war, and heinous criminals were executed by the beasts. During the Flavian age,

69 AD–96 AD, Christian citizens would likely have received their full rights, which could have been the reason that Ignatius feared that the church would intervene before he could be sentenced. If he had been sentenced to die by animal, then he probably would have been fed to animals in a local arena. In addition to the famous Coliseum in Rome, arenas that used animals existed throughout many Roman localities, so citizens from these localities were not typically transported to the Coliseum for goring. Usually members of the lower class were condemned to be eaten for crimes including murder, parricide, sacrilege, nocturnal robbery of a temple, magic, and impious rites, the last of which might have been the crime for which Christians were charged (Osiek 1981). Assuming that Christianity was a crime, or a serious crime, that could be punished using the beasts, the only evidence that could secure a conviction would be a confession (Davies 1976). Mere accusations would have been insufficient, and there would have been no right of appeal following a conviction.

Generally, there was no chance of surviving a sentence of being thrown to the animals (Coleman 1990). Public spectacles were carefully arranged to guarantee that crowds could witness executions. However, one reason that events were entertaining was because there was no certainty that animals would be interested in attacking, wounding, or killing criminals. Sometimes criminals would be restrained just beyond an animal's reach in order to frustrate the animal and increase the crowd's anticipation. Other times a criminal might be dragged while tied to an animal, for example, a boar. This could be dangerous for the *bestiarius* ("beast handler"), who might be gored in the process of tying a criminal to a beast. Occasionally, if animals refused to attack people, then criminals were granted reprieve.

Though not an account of a Roman execution, the biblical story of Daniel in the lions' den serves as a good example of reprieve following animals' abstention. In the Bible the king issued an irrevocable edict that for one month any prayer to gods or people other than the king would result in capital punishment by the offender being cast into the lions' den (Dan 6:6). Upon learning about the edict, a member of the royal court, Daniel, went home and prayed three times per day to his god. Eventually a group of men entered his house and caught him praying; then the group asked the king to execute Daniel. The king was hesitant, but since he could not reverse the edict, he ordered the punishment. Daniel was tossed into a den of lions. A stone was used to cover the mouth of the den, then it was sealed using the king's and nobles' rings to ensure that the den would not be breeched throughout the night. At dawn the king, upset by Daniel's predicament, released Daniel. The fact that the lions did not eat Daniel signified that he had not wronged the king. Thus, the original accusation was presumptively false. The group who falsely accused Daniel was condemned to the lions' den by the king. The men, along with their wives and children, were thrown to the lions. The lions crushed all of their bones before they reached the den's floor.

Arenas were also used as slaughterhouses (Coleman 1990). In Roman slaughterhouses crowds sympathized with the animals and cheered for them. Executions often served as midday breaks between other entertainment events in which there may have been some chance for survival, for example, gladiatorial contests. During some morning events people could be thrown to beasts, like lions and bears, but the early morning events were not as sensational as the evening spectacles (Coleman 1990; Osiek 1981). Feeding criminals to animals was a form of entertainment similar to setting people on fire or hoisting criminals on crosses (Coleman 1990). Though it was less exciting than the gladiators' fights, it was more exciting than slower forms of death, like crucifixion. To add excitement to crucifixion, criminals might be crucified and then fed upon by a bear and birds.

Arranging for animals to kill criminals was the costliest and most difficult form of execution to implement in Rome (Coleman 1990). Ensuring the availability of beasts sometimes delayed what were otherwise to be prompt executions. Prisoners of war were said to be the most deserving of gruesome fates, followed by serious criminals. Thus, by the time any martyrs were to be executed, it would be possible for animals to already be in limited supply. Martyrs glamorized the possibility of being killed by a leopard or another exotic beast, so when that option was frustrated by logistics, martyrs had to resign themselves to die in less interesting ways. When martyrs were gored by animals, the gushing blood represented a second baptism, thereby further exalting this method of martyrdom.

In very public enactments meant to depict bestiality, a female prisoner's genitals could be smeared with vaginal secretions produced by an aroused cow (Coleman 1990). A bull would rape the female prisoner, and possibly damage her internally. Afterward she would be executed with a sword. Mythologizationshave assigned to the audience the belief that the bull is actually a powerful bipedal male disguised as an animal.

Sometimes crowds felt great empathy for animals. In one case people sensed something human about elephants in an arena, and the crowd was not excited to see elephants being forced to crush convicts (Cagniart 2000; Coleman 1990). The crowd members were captivated by the presence of the elephants but did not cheer because they were overcome with compassion (Coleman 1990).

Dogs have been used to devour convicts for thousands of years. In Rome convicts were dressed in animal skins and thrown to dogs (Coleman 1990). During the Haitian Revolution the French hunted revolutionary slaves using dogs (Gates 2013). Dogs were permitted to extensively maul and eat the revolutionaries. Even as recently as the slavery era in the United States, escaped slaves were tracked and could be torn apart and partially consumed by dogs.

War

Animals are warriors, weapons of war, and victims of war. It is not difficult to imagine that trained and domesticated animals can easily become victims or heroes during specific battles. What may be more difficult to understand is that animals have regularly been converted into weapons of war throughout history.

A number of militaries have attempted to use animals such as cats, dogs, and snakes as projectiles of devastation. Numerous empires have used bees as weapons of war (Bérubé 2000). During World War II the Germans investigated using rat carcasses to explode British boilers, and the US military investigated releasing bats to spread napalm on trees and houses in Japan (BBC 2013; Glines 1990). The United States also investigated whether it could ensconce pigeons trained to peck at screens into the nose of missiles to better guide the missiles to their targets (Vargas 2005). Also during World War II, members of the Imperial Japanese Navy fed civilians and Allied forces to sharks (Blundell 2008). In Chile General Pinochet trained dogs to rape political prisoners (Adams 1999). During the time between the Persian Gulf War and the Iraq War, Iran became armed with Soviet-trained mercenary dolphins (BBC 2000). Killer dolphins are trained to attack using harpoons, but the mammals are also equipped to take prisoners to the surface. Because they are capable of distinguishing friendly submarines from enemy vessels, dolphins can become suicide bombers.

Animals are often used as suicide bombers. In 2003 People for the Ethical Treatment of Animals (PETA) was criticized when it sent a letter to Yasser Arafat following a suicide bombing in Israel (PETA

2003). To accomplish the bombing, a person linked with the Palestinian Liberation Organization (PLO) strapped explosives to a donkey who was used as a suicide bomber. The blast did not injure any people. In its letter PETA asked Arafat to persuade his followers and allies to refrain from intentionally using animals as weapons in the future. Some people decried PETA's letter as insensitive, even though many people can recognize that blowing up a donkey is a criminal act of animal cruelty. The Revolutionary Armed Forces of Columbia (FARC) has detonated animals throughout Columbia on a number of occasions (BBC 2003). Later in the same year that the PLO exploded a donkey, FARC strapped explosives to a horse that exploded and killed several people in a market. When a Columbian farmer refused to lead an explosive-laden donkey into a market in 2011, FARC sewed his mouth shut, stabbed him, and amputated his fingers (Daughterty 2012). In 2013 a suicide bomber in Afghanistan rode a donkey into a NATO military convoy (Khan 2013). The detonation killed several people and the donkey. Animals used as bombs are literally converted from living creatures into bomb shrapnel. This use of animals as weapons seems to lag behind more popular and contemporary attitudes about animals in war.

War animals are trained for a variety of jobs, which can routinely include service as a weapon. Their roles as protectors vary, yet their presence consistently serves as armament. For example, dogs are chained to fences surrounding Israeli Air Force bases (Lior 2012). The Animal Cruelty Law, Israel's secular cruelty legislation, dictates the treatment of these war dogs by including requirements for shelter, amount of terrain, and limitations on the duration of duty shifts. In the US Armed Forces, war dogs may perform highly specialized duties, for example, as paratroopers, messengers, rescuers, or bomb-detectors (United States War Dogs Association 2013). War dogs have typically received protection from other soldiers as well as shelter and military gear, for example, camouflage or gas masks. Yet, they can also be readily mobilized to injure the enemy. Nevertheless, the recent trend throughout militaries has been to treat animals as warriors and veterans rather than merely as inanimate weaponry. Veteran canines, for example, may be treated for post-traumatic stress disorder (PTSD) like humans; they may be adopted to loving homes or police forces, receive honors, or become subjects of national monuments (Perry 2012; Public Law 110-181, § 2877, 2012). Honoring and accommodating war animals' roles as weapons, warriors, specialists, and companions is on the rise.

In the Home

Dogs are regularly used to defend the home. Their presence can ward off intruders. Even signage warning intruders about the presence of a dog may deter unwanted trespassers. It is not uncommon for jurisdictions to require trained guard dogs to be registered with local authorities for the dog's own protection. For example, in California all guard dog companies must register each dog placed in a home (Cal. Health and Safety Code § 121910, 2013). The fire department and state, city, county, and local law enforcement must be informed about the dog. These measures ensure that dogs can be registered in emergencies, and that police are aware of the animal for the safety of everyone involved, including the dog.

Each year numerous cases are reported in which burglars enter a home and encounter a dog who scares away the intruder, bites the burglar, or, in some cases, subdues the invader. Some dogs have legally killed intruders. Legal principles hold the home to be inviolable; thus, a dog's defense of the home is usually permissible. Jurisdictions by and large would allow a dog to bite in defense of the home. However, this area of law becomes murky depending on the reason that a dog attacks. For example, if an armed burglar enters a home and attacks an occupant, then a dog's biting or possibly killing the burglar would likely be legal in most jurisdictions. However, not all jurisdictions authorize use of lethal force for home invasion if the burglar does not threaten or attempt to use lethal force. Thus, the lawful amount of force that can be unleashed by a dog may be determined under the totality of the circumstances.

Facts become especially important in determining the legality of a dog's defense of the home when the bitten party claims that no invasion occurred. Common examples are when a person who has been bitten claims to be privileged or an invitee, or when the person claims that the dog exited the property and then inflicted the bite. For example, in Ohio, police were called by a man whose leg had been bitten by a dog (Dig Heir 2012). The man told police that he was walking on the sidewalk when a dog exited a fenced yard and bit him. The owner of the house found the front door had been opened. A neighbor claimed that the man who was bitten had trespassed into the yard. The neighbor had not seen the dog bite the man in the yard but also had not seen the dog exit the yard. The dog was seized by the county dog warden even though the owner reported a breaking and entering. The dog owner was charged with "failure to confine" and "failure to vaccinate" for rabies since the owner could not produce proof of current vaccination within two days of the bite. The first charge was dropped, and the second charge was settled with a fine. Local authorities held a hearing about the dog and determined that the dog was not dangerous, vicious, or a nuisance.

Though procedure and policy are jurisdictionally specific, the fact-centered problem of defensive dog bites is rather generalizable. For example, in Germany two dogs were seized after they inflicted several bites on a woman who entered their home when the homeowner was not home (Eims 2012). The dogs were seized and labeled as "potentially dangerous" because the woman claimed that she was a friend of the homeowner and was privileged to enter the home when she knew that the owner was not home. The owner of the dogs had been fined several times for allowing the dogs to run loose. Thus, that evidence could be used by the homeowner to demonstrate that on one hand her dogs impermissibly ran loose but they never bit anyone outside the home. Yet, on the other hand, the evidence could be used by the victim or the government to show that a pattern of recklessness dog ownership and the dogs' unruly behavior led to the dog bites.

One general defense to trespass is necessity. Sometimes people are forced to trespass onto private property due to exigent or life-threating circumstances. In these cases the law makes a limited exception to trespass so that people are not forced to choose between following the law and saving their own lives. As long as trespass only occurs during the emergency, but not before or after, then it is defensible. If a dog defended a home under these circumstances, and bit someone who claimed a necessity defense, the totality of the circumstances may determine the outcome.

Sometimes dogs are attacked when people defend themselves against dogs. It is not uncommon for "man's best friend" to die protecting a human companion. Sometimes a dog's demise might be lawful. The facts of the case are significant in this gray area. Some considerations are whether a person was intruding or was on the premises legally and the kind of threat the invader posed in the home. A homeowner may not be authorized to command a dog to kill an unarmed intruder in one jurisdiction, but may be allowed to do so in another. A dog who bites or attempts to kill legally cannot be attacked in response. However, a privileged person may repel a dog attack using lethal destruction if it is a matter of life or death (*Devincenzi v. Faulkner*, 1959; Phillips 2013; *State v. Smith*, 1911). Destruction must be in response to imminent threat. It cannot be premeditated, and it cannot be in response to an attack that has ceased or occurred in the past if threat is no longer imminent.

It is not uncommon for police officers who feel threatened to kill dogs during warranted searches. Police may exercise discretion when determining whether an animal is attacking or threatening. Police need not wait until an animal has begun to bite before deciding to shoot a dog. Police are trained to injure, not kill, attacking animals. However, dogs sometimes die during warranted searches. Animal welfarists have argued that attacking dogs ought to be tasered or sedated rather than killed. Unfortunately, dogs also die during illegal searches. Yet, police are immunized when they serve warrants or conduct searches on the wrong property. For example, in Texas, police entered the backyard of a dog trainer in a mistaken attempt to serve a warrant for an expired vehicle registration to a person who did not live in that home. Two dogs approached the officer. The officer claims that the dogs were growling, so he fired three shots, striking one dog in the back. The shot was not fatal. The homeowner claimed that the dogs, who are highly socialized, were investigating the officer, not attacking or growling. In order to characterize the officer's actions as reckless, the homeowner called attention to the fact that a terminally ill six-year-old child was just next to the dogs when the shots were fired. Many times violent police encounters with dogs who are defending homes conclude with an officer permissibly discharging a weapon.

Personal Weapons

People may use animals as blunt objects by striking others with an animal's body; may order animals to attack; or may use animals, for example, as lethal machines. For example, a drunk man in Germany used a swan to beat another man (Spiegel 2009). Following the attack on the swan, the swan flew away unharmed, but the attacker continued to use objects to beat the victim, who also escaped unharmed. The attacker received a two-year suspended sentence for the attack. A drunk man in Massachusetts was charged with cruelty and domestic violence for beating his girlfriend with a python (Fox News 2012). His girlfriend was sitting in the bathtub when the attack occurred. Following the attack, which bruised the woman, the man dumped the snake into the bathtub and the snake died. Because the snake allegedly belonged to the victim, the offender was charged with larceny over $250 and wanton and malicious damage over $250.

Sometimes animals' bodies are transformed into weapons, for example, ivory swords. On occasion, this weaponization of corpses is taken a step further when entire corpses are used as weapons. For example, a man in Georgia was charged with aggravated assault, aggravated animal cruelty, animal cruelty, and battery when he beat his girlfriend's Pomeranian and then snapped the dog's neck and used the dog's corpse to beat his girlfriend (Walsh 2012). Chapter 12 further discusses domestic violence and animals. This clear link between the weaponization of animals and domestic violence is not solely present between partners but also between parents and children. For example, two legal guardians in Florida were each sentenced to twelve years in prison for manslaughter, third-degree murder, and child neglect (WCTV 2011). The pair starved a nearly nine-foot boa constrictor for a month and then allowed the snake to constrict and kill their toddler in her bed. Months before the attack the couple had tested positive for drug use. The snake, which was unlicensed, was voluntarily surrendered by the pair to Florida Fish and Wildlife Conservation Commission (FWC). The boa constrictor was entered into evidence and then donated to a caretaker. A veterinarian who treated the snake found that the snake had been stabbed.

The use of animals as weapons is often premeditated. For example, in England a man used a dog to trap and attack a teenager in a park (*Guardian* 2010). The victim was stabbed six times after he was incapacitated by the dog. To identify the dog, police used new dog DNA technology that can be used to identify any dog-attacker with a probability of a billion to one. Dog DNA is further discussed in chapter 20. This crime reflects a growing trend for youth to arm themselves with dogs in England (Davis 2010). Under the Dangerous Dog Act, threatening dogs may be seized, and in recent years the number of dogs seized from youth has soared. Employment of dogs as weapons seems to directly correlate with the increase in dogfighting enterprises. Another example of premeditated weaponization is the case of the famous US mafia hitman known as Ice Man. Ice Man would beat victims until they were bloody (HBO 2001). Then he would bind and abandon victims in rat-infested areas, for example, caves. Rats would feed on victims until they died. Ice Man once videotaped a victim being eaten alive by rats over the course of a couple days. These horrific crimes demonstrate a possible trend for private animal weaponization to occur in conjunction with other crimes.

Conclusion

Cruel means and ends have been employed by humans who use animals as weapons. The harm resulting to humans and animals is excessive, senseless, and illegal. However, proper utilization of animals as weapons has proven effective and heroic. Throughout history humans have demonstrated some enjoyment of or appreciation for animals acting as weapons. In contemporary society animals used as weapons in war or in the home are often valued and respected. This relationship can present ethical or legal conundrums under the totality of the circumstances.

References

"1st National Monument for War Dogs Honors Four-Legged Pup Soldiers of World War II and Beyond." 2012. Fox News, October 30. http://www.foxnews.com/travel/2012/10/30/1st-national-monument-for-war-dogs-honors-four-legged-pup-soldiers-world-war-ii/.

Adams, C. J. 1999. "Women-Battering and Harm to Animals." In *Animals and Women: Feminist Theoretical Explorations*, ed. C. J. Adams and J. Donovan, 68. Durham, NC: Duke University Press.

"Animal Cruelty: Man Uses Live Swan to Beat up Victim." 2009. Spiegel Online International, May 27. http://www.spiegel.de/international/zeitgeist/animal-cruelty-man-uses-live-swan-to-beat-up-victim-a-627139.html.

Bérubé, C. 2000. "War and Bees: Military Applications of Apiculture." *BeeKeeping.com*. http://www.beekeeping.com/articles/us/war_bees.htm.

Betts, K. 2013. "Central Texas Dog Shot by Police Officer after Warrant Mix-Up." *KVUE News Austin*, June 19. http://www.wfaa.com/news/texas-news/212185641.html.

Blundell, N. 2008. "A Summary of Slaughter at Sea: The Story of Japan's Naval War Crimes." *Courier-Mail*, April 26. http://www.ourcivilisation.com/smartboard/shop/banzai/seakill.htm.

"British Special Operations Executive (SOE): Tools and Gadgets Gallery." 2013. BBC. http://www.bbc.co.uk/history/worldwars/wwtwo/soe_gallery_05.shtml.

Cagniart, P. 2000. "The philosopher and the Gladiator." *Classical World* 93, no. 6:607–18.

Cal. Health and Safety Code § 121910 (2013).

Coleman, K. M. 1990. "Fatal Charades: Roman Executions Staged as Mythological Enactments." *Journal of Roman Studies* 80:44–73.

"Couple Gets 12 Years Each in Toddler Snake Strangulation Case." 2011. WCTV, August 24. http://www.wctv.tv/home/headlines/49729362.html.

Daugherty, A. 2012. "FARC Torture Farmer over 'Donkey Bomb': Army." *Columbia Reports*, February 24. http://colombiareports.com/farc-torture-colombian-farmer-over-donkey-bomb/.

Davies, S. L. 1976. "The Predicament of Ignatius of Antioch." *Vigiliae Christianae* 30, no. 3:175–80.

Davis, R. 2010. "Are Dogs the New Weapon of Choice for Young People?" *Guardian*, February 16. http://www.theguardian.com/society/2010/feb/17/dangerous-dogs-as-weapons.

Devincenzi v. Faulkner. 174 Cal.App.2d 250, 254-5 (1959).

Eims, P. 2012. "Two German Shepherds Await Fate after Biting Intruder." *Examiner*, January 27. http://www.examiner.com/article/two-german-shepherds-await-fate-after-biting-intruder.

Gates, H. L. 2013. "Did Dogs Really Eat Slaves, Like in 'Django'?" *The Root*, January 14. http://www.theroot.com/views/did-dogs-really-eat-slaves-django?page=0,0.

Glines, C. V. 1990. "The Bat Bombers." *Journal of the Air Force Association* 73: 10. http://web.archive.org/web/20080531082803/http://www.afa.org/magazine/1990/1090bat.html.

"'Horse bomb' hits Colombia town." 2003. BBC, September 11. http://news.bbc.co.uk/2/hi/americas/3098746.stm.

"The Ice Man—Richard Kulkinski." 2001. HBO.http://www.youtube.com/watch?v=jjTYwZKuyBs.

"Iran Buys Kamikaze Dolphins." 2000. BBC News, March 8. http://news.bbc.co.uk/2/hi/world/middle_east/670551.stm.

Khan, Z. 2013. "Donkey Bomber Kills 3 NATO Soldiers in Afghanistan." *Muslim Times.* http://www.themuslimtimes.org/2013/07/countries/afghanistan/donkey-bomber-kills-3-nato-soldiers-in-afghanistan.

"Killer Who Used Dog as Murder Weapon Jailed for Life." 2010. *Guardian*, March 19. http://www.theguardian.com/uk/2010/mar/19/dog-killer-chrisdian-johnson-sentence.

Lior, L. 2012. "Israel's Animal Cruelty Law Improves Conditions for IAF Guard Dogs." *Haaretz.com*, August 28 http://www.haaretz.com/news/diplomacy-defense/israel-s-animal-cruelty-law-improves-conditions-for-iaf-guard-dogs-1.461067.

Osiek, C. 1981. "The Ransom of Captives: Evolution of a Tradition." *Harvard Theological Review* 74, no. 4:365–86.

People for the Ethical Treatment of Animals (PETA). 2003. "PETA's Letter to Yasser Arafat." Everything2.com. http://everything2.com/title/PETA%2527s+letter+to+Yasser+Arafat

Perry, T. 2012. "Military's Dogs of War Also Suffer Post-Traumatic Stress Disorder." *Los Angeles Times*, November 26. http://articles.latimes.com/2012/nov/26/nation/la-na-military-dogs-20121126.

Phillips, K. M. 2013. "Self Defense When a Dog Attacks a Person." *Dog Bite Law.* http://dogbitelaw.com/.

"Police: Massachusetts Man Used Pet Python to Attack Woman." 2012. Fox News, November 3. http://www.foxnews.com/us/2012/11/03/police-massachusetts-man-used-pet-python-to-attack-woman/#ixzz2dc27sHK8.

Public Law 110-181, § 2877 (2012).

"Single Mom Asks Public for Support after Dog Bites Alleged Home Intruder." 2012. Dog Heirs, October 8. http://www.dogheirs.com/dogheirs/posts/1982-single-mom-asks-public-for-support-after-dog-bites-alleged-home-intruder#odbDQla1cpcPP1fb.99.

State v. Smith. 156 N.C. 628, 72 S.E. 321 (1911).

United States War Dogs Association. 2013. http://www.uswardogs.org/.

Vargas, J. S. 2005. "A Brief Biography of B.F. Skinner." *B.F. Skinner Foundation.* http://www.bfskinner.org/bfskinner/AboutSkinner.html.

Walsh, M. 2012. "Dog's Worst Friend: Man Kills Dog, Beats Girlfriend with Body." *New York Daily News,* August 9. http://www.nydailynews.com/news/crime/dog-worst-friend-man-kills-dog-beats-girlfriend-body-article-1.1133139#ixzz2dc8sRIJt.

19

Animals: Comparative Criminal Justice Systems

Introduction

Each jurisdiction is responsible for formulating laws and policies to protect and regulate humans and animals. Local, state, provincial, regional, national, and international authorities may govern or influence commerce, private affairs, and public or government actions involving animals. Laws in various jurisdictions sometimes overlap, are absent or silent, or fail to effectuate a desired goal. Nations and their jurisdictions may serve as examples for one another. Failures and advances in particular areas of animal welfare are made throughout the world. Careful attention to other jurisdictions' limitations and progress can illustrate beneficial or unbeneficial policies and effective modes for implementing change.

In the Middle

Cases, laws, and welfarist literature seems to indicate that the United States is neither the most evolved nor the cruelest society. American criminal justice policies toward animals lag behind other countries but also lead the way in some regards. Every year jurisdictions within the United States improve the criminal justice system's response to animals. Depending on the jurisdiction's starting point, these heightened responses may innovate progress or may still lag behind other domestic or international jurisdictions. For example, several states and municipalities prohibit animals from being locked in hot or cold vehicles without proper ventilation or heating, respectively (Schultz 2013). Jurisdictions with hot-car legislation also permit law enforcement or animal control to break car windows to free animals who would likely die from heat stroke or exposure in a short amount of time. The majority of states and municipalities officers might be authorize officers to use discretion or arrest for cruelty or neglect, but they fail specifically to authorize or require police or animal control to rescue animals in hot or cold cars by breaking windows. Police are aware of the dangers of leaving dogs in hot cars. A few police departments have installed heat sensors in their vehicles to prevent canine officers from overheating (Davis 2012). Lack of hot-car legislation is not necessarily due to oversight or absence of this problem. Some councils and legislatures have failed to pass proposed laws even though proposed standards seem basic and completely justifiable (Schultz 2013).

A few states have permitted animals to be classified as "victims" so that particular remedies previously reserved for human victims will be available to animals (Heiser 2012). Due to their status as quasi-property, animals are not usually considered to be victims. However, in a few mass-neglect cases, courts have held that each animal counted as a separate victim. Mass neglect is discussed in chapter 17. Because each animal was considered to be a victim, offenders were ordered to pay a fine for each neglected animal. Without progressive applications of the law in some jurisdictions, neglectful owners might only be required to pay a single fine or face a single charge if all the animals are neglected simultaneously. This implementation is a huge bridge between the status of human and animal victims in the criminal justice system, but it also calls attention to the fact that throughout the United States a person may neglect numerous animals at once but only face a single misdemeanor charge.

Uneven approaches within the criminal justice system might be plagued with drawbacks, but they typify democratic lawmaking processes that require separation of powers and state sovereignty. Generally speaking, jurisdictions are neither cruelty-free nor completely cruel. In other nations legislatures or councils have created far greater protection for some animals. Each country is a mix of commercial, moral, and cultural expectations and customs, laws and politics, species preferences, enforcement variations, and enforcement resources that influence how animals are treated and protected.

Leaders

Pioneering efforts within the criminal justice system to reduce animal mistreatment appear on every continent (Brels 2013). The European Union promotes animal welfare in many contexts. Outstanding examples are that throughout Europe—the international epicenter of fashion and beauty products—animal testing for beauty products is illegal, and genetic modification of dairy cows with hormones is also illegal (European Commission 2013). Specific examples within the European Union include a jurisdiction within Italy that criminalizes keeping fish in bowls because water is unfiltered (Agence France Presse 2004). In another jurisdiction dog owners cannot mutilate or dye dogs for aesthetic reasons, and they must walk dogs at least three times per day (Reuters 2005). Abandonment of dogs while owners are on vacation can be severely punished. That same jurisdiction prevents fish from being transported in plastic bags.

Certain countries have taken great strides to reduce cruelty. Many of these efforts exceed domestic efforts. Some do not exceed US protections for animals but represent leading efforts within their regions. In the Philippines animal mistreatment and infliction of pain or suffering on an animal is illegal, though enforcement is not proactive. However, legislation in the Philippines prohibits habitat destruction and killing any animal for any reason other than for food or a few other enumerated exceptions (Favre and Hall 2004). Israel's legislation and enforcement are not particularly cutting-edge, but a nonprofit animal control organization, Animal Guard, enforces laws and attempts to deter cruelty through several tactics including by training law enforcement, speaking in schools and on Israeli Army bases, and instilling love for animals in society (IADF 2013). Costa Rica already bans circuses and sport hunting, and now has closed all zoos on cruelty grounds. Animals in zoos will be rehabilitated, adopted, or returned to the wild (Romo and Shoichet 2013). South Africa limits the content of commercials as a strategy for deterring cruelty (Kuch 2013). Advertisers may not cause pain or distress to animals, and they are forbidden from producing advertisements that may reasonably be believed to condone or promote cruelty or any irresponsible treatment of animals.

Lagging Behind

In most countries animal abuse is routinized in some form, but in a few countries, widespread abuse is completely ignored overall or within certain industries. Abuses occur within greater systems that implement certain protections for animals in these jurisdictions. In India, for example, killing cows is illegal in the majority of states, but where it is legal cows are starved, dragged by facial piercings, marched for miles in oppressive heat, and packed so tightly into trucks that their bones break (Popham 2000). Portugal theoretically supports private welfare organizations and requires municipal licensing for commercial use of animals, but the government does not enforce anticruelty policies or laws, which are few and far between (Favre and Hall 2004). For example, in Portugal, cats and dogs may be eaten. The process of mulesing requires farmers to pull out large chunks of wool and flesh from sheep's backsides in an attempt to prevent and remove maggot infestations (PETA 2013). Industry standards require no training for the performance of this surgical procedure (Matthews n.d.). Thus, the practice should be outlawed or regulated by the government. In 1635 Ireland passed legislation that banned the practice of pulling wool from a live sheep, which demonstrates long-standing governmental concern about mulesing (Kelch 2012). Almost four hundred years later, Australia continues to allow mulesing.

Conclusion

Thorough cross-cultural comparisons of historical and contemporary relationships between humans and animals must consider attitudes and values. Comparative analyses tend to consider effects of local religious history or practice on understanding of human stewardship or dominion over animals. Factors may be viewed *in toto* or in consideration of nations' progress toward humane treatment of animals. However, treatment of animals, adherence to policies and agreements, and attempts to innovate and enforce laws may be reviewed generally. Compared to other nations, the United States is a pioneer and leader in some senses, but in other areas the United States has failed to take the furthest strides possible.

References

Brels, S. 2013. "Animal Welfare Protection Laws in the World." *Animal Legal and Historical Center*. http://www.animallaw.info/nonus/articles/art_pdf/arbrelssabine2012.pdf.

Davis, V. T. 2012. "Protecting Dogs Who Save Others." *My San Antonio*, August 26. http://www.mysanantonio.com/default/article/Protecting-dogs-who-save-others-3816798.php.

European Commission. 2013. "Health and Consumers." September 12. http://ec.europa.eu/consumers/.

Favre, D., and C. F. Hall. 2004. "Comparative National Animal Welfare Laws." *Animal Legal and Historical Center*. http://www.animallaw.info/nonus/articles/arcomparativenationalwelfarelaws.htm.

"Inside the Australian Wool Industry." 2013. People for the Ethical Treatment of Animals (PETA). http://www.peta.org/features/inside-the-australian-wool-industry.aspx.

Israel Animal Defense Force (IADF). 2013. http://www.animalpolice.org.il/?CategoryID=201&ArticleID=135.

"Italian Town Outlaws Goldfish Bowls." 2004. Agence France Presse, July 26. http://www.freerepublic.com/focus/f-chat/1178364/posts.

Kelch, T. G. 2012. "A Short History of (Mostly) Western Animal Law," pt. 1. *Animal Law* 19:23.

Kuch, C. 2013. "Perception, Reality, and The Law." *National Councils of SPCA*, September 6. http://www.nspca.co.za/#%2FNews%2F2630%2FPerception%2C-Reality-and-the-Law.

Matthews, R. (n.d.) "The Impacts of Mulesing Alternatives on Sheep Welfare." http://vip.vetsci.usyd.edu.au/contentUpload/content_3231/Rebecca-Matthews.pdf.

Popham, P. 2000. "How India's Sacred Cows Are Beaten, Abused and Poisoned to Make Leather for High Street Shops." *Independent*, February 14. http://www.independent.co.uk/news/world/asia/how-indias-sacred-cows-are-beaten-abused-and-poisoned-to-make-leather-for-high-street-shops-724696.html.

Romo, R., and C. E. Shoichet. 2013. "Costa Rica to Close Zoos, Release Some Animals." *CNN*, August 8. http://www.cnn.com/2013/08/07/world/americas/costa-rica-zoo-cages

Schultz, M. 2013. "House OKs Bill to Let Officers Remove Dogs from Hot Cars." *News Observer*, July 19. http://www.newsobserver.com/2013/07/19/3038300/house-oks-bill-to-let-officers.html#storylink=cpy.

"Walk Your Dog Three Times a Day or Be Fined, Says Turin." 2005. Reuters, April 25. http://www.enn.com/top_stories/article/11880.

20

Extremes

Introduction

The presence of animals in society and the criminal justice system is complex. Some relationships between humans and animals are traditional or well-established under the law. However, the majority are in a state of flux as laws progress to further protect and include animals. Certain interactions far exceed traditional relationships and venture into extremes. Animals used in sophisticated strategies have produced strange, cutting-edge, or unheard-of results. When driven to extremes, animals may react unpredictably or humans may use animals in bizarre ways. Extreme relationships demonstrate how the criminal justice system must constantly be prepared to respond to new scenarios.

Cutting-Edge Technology

Animals have become involved in the use of extremely sophisticated technology in the criminal justice system. One increasingly common way that animals are involved is in DNA evidence (Boyle 2013; Cusack 2015). Cat and dog fur can attach to clothing and be left at crime scenes. When investigators discover animal fur at crime scenes, they analyze mitochondrial DNA signatures, which are uncommon identifiers that are passed genetically from animals to their young. Cat and dog DNA databases allow investigators to compare signatures to hundreds or thousands of other animals to support their theory that DNA must have come from a particular suspect's animal companion. Another example is in Capri, Italy, where improperly discarded dog waste discovered in public areas undergoes DNA testing (Aldern 2011). The source of the waste is identified, and then owners are forced to pay several thousand dollars in fines. A couple dozen apartment complexes throughout the United States independently conduct DNA testing of dog feces (*Huffington Post* 2011).

Other technological innovations have assisted in curbing dog waste violations. For example, in Brunete, Spain, members of the neighborhood watch casually converse with animal owners who allow their animals to defecate in public without cleaning up after them (Gates 2013). Volunteers identify the dog's name and research it in a town database. The database provides volunteers with the owner's address. Volunteers will collect an offending dog's feces and mail the dog's waste to the owner. Relentless infractions have resulted in at least one dog park in the United States opting to utilize cutting-edge technology to avoid any temptation to recklessly litter (*Green Diary* 2013). After dogs defecate at the dog park, owners place feces into a receptacle that converts the feces into methane to power a lamp at the dog park.

High-tech surveillance may be used to protect animals and the home. In one case an animal's instincts prompted others to install surveillance. A family's dog began behaving aggressively toward the family's babysitter (Ciampanelli 2013). Because the parents trusted their animal companion, they became suspicious of the babysitter. They conducted undercover surveillance by videotaping the babysitter when they were not home. The parents learned that the babysitter had begun physically abusing their child. Without the dog alerting them to the abuse, they would not have used technology to discover and document the abuse, which led to criminal charges against the babysitter.

Far-Fetched Defenses

Some people have concocted far-fetched schemes in order to blame animals for crimes. For example, a man in Germany used his dog on appeal against a murder conviction (*Cape Cod Times* 2012). The defendant claimed that his dog accidentally smothered his wife after she passed out drunk on the bathroom floor. Another man was arrested for planning to extort and kill a wealthy victim (*Daily Mail* 2012). The offender planned to electrocute the wealthy victim in a bathtub by tossing an electronic appliance into the water with the victim. The offender thought that by electrocuting a cat with the victim, the cat would be blamed for accidentally knocking the appliance into the tub. The offender was thwarted before he could kill the victim or the cat. Country singer Mindy McCreedy did not blame an animal, but she may have killed a dog who revealed that she could be guilty of a crime. After her boyfriend suffered a fatal gunshot wound, McCreedy told authorities that her boyfriend committed suicide (Burgess 2013; Quigley 2013). She remained a person of interest after her late boyfriend's dog located the bullet that had killed him. McCreedy killed the dog and herself. Some media outlets wondered whether this was an act of revenge against the dog for finding the bullet that could possibly reveal that she murdered her boyfriend.

Food

Food is frequently linked with a variety of crimes. For example, animals can be used to poison people. In Illinois a man was arrested and for attempting to poison his wife with puffer fish poison (CBS 2011). First, the offender made false claims to the Internal Revenue Service so as to take out a twenty-million-dollar life insurance policy on his wife. Then he assumed the alias of a researcher and ordered rare puffer fish poison from a research lab through the mail. The lab informed the Federal Bureau of Investigation, and he was arrested before he could marry his wife. Similarly, in China the deputy director of agriculture in a town was investigated when a tycoon died after eating cat soup with the director (Yiu 2012). At first, it seemed that the soup was rotten, but authorities discovered that the director was familiar with local poisonous herbs, which he may have used to poison the tycoon's cat soup.

Anecdotally, it is said that if humans die, then their animal companions may eat them if they lack access to other sustenance. Usually this is not an animal's fault, and authorities do not destroy ravenous animals if they did not cause a person's death. In a particularly gruesome example of animals eating an owner, a man in Indonesia abandoned seven companion dogs for two weeks while he went on vacation (*Inquisitr* 2011). When he returned the starving dogs killed him, tore apart his body, and ate him. When police arrived the dogs were so wild that they had to paralyze the animals prior to entering the property. In that case, had the man survived, he likely would have been charged with neglect.

Conclusion

Extreme situations involving animals affect the criminal justice system. Extreme, advanced, and shocking possibilities will continue to filter into the justice system. Some of these extremes will help law enforcement and the justice system to better respond to infractions and crimes. However, some extremes will continue to shock public conscience or challenge common understandings of human-animal relationships.

References

Aldern, N. 2011. "Capri to DNA Test Dog Waste." *Italy Magazine*, April 13. http://www.italymagazine.com/italy/pets/capri-dna-test-dog-waste.

Boyle, A. 2013. "Elementary, My Dear Fluffy: Cat DNA Solves Another Homicide." *NBC*, August 14. http://www.nbcnews.com/science/elementary-my-dear-fluffy-cat-dna-solves-another-homicide-6C10913900?ocid=msnhpandpos=6.

Burgess, T. 2013. "Mindy McCready Shot Dog: Both 'Found Dead Next to One Another.'" *Examiner*, February 18. http://www.examiner.com/article/mindy-mccready-shot-dog-both-found-dead-next-to-one-another.

Ciampanelli, P. 2013. "Dog Saves Child from Babysitter Abuse." *Paw Nation*, September 12. http://www.pawnation.com/2013/09/12/dog-saves-child-from-baby-sitter-abuse/?icid=maing-grid7%7Cmain5%7Cdl4%7Csec1_lnk3%26pLid%3D374015.

Cusack, C. M. 2015. *Criminal Justice Handbook on Masculinity, Male Aggression, and Sexuality*. Springfield, IL: Charles C. Thomas.

"DNA Testing Dog Poop: Apartments Get Serious about Tracking Down Owners Not Cleaning up after Pets." 2011. *Huffington Post*, June 24. http://www.huffingtonpost.com/2011/06/24/dna-testing-dog-poop_n_884060.html.

Gates, S. 2013. "Town Mails Dog Poop Back to Negligent Owners in Spain." *Huffington Post*, June 5. http://www.huffingtonpost.com/2013/06/05/town-mails-dog-poop-spain_n_3390191.html.

"Indonesian Man Eaten by Starving Pet Dogs." 2011. *Inquisitr*, September 8. http://www.inquisitr.com/139936/indonesian-man-eaten-by-starving-pet-dogs/.

"Man Admits to Buying Puffer Fish Poison in Plot to Kill Wife." 2011. CBS, August 3. http://chicago.cbslocal.com/2011/08/03/man-admits-to-buying-puffer-fish-poison-in-plot-to-kill-wife/.

"Man 'Planned to Extort a Wealthy Former Attorney Then Electrocute Him in the Bath—And Frame the Cat as The Culprit.'" 2012. *Daily Mail*, December 5. http://www.dailymail.co.uk/news/article-2092518/Man-planned-extort-wealthy-attorney-electrocute-bath--frame-cat-culprit.html.

"Man Says Overweight Pet Dog Suffocated Wife." 2012. *Cape Cod Times*, January 18. http://www.capecodonline.com/apps/pbcs.dll/article?AID=/20120118/NEWS11/120119761/-1/rss04.

"Park Spark Project Utilizes Dog Poop to Power Lamppost Onsite." 2013. Green Diary. http://www.greendiary.com/park-spark-project-utilizes-dog-poop-to-power-lamppost-on-site.html.

Quigley, R. 2013. "Mindy McCready Breaks Down as She Insists She Did Not Murder Her Lover—But Says She 'Doesn't Know' If He Was Killed or Shot Himself." *Daily Mail*, January 29. http://www.dailymail.co.uk/news/article-2270145/Mindy-McCready-says-did-murder-lover-admits-doesnt-know-murdered-committed-suicide--revealed-did-attend-memorial-service.html.

Yiu, K. 2012. "Death by Cat Meat: Chinese Billionaire Poisoned." *ABC*, January 5. http://abcnews.go.com/blogs/headlines/2012/01/death-by-cat-meat-chinese-billionaire-poisoned/.

21

Conclusion

Animals in the criminal justice system may be treated as victims, objects, victimizers, weapons, family members, property, officers, war heroes, rescuers, supporters, and service animals. This list is not comprehensive, and these roles may not be discrete. A single animal may be vulnerable, valuable, protected, and neglected depending on situational context. Human-animal relationships define animals' roles, and animals' roles may be qualified by species, numerosity, utility, domestication, attractiveness, and other qualities. Humans' roles in human-animal relationships may be qualified by local opinions about the environment and animals, religion, morality, caretakers' obligations, legal duties, and systemic responses. Thus, an animal's status may be relative within context or role.

Systemic responses and polices for working animals, domesticated animals, animal companions, exotic animals, and wild animals may vary widely between jurisdictions. Each jurisdiction's laws and protocols may be a patchwork created by various sources of authority including case law, health codes, criminal codes, administrative codes, local ordinances, civil procedure, discretionary law enforcement actions, nonprofit organizations, attorney general opinions, and other sources. Nonprofit organizations may satisfy governmental roles, or they may compliment governmental efforts. Nonprofits may operate in conjunction with or in lieu or local, regional, national, or international policies. Some organizations focus on protecting certain animal species, while others operate to protect or bring awareness to particular human-animal relationships or roles.

In some situations legal responses to animals may result from rights available to animal owners, but at other times responses may directly address individual animals in a manner traditionally used to protect humans or to resolve problems affecting humans. Thus, context may be determinate of responses. Factors influencing policy design and implementation may include species-specific problems, professional protocol, relevant scientific or scholarly data, geographic location, and resource availability. Tradition is a major influence on treatment of animals in the criminal justice system, industry, and society. Responses to animals may be based on traditional morality, religion, speciesism, commerce, and other major societal influences. Tradition maintains the status quo, and in many cases law upholds tradition. Sometimes animals are protected by tradition. For example, due process for animal owners may protect animals, compassionate approaches to animal suffering may be institutionalized by custom, or traditional governments by require that certain animals be revered or spared. However, traditions that permit cruelty, abandonment, or neglect are likely to continue in the absence of progress or change. Thus, questions arise about how to best recognize animals' current roles and needs, idealize change, generate impetus and necessary community buy-in, and implement new policies.

Inclusion of working animals in the criminal justice system may help to influence public opinion about animals' capacities, intrinsic value, and utility. Positive influences on public opinion could serve to motivate policymakers, lawmakers, and community members to implement important protections and systemic changes for animal welfare. Despite the fact that working animals have proven to have many superior abilities, they are still vulnerable to physical abuse, sexual abuse, neglect, and abandonment. However, heightened legal protections, adoption programs, retirement placement, pensions, media coverage, and public donations continue to demonstrate systemic and localized appreciation for working animals. Public awareness of animals' contribution to human society and societal appreciation for working animals serves to bridge gaps in understandings about human-animal relationships that can lead to improved treatment of animals. Increased public awareness of working animals may also deter crime, act as goodwill between the criminal justice system and the public, and inspire criminal justice members to implement programs for service animals and therapy animals.

Animals' therapeutic affects cannot be underestimated. In the criminal justice system, defendants, victims, judges, attorneys, offenders, and others benefit from animals' presence. In prison pet programs, animals, inmates, juvenile delinquents, and the public benefit from training. Inmates, juvenile delinquents, and animals learn skills, which increases their utility or desirability in society. Disabled people are benefited by service animal training, and local animal control is assisted by adoption programs. However, availability of service animals to disabled inmates or juvenile delinquents is patently lacking. That role is rarely sanctioned even though service animals are frequently trained by inmates. It is likely that these policies may improve in the future as sensitivity toward disabled Americans increases and information abounds about how to manage service animals among disabled institutional populations.

Animal populations in prisons are typically regulated. Unregulated populations may include infestations or contraband. The presence of infestations in prison may amount to human rights violations or violations of the Eighth Amendment. Contraband animals may include wild animals or animals from infestation populations groomed as pets or as couriers for contraband. Animals may be used to move contraband within corrections facilities or may be trained to transport contraband into prison. Trained animals may also be used to circulate "kites," that is, messages, in prison or to the outside. Animal courier is a traditional role that has been used during war, by criminal justice members, and by inmates throughout the world for centuries.

Utilization of massive amounts of animals may result in cruelty. Animal operations, including farms, slaughterhouses, illegal and legal entertainment industries, and puppy mills may find compliance with the law to be challenging or impossible. Yet, oversight for legal operations seems to improve and increase annually, thereby demonstrating public and societal demand for compliance. Video exposés have contributed significant knowledge about animal abuse in commercial operations, and they have generated tremendous public support for criminal justice responses. Existing laws and new laws may make dealing with large numbers of animals more onerous than cost-effective. Operations may require carefulness, substantial effort, and nuanced procedures that make systemic oversight equally costly. When cruelty is discovered by exposés or through government oversight, numerous animals may be humanely euthanized or rescued. Rescue operations and humane animal removal attest to the criminal justice system's intent to help animals despite logistical complexity and exceptional resource allocation. In some cases cost concerns, culture, and expediency may result in seemingly less compassionate responses. Culling, hunting, exterminating, and destroying seized animals demonstrate that some members of the government and society feel that killing animals may be resourceful, just, regulatable, and appropriate in many circumstances.

Some animal welfarists believe that human-animal relationships should never involve slaughter or harm to animals. Many welfarists believe that animals are entitled to personhood, equality, heightened protection, humane treatment, care, modified rights, or moral consideration. Donors who buy into these beliefs and values may supply nonprofit organizations with billions of tax-deductible dollars each year. Some organizations work with the criminal justice system and others act as animal control, but a few work against the government as "terrorists." Many organizations attempt to comply with the law to protect their 501(c)(3) status, which makes appeals to donors and legitimizes animal welfare activism as a charitable purpose. The animal welfare movement is not single-minded, but organizations' general goals to help animals and increase public awareness about animal suffering are often recognized by society and the government as being charitable purposes. Animal welfarism has pioneered and shaped many criminal justice responses. However, some newly formed criminal laws respond to animal welfare tactics, for example, undercover taping and captive animal release, that seem to defy ordered liberty or trump business owners' rights. New criminal justice opposition to radical welfarism has resulted in revised tactics among welfarists, tactics designed to assist animals, oppose systemic resistance, and comply with or circumnavigate law.

The criminal justice system continues to need improved laws, policies, emergency responses, as well as training programs for working animals, animal control, and personnel training. Some recent positive changes can serve as a model for future changes; yet, enforcement and resource distribution will be key for advancing animal welfare through the criminal justice system. Nonprofit welfare organizations may use donations and education campaigns to finance or generate interest in improved human-animal relationships, utilization of animals' skills, and systemic responses.

Treaties and international policies demonstrate worldwide awareness and willingness to participate in improved human-animal relationships. Enforcing appropriate roles between humans and animals is difficult across borders. Foreign nations may enforce exemplary policies that could influence domestic policy. Influence by foreign policies and participation in international animal welfare policies may challenge traditional notions of domestic autonomy, state sovereignty, or human dominion. Yet, traditional treatment of animals in the United States need not be eradicated by innovative criminal justice approaches. International ideals are designed to better protect domestic animals and exotic animals in the United States and abroad while considering human interests. Any liberties lessened by adherence to international policies or adoption of foreign perspectives may serve to better protect domestic and global ecosystems as well as preserve natural resources thereby extending commercial viability. Tradition could potentially be maintained by new policies; however, it is likely that only the most conscientious aspects of traditional approaches will best be able to guide future progress. Some foreign jurisdictions may adopt American traditions as globalized attitudes toward animals continue to circulate and prompt reform. Thus, US corporations doing business abroad may continue to increasingly become subject to uniform regulations and held accountable domestically. Uniformity is a central purpose of the criminal justice system. International uniformity only strengthens enforcement for every nation and increases the benefits for all jurisdictions using criminal justice systems to protect, employ, and regulate animals.

Index

Made in the USA
Monee, IL
31 August 2021

76839180R00142